Singers of the Century

Singers of the Century

J.B. Steane

Amadeus Press
Reinhard G. Pauly, General Editor
Portland, Oregon

First published in North America in 1996 by
Amadeus Press (an imprint of Timber Press, Inc.)
The Haseltine Building
133 S.W. Second Avenue, Suite 450
Portland, Oregon 97204, U.S.A.

A catalog record for this book is available
from the Library of Congress

ISBN 1-57467-009-3

Typeset by Ray Davies
Printed in Great Britain by
Redwood Books Ltd, Trowbridge

Contents

v

To Edwyn and Marie-Thérèse

Foreword

All of the singers included here are in some way special. The quality of voice, the art of its usage, the character behind it: these, or any one of them, may be sufficient to account for the specialness. It may also have to do with the taste of the times, associations of repertoire, composers, other singers, publicity or perhaps sheer good luck. All, at any rate, have made a mark, whether upon the affection of their own audiences, the wider public that knows them through their recordings, or (as is usually the case) both.

To seek out what is special in each of them has been the main purpose of these essays. Or perhaps there is a larger purpose also, namely to help keep the voices, the names and the circumstances of these remarkable people's lives in circulation. Sometimes, meeting enthusiasts with expert knowledge and huge collections on disc, tape and video, one feels that the survival of such interests is assured; but equally it happens that indifference and ignorance (even in what one might think of as high places) seem endemic, and the incomparable inheritance of recorded sound and available knowledge languishes unused. In common with most lovers of singing, I view the current state of the art with mixed feelings, often rejoicing, often regretful and apprehensive about trends that surely work against its best interests. As in most things, awareness of the past is so very important for the understanding of what we hold in our hands in the present. Knowledge and appreciation should follow, but simple awareness has to come first. The most urgent wish a writer on such a subject as this can have is that in however limited a way his work may help to promote it.

The chapters here comprise the first fifty articles in a continuing series published monthly in *Opera Now*. Reassembling them in book form has involved thought about the advantages of chronological and alphabetical arrangement, or of sorting into categories by voice, repertoire or nationality. In the end we have settled to retain the original order: it has, for one thing, the merit of surprise. As the reader will have observed, one singer follows another in an arbitrary sort of way, Emma Calvé after Richard Tauber, while Tito Gobbi precedes Dame Nellie Melba. From the writer's point of view there was much to be said for this freedom of choice, and I shall be ever grateful to the enlightened Editor who presented me with a word-limit and let me get on with it. Such self-imposed guidelines as were originally dreamt up (male and female to alternate, ancient and modern likewise, never two of the same kind, sopranos for instance, to follow in succession) shared the fate of most good intentions, with the result that I was free to pursue my own interest of the moment, spurred sometimes by a biography (Crespin, Vishnevskaya), a recording (Ivogün, Zenatello), a farewell appearance (Bergonzi, Ludwig), or a masterclass (Di Stefano, Nilsson). Sadly, in two other instances (the lamented Arleen Auger and Lucia Popp) the immediate occasion was a death. In one chapter only (Smirnov and Sobinov) have I varied the original plan and included more than one singer.

In addition to providing the element of surprise, the original order of publication also commended itself because in some degree it counteracted a tendency observable among the devotees of singers and singing: a certain exclusiveness. There are the Golden Agers who will hear no good of anybody still in the business; others, among the modernists, reject the dead diva in favour of the living; and some there be whose devotion is more or less confined to tenors. A little less chance of such selective reading arises when persons and periods are serendipitously mixed, and when the tenor-fancier turns the pages from Aureliano Pertile and Antonio Cortis to be confronted by Christa Ludwig and Dietrich Fischer-Dieskau.

Those two (Ludwig and Fischer-Dieskau), though now retired, are among the more 'modern' of the singers discussed. Later in the series I shall hope to include more of those who are still before the public, but clearly there is an advantage in being able to survey a singer's life and career as a whole. I hope it will not be thought that the inclusion of biographical and sometimes anecdotal material constitutes a gross departure from the true path of critical duty. I have written elsewhere of singers on record and on the judgment of critics in their own time. These have a place here too, but in this series I have wanted rather more to relate the artist to the human being and (in turn) the human beings to their times.

All the same, 1,500 words, which was the agreed limit for the articles after the slightly longer first five, do not amount to very much in terms of space or length, and it may well be objected that, knowing the constraints, one should adopt a more stringent and businesslike method. I quite see the force of such an argument and will duly take shelter until it passes over: I had rather travel pleasantly and arrive late (or not at all) than be hustled to follow a rigid timetable. Besides, a factual apparatus with dates and (as they say) 'suggestions for further study' is included at the end of the book. The fact is of course that these studies are also exercises in a leisurely and obsolete literary form. It used to have a section to itself in the public libraries as well as a place in the schools and colleges. Last time I attended some sort of educational conference, a middle-aged teacher of English referred to it as 'the god-awful essay'. I almost thought of dedicating this book to its memory.

Illustrations

ILLUSTRATIONS

Picture credits

(references are to the pages of this book)

Britten-Pears Library, 137 (photo Helga Sharland)
Fritz Curzon: 167, 169
Decca: 97 (photo McBean), 249
EMI: 12 (photo Reg Wilson), 27 (photo Walter Bird), 67, 93 (photo Reg Wilson)
Gramophone: 62 (photo James Abresch), 99, 113 (photo Max Erlanger de Rosen),
    127 (photo Axel Poignant), 132 (photo Hans Wild), 139, 153 (photo David
    Farrell), 155 (photo S. Lauterwasser), 157, 183, 193 (photo Clive Barda), 195,
    203, 205, 213 (photo Donald Southern), 215, 222, 225, 233, 235
Michael Henstock: 43, 45
Hislop family and Michael Turnbull: 79
Nimbus: 3, 19, 22, 32, 53, 72, 117, 122, 143, 145, 149, 207, 237
Vivienne Rendall: 243
Royal College of Music, 217
Royal Opera House, Covent Garden, 4 (photo Karossa Janos), 37, 147, 172, 179

CHAPTER 1

Richard Tauber

Among mementoes stored in the archives at Covent Garden is Richard Tauber's monocle. It is sometimes brought out on exhibition, and coming upon it then is rather like finding Schubert's spectacles in a glass display-case in Vienna. Not that the comparison should be carried too far, for Tauber, though quite a prolific composer, was assuredly no Schubert. But at the very least his monocle can claim comparable status with Pavarotti's white handkerchief. In fact it was more than that, for it represented something in the singer's personality, and was emblematic rather than incidental.

Tauber was not really a very romantic figure; but put on his white tie and tails, brush up his top-hat, lodge his monocle, and he embodied the world of the waltz-dream, the Ambassador's Ball where exiled aristocrats spoke with mysterious accents and a song sung softly on the balcony after midnight could win the hand of the Magyar princess. It was, of course, phoney. That world, if it ever existed, is not one which anybody in his senses would contemplate with anything more than a humorously-indulged sceptical nostalgia. That goes for all those operettas of Lehár which involved Tauber so intimately, and it goes (I suspect) for the tales of Old Vienna too. But Tauber was a magician among singers, a master of metamorphosis. When he sang, cheap music would glow and romantic myths became valid through sheer enchantment.

It has no doubt been said, and may well be true, that he could not have possessed this skill had it not been for his lifelong contact with much better music. His career in fact began and ended with Mozart. He made his debut at Chemnitz in 1913 as Tamino in *Die Zauberflöte*, and his final appearance was as Don Ottavio in *Don Giovanni* at Covent Garden in 1947. That had been the rôle in which his merit was first widely recognized as something well beyond the ordinary. In 1924 his Ottavio was hailed as a performance so polished and compelling that the opera almost regrouped itself, with this often weakly portrayed character as its centre. The *cantilena* of 'Dalla sua pace' ravished the ear, and the brilliance of 'Il mio tesoro' dazzled the senses. In Dresden, Vienna and Berlin he became known as the finest Mozart tenor of the age.

He was also one of the most adaptable and hard-working of singers. To

1

the standard lyric repertoire of Almaviva in *Il barbiere di Siviglia*, Alfredo in *La traviata*, Faust, Don José and so forth, he added the leading Puccini rôles (including Calaf in the German premiere of *Turandot)*, and in 1928 Florestan in some famous performances of *Fidelio* with Lotte Lehmann. There were many premieres and operas that came and went in a single season. Others, such as his Lenski in *Eugene Onegin*, Tonio in *La fille du régiment,* and even the Steersman in *Tristan und Isolde* were collector's pieces of the kind opera-goers love to have stored away in the memory-box. His musicianship and quickness in learning became legendary, especially after 1915 when he sang Bacchus in *Ariadne auf Naxos* at forty-eight hours' notice and with the benefit of only a single rehearsal with Strauss at the piano.

This is Richard Tauber as musicians prefer to think of him. He was also an accomplished Lieder singer, and if his style in *Winterreise* and *Dichterliebe* (as far as we can judge from records) was personal and romantic it was also exercised with evident intelligence and sensitivity.

But there was another side to him. In 1922 he sang at the Theater an der Wien in Lehár's *Frasquita*. The Director of the State Opera did not like it, for dignity seemed to be compromised when one of his leading singers was heard in a secondary house and in a second-rate type of music. But out of the corner of his eye the Director must also have sensed that there was something to be gained, for the Serenade in that operetta is a very catchy tune and whenever the Viennese hummed it over to themselves the voice they heard singing it in their heads was Tauber's; and so on nights when he was singing at the Opera there was a fair chance that the house would be full and business would flourish. *Frasquita*, however, was only the beginning. Lehár recognized in Tauber his ideal tenor; and he wrote *Paganini* with him specifically in mind. At its premiere in Vienna Tauber was abroad and the piece failed dismally; when it opened later in Berlin he took the lead and it triumphed. *Der Zarewitsch* followed in 1927, then *Friederike* and, in 1929, the operetta which became inseparable from Tauber and which evokes his memory even now, *Das Land des Lächelns*. Each of them had its specially designed Tauberlied ('every Tauberlied a Zauberlied' as Irving Kolodin happily put it), and *Das Land des Lächelns* had the most successful of them all, 'Dein ist mein ganzes Herz' or, still more famously, 'You are my heart's delight'.

That song became to him like the little lamb to Mary in the nursery rhyme, for wherever Tauber went that song was sure to go. At a tender age I myself was taken to a Tauber recital and though I remember little else I do recall the piteous wails which attended his announcement, at encore-time, that he would not be singing 'that song'. Lamentation turned to joy only when he also announced that not merely 'You are my heart's delight' but the whole land of smiles would be transported to our theatre in a month or so's time. For some reason I was not taken to that: I think it was put to me that it was about a Chinaman and I probably wouldn't

2

A Tauber night in Hungary

like it. And indeed its popularity was rather extraordinary. When first shown in London, in 1931, it aroused the wonder of the *Observer*'s theatre-critic, Ivor Brown, who found it almost passed belief that 'a singer with a presence so little romantic ... impersonating, if you please, a Chinese diplomat ... should be able to magnetize his audience to the top of adoration's bent'. The voice, he said, did it all: 'he smiles and chants, flourishes an arm as though he were leading the orchestra of the world's desires, and chants again.'

The song and its singer duly went round the world, though as the 1930s slouched towards their grim conclusion Germany became closed to him (for he was part-Jewish) and so all too soon did his beloved Vienna. Films enlarged his following, as did his recordings, the selections for which became increasingly 'popular' in nature. The penalty was that serious musicians began not to take him seriously. It then came as a surprise, in 1938, and in some quarters it was viewed with misgiving, when he was engaged for the season at Covent Garden. In the event he drew praise from most, yet the reviews show him to have been a marked man, everybody waiting to pounce if they found Mozart confounded with Lehár. Stephen Williams, in the *Daily Mail*, voiced the general feeling at *Die Zauberflöte* on the opening night. Tauber, he said, presented 'a virile and romantic

4

Tamino', giving 'a performance which perhaps disappointed his admirers but undoubtedly relieved his detractors .... He gave passion and character to this rather wooden-headed hero, and only once or twice during a painfully affected *mezza voce* did I feel that Mozart's grave must be suffering some disturbance.'

When he made his last appearance in the house, on 27 September 1947, the critics seem to have forgotten the grudges of those days and to have remembered only that here, in their midst and in his old rôle of Ottavio in *Don Giovanni*, was one of the great Mozart singers of the century. He was by then a desperately sick man. What it cost him to sing that night can have been equalled only by the satisfaction of being united with the company in which he had once been a star. The Vienna State Opera was on a brief visit to London, and he sang with it that night by special request. The following evening he made a last broadcast after which he went to hospital where he died on 8 January, aged fifty-six. Lehár, now seventy-eight, died later that same year.

Wonderfully (though by now we take the wonder for granted) that is not the end of the story. His last published recording, prophetically perhaps, was of a song called 'There is no end'. Records ensure that; as long, at any rate, as there are people to listen to them. Tauber's official discography runs to over seven hundred items, and there are many more than that when transcriptions from broadcasts and so forth are taken into account.

What they show above all is an artist who made everything live. Limited in range and power, increasingly subject to vowel-distortion on the high notes, his voice nevertheless could be the most seductive in the world. With it he teases and excites, plays every trick in the book and others of which he alone had the mastery. But as the years go by, the more spurious tricks recede, and the true character of the artist shapes up with stronger definition. The unique musician remains, as the man with the monocle begins to fade.

CHAPTER 2

Emma Calvé

Calvé's life was never short of incident, and when, at the age of eighty, she learned that there were people in Hollywood who might value her help in making a film about it, she approached the new adventure with all the ardour of a girl preparing for her first ball.

In the event she was disappointed. The plans came to nothing, which was perhaps as well for no doubt it would have been a terrible film. Still, there was plenty of material. She herself had supplied much of it in a first autobiography, *My Life*, published in translation in 1922 and supplemented by some memoirs, *Sous tous les ciels j'ai chanté*, completed in 1939, resonant of title if somewhat shaky in its facts.

My Life is an astonishing document. Emotionally, it cultivates the grand thrill, the verbal equivalent of the dramatic gesture, some great actress (the Duse, perhaps, whom Calvé adored) throwing an arm across her chest while the head is lifted in an expression of noble intensity. The book tells of lost loves, suffering, and the restoration of the will to live by such means as a song arising from the hearse-like gondola at deep midnight on the Grand Canal. 'In the crucible of pain and suffering, my spirit seemed to have developed a new sensitiveness, a new power of sympathy, a wider understanding of life and art.' There are the triumphs, the gratifications of fame which sometimes took a charming form as at Honolulu, where on arrival at the harbour 'we beheld a fleet of little balloons floating over the city, to each one of which was attached a large picture of myself'. At St Petersburg the enthusiasm was more alarming: officers and cadets climbed on stage, kissing and even biting her arm: ' "Fiends! Savages!" I cried. "Are you going to devour me? Let me pass." ' At which they duly conducted her to a waiting troika: that was the life.

In Rome she learned the secrets of the *quatrième voix* from one of the last castrati in the Sistine Choir. In Chicago she first heard of the Swami Vivekananda, who became her guru accompanying her on agreeable trips to Egypt and the Middle East, and whose voice she would hear giving sage advice long years after his physical departure from this world. In Constantinople she frightened the Sultan, who feared that Carmen's dance presaged an attack upon his life. In Houston, then an inconsiderable town where the Metropolitan Opera's touring train stopped for an hour, she

entertained three hundred cowboys. These 'fine strapping fellows, who greeted us with whoops and cries in true Western style', were reduced to tears ('their heads on each other's shoulders') by Melba's rendition of *Home, sweet home*, after which Calvé cheered them up with the 'dance gestures and gay grimaces' of 'a dashing Spanish air'.

Other episodes described in the autobiography suggest the stage-manager's hand, or at least the rosy spectacles of a creative memory. She was a great believer in omens, evil eyes and dreams. Her dead father appeared in a dream one night and urged a visit to Arles. The town was sufficiently near to her castle at Cabrières for this to be a practicable proposition, so she awoke the household and set off with them to arrive just as the ceremonial unveiling of a monument to the poet Mistral was finishing. On the outskirts of the crowd, she began her favourite Provençal song, 'O Magali'. The people opened a pathway for her and, still singing, she walked to the platform. Then, 'looking out over the sea of upturned faces I sang, with a complete and joyous abandon, all the Provençal songs that I knew'. She stopped when exhausted. Mistral then, 'in the warm language of the South', improvised a prose-poem of appreciation: 'You came down from the mountains .... The crowd parted to let you pass, swept back by the fire of your oncoming, your voice like a sword, a leaping flame.' The crowd eventually dispersed. It had been a memorable occasion, but had lasted rather longer than expected.

Calvé always considered herself a child of the hills and the countryside. There was also a Spanish element in her upbringing, for the family moved from the village of Decazeville to northern Spain three months after her birth in 1858. There she remained till the age of seven, emerging with a speech compounded of Spanish, Basque, French and the *patois* of all three. This had to be sorted out in the convent school at Millau. She sang almost before she spoke; she also danced, and observed the Spanish gypsies. At the convent, speech and manners were no doubt tamed, her singing too, but it was as a singer rather than as a nun that she found her vocation, and all roads led to Paris.

Three years' study there led to some concert work but not much else till 1882 when she made her operatic debut at the Monnaie in Brussels. She sang four rôles – Marguerite in *Faust*, Cherubino in *Le nozze di Figaro*, Alice in Meyerbeer's *Robert le diable* and Salomé in Massenet's *Hérodiade*. Six months with Mathilde Marchesi in Paris did not quite make her a Marchesi pupil and in fact she seems not entirely to have hit it off with the famous teacher. She sang with Victor Maurel's company in a wider repertoire, then at the Opéra-Comique and at Nice, securing an engagement at La Scala, Milan, in 1886, which proved a complete disaster, for she was hissed.

She appeared elsewhere in Italy with more success, and eventually returned in triumph to La Scala in one of her great rôles, the Ophelia of Thomas's *Hamlet*. But the fiasco forced her to restudy, this time with the teacher of whom she always spoke with most gratitude, Rosine Laborde. The other essential influence was that of the great actress, Eleonore Duse, in whose art Calvé saw something that she herself could bring to the operatic stage. And this she did. At Rome in 1891 she sang Suzel in the world premiere of *L'amico Fritz*, and though Mascagni seems not to have shared the general enthusiasm, she enjoyed a marked personal success, with a greater one to follow as Santuzza in *Cavalleria rusticana*. Then, in 1892, came *Carmen*. The first of what she (over?) estimated at three thousand performances was given in Paris, followed by London and New York, and she became quite simply one of the most celebrated women in the world.

Of her performances at the Metropolitan in 1893 W.J. Henderson of the *Sun* wrote: 'It was on the night of November 29, 1893, that we first learned to know Santuzza in *Cavalleria rusticana*. On December 20 Madame Calvé taught us the meaning of Carmen.' Her Carmen, he said, was frequently 'the exhalation of a passing mood … at other times she is as strong and as fathomless as the seven seas'. Her Ophelia he ranked as 'one of the master creations of the lyric stage. Of course her great triumph in the part was reached in the mad scene, which had been used as a piece of vocal fireworks in the concert room so often that its dramatic possibilities were not known. Madame Calvé showed us that this mad scene was one of the opportunities of a dramatic singer's career. The technical difficulties she overcame in a manner which proved that as a vocalist pure and simple she had few equals. But her conquest was in imbuing every measure with emotional eloquence, while she accompanied her song with look and action suited to the word.' The account has a familiar ring. It might have been written sixty years later about another Madame C in another mad scene, and provides commentary on the quaint notion that acting on the operatic stage began with Callas.

In later years it seems that the famous portrayals coarsened. Gramophone records afford no more than a glimpse of her real art, and even then less in the solos of Carmen than in her duet, 'Là-bas dans la montagne', which she recorded with the stylish tenor Charles Dalmorès. Here, though modern listeners will find the drawing-out of the triplets disconcerting and the unscripted high B somewhat alarming, she gives a vivid performance: in spite of its liberties (or perhaps partly because of them) I have come to find it the most fascinating and even the most right-feeling of all recorded performances of the scene. Her most amazing record is that of a song called 'Ma Lisette', where the head-voice sustains soft high notes of unearthly and most beautiful quality. Nor would I be without her 'Old folks at home', with its magically softened tones echoing 'all de world am sad and dreary' in a way to make the cowboys weep.

There are some fine, clear and firm-voiced records made around the age of sixty, and she continued to give concerts to audiences who, as the *New York Times* put it in 1922, were appreciative of the things she did do and indulgent towards those she did not. She was an indefatigable teacher at her château ('Madame was always first one up in the morning', the girls reported). And two days from her death, near the end of a long and harrowing illness, she made a last record. In it she reads from her autobiography a passage recalling the day in 1916 when she sang the 'Marseillaise' to ten thousand New Yorkers and with a *poilu*'s helmet in her hands, borne aloft by the multitude, collected dollars for war-ravaged France.

France, said the Mayor of Millau shortly after her death in 1942, would never forget her, and her grave in Millau would become a place of pilgrimage and welcome for lovers of art the world over. In the Hotel Emma Calvé a few years ago an offhand woman gestured towards a wall where I found a dingy typewritten information-sheet. In the cemetery the keeper managed to find the grave and apologetically murmured something about the inconveniences of dying in wartime.

Calvé as Ophelia in *Hamlet*

CHAPTER 3

Elisabeth Schwarzkopf

I imagine that every prima donna from Faustina and Cuzzoni onwards has had, or might have had, a drawer labelled 'Commendatory verses'. Schwarzkopf, distinguished in this as in all else, could at least claim for hers a piece of work by a real poet. 'Elisabeth Schwarzkopf in New York' is the title of a sonnet by Robert Lowell (a sonnet in as far as it is fourteen lines long, and has two themes or subjects brought into some sort of relationship).* The trouble with real poets, especially those of the present century, is that they are not always entirely easy to understand. I personally would not be eager to paraphrase Lowell's thoughts here, but his description at one point is strikingly vivid and in turn suggests lines of thought which, if not the poet's own, may in a roundabout way lead us back to him.

'Cardigans', of all unpoetic words, is what fixes it. 'La diva...', he says, 'roughs it with chaff, and cardigans at recordings'. In between the noun-subject and the verb he summons up briefly a little picture of her in public performance (Carnegie Hall or the Metropolitan): 'crisped, remodelled for the boards'. But just now he has seen her in a recording session, presumably the one in New York with Glen Gould, where (again presumably) he was an invited guest. In the studio she is not 'la diva' but a working woman. The glamour of the great singer from Europe, the expensive hair-do, the elegant gown, the sophistication of beauty – unattainable as in a Dietrich or Garbo – are all in limbo: here is a sturdy, middle-aged woman, engaged with everybody else in the job in hand, and wearing a cardigan.

Poets are creatures of wonder. That is, they see things which are observed at the time by ten, fifty, a hundred pairs of eyes, but the poet's is the mind in which the wonder of prosaic fact lingers and glows into words. Lowell stays a little longer with the ordinary sight of the working, middle-aged woman 'roughing' it. She might, he ruminates, be the visiting friend or relative (everybody has one) who 'is no trouble' and lends a hand with the washing-up: 'like anyone's single and useful weekend guest'. And if you

---

* References here are to the poem in its revised form, *Midwinter* (no. 7), *Notebooks*, Faber 1970.

11

said to a neighbour casually dropping in for a cup of coffee 'Let me introduce you – Elisabeth Schwarzkopf', you would see the neighbour's well-mannered face adjust, to superimpose the glamorous image of 'la diva' on the unmade-up, cardiganed guest thus presented.

The poet has caught at a truth (I also have been at a recording session and know what he means, in this part of his poem at least). Schwarzkopf herself must have a keen, and I should think interesting, conviction about identities. The working woman dresses for work, and a singer's work is perhaps 75 per cent (more?) practice, preparation and rehearsal. The public self is another thing. In some sense, 'Schwarzkopf' was a creation, a work of art in itself. The standards which she and her husband set so rigorously in music were also embodied in this creation. Schwarzkopf's appearance on the concert platform told of standards that already had something of the past about them. It had nothing to do with the contemporary age of casual dress and anyhow-hair, of pop-culture whether manifest in manner or manners, expression in the eyes or set of the mouth. There was a time, not so distant, when people admiring the quality of some household article or piece of furniture would say 'Ah, that's a bit of good pre-war'. Or perhaps readers will remember how in *Nineteen Eighty-Four* Winston comes upon a pad of particularly fine, creamy writing-paper and delights in it because he knows it must have been made in the age before the Revolution. There was some feeling of that sort about Schwarzkopf's presence on the concert platform.

This was what she and Walter Legge, but he particularly, wanted the post-war public to have. He, married to Schwarzkopf in 1953, was also married to an idea, or ideal, which he had preserved since early youth, that of great singing. In the 1920s he was one of the gallery-queue people for the summer seasons at Covent Garden: there are only a few of them left now, but many remembered him, his idealism and his ambition. He was also nurtured from early days on the gramophone records of great singers, and these (records of Titta Ruffo, Sigrid Onegin, Renato Zanelli, Meta Seinemeyer and so forth) remained throughout life as a kind of fuel-resource, something that would always set the idealism freshly aflame. In the young Schwarzkopf he knew he had met a singer, perhaps *the* singer, capable of upholding this tradition. She had the voice and technique (he was an expert judge of both); she had a strong personality; she would never be merely Trilby to his Svengali, but had the intelligence to make artistic collaboration fruitful, forming, as he said, 'the longest and happiest musical association of my life'.

It is worth recalling just how varied and satisfying a career Schwarzkopf's was. We tend to remember the recitalist at the expense of the opera singer (naturally, because she continued in concert work until 1979, having retired from opera eight years earlier). The Vienna Opera heard her originally as a soprano *leggiero* (and Legge heard her first as Rosina in *Il barbiere di Siviglia*); she became their Donna Elvira and later a triumphant Fiordiligi. Elvira and the Countess at Salzburg, Eva at Bayreuth, Anne Trulove in the premiere of *The Rake's Progress* at Vienna were special events; repertory appearances at Covent Garden in operas as diverse as *Die Zauberflöte* (an exquisite Pamina), *La traviata*, *Rigoletto*, *Manon*, *Der Rosenkavalier* (as Sophie) and *La Bohème* were bread-and-butter for a few years from 1947 on. A chapter sometimes overlooked concerns Schwarzkopf at La Scala. She made her house-debut there, predictably enough perhaps as Countess Almaviva, at the end of 1948, then sang Elisabeth in *Tannhäuser*, followed by Anne Trulove in 1951 and her first Marschallin in '52. *Lohengrin*, *Pelléas et Mélisande* and *Faust* were other collector's pieces, as were staged performances of Orff's *Carmina burana*, *Catulli carmina* and *Trionfo di Afrodite* under Karajan. For many years she appeared regularly at the San Francisco Opera, and in 1965 made her long-deferred debut at the Met, as the Marschallin, with a gala some days later comprising three first acts and three prima donnas to go with them – Schwarzkopf in *Der Rosenkavalier*, *La Bohème* with Tebaldi, and Sutherland in *La traviata*. Schwarzkopf's retirement from the stage was also in Act I of *Der Rosenkavalier*, at La Monnaie in Brussels, fulfilling a promise made years earlier that this was where she would take her leave.

'Die alte Marschallin' is a phrase Lowell remembers. 'Wo ist Silvia' he chants, presumably to represent Schwarzkopf in the concert hall; and the phrase from *Der Rosenkavalier* would have recalled her appearances at the Met. Of course, at that time neither the Marschallin nor Schwarzkopf herself could be described as 'die Alte'. But 'I have been young and now am old', as the Psalmist says, and Schwarzkopf, unthinkably (like the Marschallin contemplating her future self as 'die alte Fürstin Resi'), has passed seventy.* Again the matter of identity arises. Her rôle now is teacher, again with its own costume: not the voluminous gown of the prima donna or the cardigan of the woman at work, but the austerity of the professor.

Television viewers may remember an interview four or five years ago in which Schwarzkopf discussed her teaching. If my memory is correct, she was dressed with extreme simplicity and in black: it struck me then that here was a survival of the real old German school, where the teacher teaches: no jolly-jolly do-your-own-thing and call-me-Betty, but instruction from a position of authority. The camera, as it came in for its close-up of the face, showed a beauty ensured by bone structure that time cannot touch. And there were also humanity and humour behind the severity. But essentially this was another reminder of the European tradition that Schwarzkopf personifies, in this instance one in which mastery is passed on by those who have acquired it, in an exacting school where the only certain reward is that of hard work towards high standards.

* This was at the time of writing. Schwarzkopf was born on 9 December 1915.

14

Her own standards, as singer and teacher, have been directed towards matters of musical understanding and interpretation. Behind that were her purely vocal qualities: in all those years I never heard her produce a note with any suspicion of wobble, and it was rare for the tone not to be pure and radiant. No doubt it was this purity of sound that gave Lowell a sensation of 'trembling like water-ivy down my spine'. Again the poet finds special words for the common experience. He also makes it clear (if obscurely) that the cause of the *frisson* goes deeper. It has to do, I think, with the thrilled awareness of a high European culture. Whether as the working woman in cardigans or as *la diva* 'remodelled for the boards', Elisabeth Schwarzkopf is perceived as its representative. Here she is, a living presence in New York: the art she embodies is itself the embodiment of that culture.

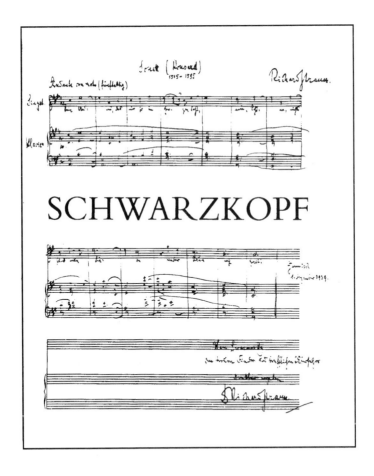

CHAPTER 4

Feodor Chaliapin

Genius: The word lay spread in infinite repetitions thick upon the ground where Chaliapin trod. Eventually all the many individual, true and spontaneous tributes came together to form one great placard, which would hang upon him for eternity. Sometimes, squinting in an uncertain light, the eye seemed to make out another word in its place: perhaps it said 'Showman'. Occasionally that too appeared to change and may have read 'Child' or even, though in tiny print so that only those nearest to him could make it out, 'Big Baby'.

But about the genius there was and is no doubt. Though he was always described as being an artist whom you had to see, we, who must go mainly by the evidence of our hearing (and that at a second remove, through gramophone records), have instant assurance of his greatness. Sight is not entirely denied evidence either, for turning the pages of his biography we can look at the photographs. These show not so much Chaliapin as perhaps two dozen different Chaliapins, or rather two dozen different people incarnate in him. This is not just an illusion created by skilful make-up: even in immobility, expression and posture tell unmistakably of separate characters, complete identities.

On one page, the careworn brow of faithful old Susanin accepts defeat, the cheeks gaunt, the eyes sleepless, the overcoat now too big even for his giant frame, the hand alone telling of determination as it clasps the stick that has helped him on his journey through the snow. Turn the pages and there, mouth turned down at the corners, eyebrows raised, head held high, Don Basilio glances in cynical scorn. Don Quichotte's eyes pop in response to the open book on his knee, the tufts of white hair airy as the ideas now possessing the credulous mind; the spiked moustaches tell of youthful aspiration, and the stringy neck shows old mortality marked out by time. Stooped and aquiline, Ivan the Terrible keeps an ever-wary eye suspiciously alert. Windblown and in rags, the Miller of Dargomyzhsky's *Rusalka* has madness rife in the tension of his hands as in the wildness of his eyes. Dosifei of the Old Believers comprehends the inexorable will of his terrible God. Salieri, with straggly hair and weakly dropping jaw, perceives another kind of horror. Méphistophélès sings his serenade with

16

Chaliapin as the Miller in *Rusalka*

17

mouth crooked as his soul. Boris Godunov stands by the side of his throne in a last agony of body and spirit.

Years ago, a broadcaster told how as a youngster he had been taken to see Chaliapin in *Boris Godunov* at Drury Lane. He was immensely impressed by all those tall Russians and their magnificent bass voices. 'Is this him?' he would ask. 'No, no, not yet' came the answer. But with each new soloist (and there are quite a few before Boris' entry) he kept asking, only to be told: 'When it's him, you'll know'. And so it was: the great figure, the great voice, the personal magnetism. 'When Chaliapin moved, the whole stage moved with him,' Ezio Pinza wrote, thinking back to performances at the Met where he had sung the rôle of the monk Pimen and so for one scene shared that shifting stage with the great man. Others recount how at rehearsal of the Clock Scene in Paris the hallucination was so real that people stood on their seats to make out what it was that the Tsar saw so clearly and with such terrorstricken eyes.

Much has been written about Chaliapin. Because he was so eminently an actor-singer and his appearance on-stage made such a vivid impression, he was an easier and more rewarding subject for the writer than those who were singers first and foremost. Moreover, before the First World War, he was part of a movement, exciting in its newness and promise. One who catches the special thrill is the publisher Victor Gollancz, whose memoirs, *Journey Towards Music*, have 24 June 1913 as a great landmark. To the London public, not only Chaliapin, but *Boris Godunov* itself, was new. 'The sense of anticipation in the gallery that night was keener than at any performance I had ever attended, the premiere of *Elektra* not excepted.' The blazing richness of the stage production, the colour and resonance of the choral singing, later in the season the splendour of the Russian ballet, and of course the presence of Beecham, the magician who had made it all happen: everything has its place in Gollancz's narration, but the memory of Chaliapin still towers above the rest. 'You might perhaps have thought that it was not acting at all but superb natural dignity, had it not been for the scene with the chiming clocks, and for the death scene at the close.' The voice, as he says, was 'less easily describable' but he suggests 'something of the look of a flame rising high and steady but with a little smoke about it' or 'think of autumn at its gravest and most beautiful; of words deep with compassion; of Casals' cello, that above everything: for Chaliapin had all the qualities of a great singer and something extra as well, something I have found, among musical executants, in Chaliapin's singing and Casals' playing almost alone.' Beyond this, alas, he too admits defeat and has to resort to 'some unanalysable residue in the voice and way of singing [that] made him unique'.

Those were Chaliapin's kingly days. Later, though 'genius' was tagged to him more resolutely than ever, all was not quite as before. More of his appearances took place on the concert platform, and he needed a stage.

18

Chaliapin in three roles: *above* as Boris Godunov;
left above as Basilio in *Il barbiere di Siviglia*;
left below as Varlaam in *Boris Godunov*.

His instinctive solution was to introduce an operatic element into his recitals, not so much in the repertoire as in the style. First, an element of surprise was created by his unusual programmes: that is, there *was* no programme, but a book containing the texts of roughly a hundred items from which he would announce his choice. Then there was his platform manner, which involved a lot of gesturing, conducting the accompanist, and walking about. In the postlude to *The Two Grenadiers* of Schumann he would sometimes stagger off to die quietly in the wings. Critics also became speedily disillusioned with what they called the 'hymnbook' method of programming: they felt that the songs which came up most regularly were those in which they could see least musical value, and when

19

something more in their line, such as Schubert's *Ständchen* or *Der Doppel-gänger*, was announced they would find it maltreated in some way that would not have been tolerated had not genius so evidently been in question.

In opera too there was a growing sense that he was exhibiting a solo turn. His voice now seemed smaller, less regal. In *Il barbiere di Siviglia* he 'lifted Basilio to a prominence that he never enjoyed in this opera before. So much can a great artist achieve without detriment to the balance or the consistency of a dramatic ensemble.' That was Herman Klein's charitable view in his retrospect for *Gramophone* magazine in 1926. He went on to describe Chaliapin's originality, staying back on his supposed expulsion after 'Buona sera', singing a kind of drone till it drew attention and then being forced out as he was thought to have been in the first place. As Méphistophélès in 1928 he seemed more certain of his position as principal attraction than of his words or other details of the opera. His call to the conductor across the footlights ('Plus vite! Plus vite!') was widely reported, as was the unexpected success of the young American baritone John Charles Thomas as Valentin. Even in his great rôle of Boris some felt that this style of acting, in theatre at least, had gone out with Beerbohm Tree.

Behind the scenes he could also be difficult. At the Met once in *Don Quichotte* he arrived somewhat precipitately on horseback, the horse, it was said, having been jabbed in the flanks by a disgruntled stagehand. Going through that opera for the first time in piano score with the composer, the big man had wept so copiously that Massenet had to remind him that there would be plenty of time for blubbering at a later date onstage. In private life too he could be a trial, as once when he waded out sufficiently far into the sea to attract attention without getting too wet, and complained to his rescuers that nobody loved him.

But this was a man who had known real cold and hunger. He came from the backstreets of Kazan. He had starved, begged, worked and observed. He came through to St Petersburg and Moscow, broke the moulds of conventionality and became the embodiment of a new and living school of Russian opera. In the West he transformed the view of what an opera singer might be. He *sang*, certainly, and often his status purely as a singer has been underestimated or taken for granted. He also breathed into his characters an intensely vivid life, and it was in this that his genius lay.

CHAPTER 5

Amelita Galli-Curci

Readers of Nancy Mitford's *The Pursuit of Love* will remember Uncle Matthew whose up-in-the-morning-early *aubade* was a selection on his great horn gramophone of the recordings of Madame Amelita Galli-Curci. More often than not it was 'Lo, here the gent-el la-ark' that regaled the household, but sometimes they awoke to 'Una voce poco fa' or the Mad Scene from *Lucia di Lammermoor*. But then came a terrible day. The celebrated soprano arrived on these shores, and Uncle Matthew went to Liverpool to hear her. He returned deeply reticent of his experience, and the gentle lark was heard no more.

It is a sad little tale and has the ring of truth. Galli-Curci came to Britain for the first time in 1924 and expectations ran feverishly high. The Albert Hall, it was said, sold out on the opening of the box-office eight months before the first concert. Uncle Matthew was not alone in his devotion to her recordings. Every house in the land, where a wind-up gramophone could be afforded (or tolerated) and where there were any aspirations towards the possession of a 'celebrity' label, had its Galli-Curci. Tales of her triumphs abroad made news in the *Daily Mail* if not in *The Times* and, through this marvellous new medium which brought the celebrity into the home, the brilliance of her technique and the purity of her tones were manifest. But things were not always quite the same in the flesh.

Not that Galli-Curci was a creation of the gramophone record: hers was a genuine opera-house success. Her triumph at Chicago on 18 November 1916 was like Joan Sutherland's in London on 17 February 1959, a once-in-a-lifetime operatic happening when, with a contagion of excited conviction, everybody (except the crusty few) says 'To hell with inhibitions about cliché and rash judgements, I will stake my bottom dollar that this day a star is born'. There had been no advance ballyhoo and the furore was not a one-off, never-quite-so-good-again occasion; in one performance after another, season by season, she gave all that was expected of her, and more.

She was indeed a lovely and distinguished singer, but disappointments did arise. One no doubt had to do with the recordings. The voice beamed into the drawing-room with such brilliance and was so exceptional in respect of range, accomplishment, beauty of tone, and individuality of

style that people assumed it must be exceptional in volume too. It was not; and though many listeners have testified to its celestial quality particularly in the quieter lyrical passages of an opera such as *La traviata* (which she sang for her debut at the Metropolitan in 1921), hers was not, in the great spaces of that auditorium at any rate, a voice for thrills in sheer brilliance of projection. Also, in many countries (such as Britain) she was heard not in opera but only in recital work, which limited her scope for presenting the Galli-Curci people had come to know through her operatic 'coloratura' records. And finally there was the physical fact of a goitre, a throat tumour which was removed in 1935 but which had apparently been growing for fifteen years.

It seems extraordinary that this was not dealt with earlier. Fifteen years takes her back to 1920 or '21, the crucial time when the call to the Met came, and with that, the opening night of the first season without Caruso, when she must have felt like one sitting on top of the world. But her biography (*Galli-Curci's Life of Song* by C.E. Le Massena, first published in 1945) is unusually frank: she had 'kept on until there was insufficient room for proper breath passage to ensure full tone production' and 'only by potent will-power did she secure enough volume to get them [her tones] across to her audiences'. It explains a feature of her later recordings, that the high notes have lost body and penetration; and even the later pre-electrical recordings have an occasional fallibility in intonation around the note F at the top of the stave.

But, whether through the independence of spirit that was in other ways a great strength, or from whatever cause, she seems to have lacked a wise directing influence in her career. Was it ever there? Her beginnings were unorthodox. She was brought up in a musical family and studied the piano, till one day Mascagni came to the house in Milan and during an intermission in his endless talk heard the girl play and sing. He recommended that she should be a singer rather than a pianist, and in her mind that decided it. She taught herself, diligently and with intelligence, evolving a composite method of her own and eventually preparing the rôle of Gilda in *Rigoletto* for her debut. That was at Trani on Boxing Day, 1906, when Galli-Curci was 'officially' seventeen, or, accepting the more probable 1882 as the year of her birth, twenty-four. By trial and error, with experience and cautiously growing repertoire, she sang world wide. Originally 'Amelita Galli', she married the Marchese di Sineri and added his name of Curci to her own. Increasing success in South America led to an engagement in Chicago and so to the great day (also her birthday) in 1916 when the cheering began in earnest and the whole world came to hear of it.

So far so good: ten years from debut to stardom sounds about right. The next ten (despite the Marchese being found, metaphorically, with his hands in the till so that separation was followed by divorce) were the years of triumph: a fame and adulation that is hard now to imagine (but perhaps

Pavarotti's in our own time comes nearest). Even then the need for wise direction was clear. It was not only a question of the throat-ailment. Her operatic repertoire remained small, limited to roughly a dozen lyric-coloratura rôles. Years ago, indeed, in South America, she had sung Sophie in *Der Rosenkavalier*, but there was no chance of that now, nor of expanding the *bel canto* repertoire, for these operas had not been redis-covered. So there remained the very different world of the concert hall, and we are back in the year 1924, with the first British tour and the sad experience of Uncle Matthew.

ALEXANDRA PALACE
WOOD GREEN.

Saturday, NOV. 22 at 8

GALLI-CURCI
CONCERT

(By arrangement with Messrs. EVANS & SALTER, of New York).

STEINWAY GRAND PIANOFORTE.

TICKETS (including Tax): **21/-, 14/6, 12/-, 8/6, 5/9 & 3/6**

NOW ON SALE at the BOX OFFICE ALEXANDRA PALACE, N.22

LIONEL POWELL & HOLT, 6, Cork Street, London, W.1.

ROYAL ALBERT HALL
Manager - · HILTON CARTER, M.V.O.

Saturday, NOV. 29 at 2.30

EXTRA RECITAL
by Madame AMELITA

GALLI-CURCI

(By arrangement with Messrs· EVANS & SALTER, of New York).

STEINWAY GRAND PIANOFORTE

Tickets (including Tax)— **NOW ON SALE**

Reserved: Stalls 21/-, Arena 15/- & 12/-, Balcony 7/6, Lower Orchestra 7/6

Unreserved: Orchestra 5/9, Gallery Promenade 3/6.

May be obtained at the BOX OFFICE, ROYAL ALBERT HALL, LIBRARIES, USUAL AGENTS, and of

LIONEL POWELL & HOLT, 6, Cork Street, W.1

A stamped addressed envelope must accompany all applications for Tickets by post.

Booking Telephone: Regent 600.   Box Office open 10 to 5.   Saturday 10 to 12.

A more articulate British devotee, also disappointed and perplexed, was Compton Mackenzie. In his new magazine, *The Gramophone*, he said that he could face old age with equanimity if he had as many records of Galli-Curci as of Caruso. But he too travelled to hear her in person, and found that, for one thing, nobody seemed to have taught her how to take the stage. She entered like a mouse that had taken the wrong turning. Or, putting it another way, she gave the audience no time to realize her presence and to respond: she looked charming, with her red rose, black hair and golden shawl, but you had just about become aware that something bright had arrived when she began to sing. Moreover, she sang songs, modest, uneventful little things, and not till the end, with Dinorah's *Shadow Song* from the opera by Meyerbeer, did the audience fully realize that Amelita Galli-Curci was in their midst. Later, when he met her, Mackenzie suggested that she sing 'Casta diva': did she ever include that in her concert programmes? No: the idea seemed to her to be quite daring and original. She had by then married her nice, good, gentle accompanist, Homer Samuels. What she probably needed was a Walter Legge.

CHAPTER 6

Tito Gobbi

Gobbi's voice was one of the most beautiful I ever heard. If the reader rightly detects a note of mild defiance in that, it must be because both of us know that beauty of sound was not among the qualities most conspicuously attributed to him.

For one thing, he paid the usual price of the actor-singer (Chaliapin being the prime example): people were so busy looking at him that they almost forgot to think about what they heard. He himself was partly responsible. Particularly in later years, almost everything he did emphasised the actor and neglected the singer. On television we saw him change himself stage-by-stage into old fatguts Falstaff, or, affixing the important nose and arching the eyebrow, he became supercilious Scarpia, a man of brute power and aristocratic manners such as all Rome might fitly bow before. These were the things he discussed in his writings. *My Life* (1979) and *Tito Gobbi on his World of Italian Opera* (1984) make interesting reading, but there is more of theatre in them than of music; more character than *cantabile*. That went to some degree for his singing too. Often he put his voice to purposes in which sheer beauty of sound played only a very limited part. Sometimes this could be defended as a deliberate feature of the performance: the quest for dramatic truth. At other times the roughnesses (they were of varied kinds) seemed to result from a technique and sense of style that were in part faulty. But the material, the natural timbre, of the voice was quite another thing. It was rich, vibrant, characteristically Italian, yet personal too, and quite exceptionally beautiful. I think I became conscious of this one night, halfway through *Don Giovanni*. It must have been in the Serenade or 'Là ci darem la mano', but it suddenly came like a revelation that this was a voice I was going to thirst for when it was no longer with us.

And that is true: if the genie of the magic lamp or the operator of the time-machine were to offer a voyage back to hear one voice from past 'live' experience, I would ask for Gobbi. At least, it might be a toss-up between him and Corelli (they were both voices you wanted to *drink*); but Gobbi would call most on the affections provided that he was not singing too loudly or too high, too emphatically or too much 'in character' for that darker tone, with its sweet-sad vibrations, the potent, very distinctive

vowel-sounds, to come through. Even now, the inner ear can *just* manage to recapture the sound as it was (not the sound on records, though they are faithful enough); but how it yearns to catch, if only for a moment or two, the physical sound itself.

Of course, one can quite understand why it was that in his books, talks and classes, so much was said about characterisation rather than singing; quite apart from the interest involved, it is so much easier to talk about. So also, as a member of his audiences, when one thinks back to those many nights when he was there – an almost inevitable figure onstage in certain operas, yet never so familiar that one lost the sense of distinction – it is the visual memory that survives most readily. As Iago he stands in front of a pillar in the quartet of Act II, his eyes slyly watchful of the others, his lips curling with a sort of complacent disdain. As Scarpia there was something curiously froglike about him. Not in the arrival, 'Un tal baccano in chiesa!' – *that* was a moment, to be sure: the presence, the timing, oh and the timbre of the voice, all (in the literal sense) terrific. But in the presence of Tosca, as the manners of the courtier lent a hideously ingratiating aspect to the police-state tyrant, so the large eyes, the wide mouth and lithe posture suggested a peculiarly repulsive and threatening man-size frog.

Was he in fact such a great actor among opera-singers? I'm not absolutely sure that he was, for I can't remember being moved in the theatre (as I certainly have been while listening to his recordings) by his Boccanegra, his Michele in *Il tabarro*, even his Rigoletto. He always commanded attention, that was true; and everything was the strongly concentrated product of thought and feeling, often with real insight. His insights are there on the printed page too. For instance, I don't think that it had ever occurred to me that Rigoletto's emotions on being reunited with his daughter in the Duke's palace are intensified by the pain of her seeing him in his jester's attire and so realising the nature of this occupation that he has kept secret from her all her life. Gobbi makes the point very effectively, and it is one of many. Yet I don't quite recall being moved by it in the theatre, and Andrew Porter's account in *Opera* (August 1956) may suggest why. He pays tribute to what was impressive in Gobbi's performance both vocally and dramatically, but remarks that 'it had no living relationship to the others onstage. The courtiers, Gilda herself, might have been so many stage-props supporting a pre-set interpretation .... It was a tremendously "ham" performance, yet guided by intelligence.'

'Ham', even if mitigated by 'intelligence', is a harsh term, but it was directed at Gobbi more than once. 'You are not *prosciutto*', Walter Legge said to him: 'You are *prosciuttissimo*'. Perhaps the one moment of that Covent Garden *Rigoletto* to remain clearly in my own memory was also 'ham', but if so, like the March Hare's butter, it was the best. As Monterone passes through on his way to execution he denounces the injustice and Rigoletto turns to face the audience like a man inspired, and promises

Gobbi as Rigoletto

vengeance: 'un vindice avrai'. Gobbi gave the E flat from an open throat, with all that fine resonance, and held it, eyes glaring, mouth fierce, before coming down into the 'Si, vendetta'. At such points, 'ham' or not, he could be tremendous.

There were others of a quieter nature: those lines, for instance, at the end of *Gianni Schicchi* where the old rogue addresses the audience, saying that though Dante consigned him to the Inferno he hopes they themselves might take a more tolerant view. The rich tones of the singer's speaking voice warmed the whole house, and we all smiled, applauded and turned out happily to make our ways home. In more complimentary vein, Legge called Gobbi's 'the acting voice' (and Gobbi quotes that one in his memoirs). It implied of course that he was especially adept and useful as a recording artist, very much the male counterpart of Callas. If a 'highlights' disc were issued which included excerpts from the operas these two recorded together, it might indeed be almost too much of a good thing in its intensity. In addition to the scenes from *Tosca* there would be *Rigoletto*, *Un ballo in maschera*, *Aïda* (an incomparable Nile duet), *Lucia di Lammermoor*, *Pagliacci* and, not to be forgotten, one of Callas' rare excursions into comedy, *Il barbiere di Siviglia* under Alceo Galliera, the version which still, to my mind, tops the list as far as wit, character and vitality are concerned. His *Falstaff* with Karajan also remains supreme, and for Gobbi's part in it (though he had a voice that was less susceptible to Falstaffian make-up than was his figure) you can take almost any phrase,

29

at random, and compare it, also at random, with others in the part, and every time the process will demonstrate the completeness of Gobbi's performance.

He had one of those hauntingly individual voices which leave their imprint on phrases and arias. For anybody brought up on Gobbi's recordings it is almost impossible to hear (mentally) another voice in certain of Michele's phrases in *Il tabarro*, or Rodrigo's in *Don Carlos*. Yet, broad as his recorded repertoire is, it still has some notable gaps. It would, for example, have been good to have his Jack Rance in *La fanciulla del West* (and that was a part he had some interesting things to say about, stressing the need to see the man from inside, where, presumably, he does not register as 'the villain'). An aria in which I can always hear his voice, though as far as I know he never sang it, is Barnaba's 'O monumento' in *La Gioconda* (that phrase about the Doge, 'un vecchio scheletro', and then the inspired hailing of the true ruler of Venice, the spy). But the most grievous omission is undoubtedly his *Wozzeck*.* In 1942 he sang the rôle in the first Italian performances of the opera, and repeated it at La Scala in 1952, when Mitropoulos had to appeal to the audience for quiet and co-operation. Gobbi involved himself in this 'martyrdom of flesh and spirit' (as he describes Wozzeck's condition, living in 'an atmosphere of pain and torture') with a seriousness that at times alarmed his wife, who years later showed him a postcard he wrote to her, incoherent in expression and initialled 'W'.

Among the less predictable of his choices for recording are some songs. Respighi's *Nebbie* is one to look for, wonderfully evocative both of the words' sense and of the singer as we heard him in the flesh. The rise and fall of the notes as in a scale exercise reminded me that I once heard Gobbi warming up for the evening's performance at Covent Garden. There were still some people from the vegetable market around, and as I stood in the street, listening and looking towards the dressing-room, one of the barrowmen observed me with some wonderment. 'You a fan?' he asked. A few others had stopped too. ''E's a fan', the man explained; and for a moment all the faces turned towards that open window to catch some notes of the warm south.

---

* Pirated recordings exist of passages broadcast from Rome on 28 September 1954; there are also scenes from *La fanciulla del West*.

30

CHAPTER 7

Nellie Melba

Melba was immense: not with the physical attributes of the joke-prima donna, nor with a voice that would rank among the loudest or highest, but with a style of being, an outsize reputation, an assumption of almost universal command, based on what many would consider a tiny area of achieved and acknowledged perfection.

She was a struggler, and at the end, in her five weeks of fatal illness, she put up what was described as an astonishing fight for life. Always, it seems, whatever was heroic and noble about her got caught up in the mundane and faintly ludicrous: according to her doctor, she died of an infection contracted in England from eating watercress. But her funeral was grand as any Meyerbeer opera, a stately progress befitting one of the giant figures of the nineteenth century: a Wellington, a Lincoln or a Tennyson.

She died in Sydney on 23 February 1931, and as the cortège made its two-hundred-mile journey to Melbourne it was reported that 'at every place of habitation homage was paid to the great singer by her countrymen and countrywomen, and children attending the bush schools stood at attention'. In Melbourne, though the day was unbearably hot, thousands waited around the railway station. Representatives of the Governor-General, the Government and the municipality stood bare-headed. At the funeral, more than five thousand people passed the coffin in the Scots church, and more than five hundred wreaths covered the catafalque. The flags stood at half-mast, traffic was stopped, the twenty-three-mile route to Lilydale cemetery was lined with people, and eventually the Lilydale Boy Scouts, known as 'Melba's own', sounded the Last Post.

All of this was reported in the London *Times*, which also had a leader on her. The anonymous writer mused on the name. It was not, of course, her baptismal name (she was Helen Porter Mitchell), while in print and on formal occasions she became Dame Nellie. But, as *The Times* said, 'in memory and in speech that comes straight to the lips, never anything but Melba ...'.

So what *was* this 'Melba'? Factually, she was an Australian girl, daughter of a Scottish settler at the time of the gold rush who married a musical wife. Their daughter played the piano and the organ, took singing lessons,

and by 1884 was noted in a local paper as singing 'like one out of ten thousand'. Marriage did not prevent her from sailing for London, where Sir Arthur Sullivan held out hope of a small part in one of his operas if she were to undertake a period of further study. This sent her to Paris and to the great Mathilde Marchesi: 'Salvatore! Salvatore! enfin j'ai trouvé une étoile' she is supposed to have called out to her husband having heard the twenty-five-year-old Australian sing her party-piece. After nine months (not long enough, according to Marchesi) the newly-named 'Melba' made her debut in *Rigoletto* in Brussels, where her success was immediate and extreme.

Covent Garden did not fall into her lap on first acquaintance in 1888, but the Paris Opéra did the following year and, domino-like, London, St Petersburg, Milan and New York capitulated each in turn. She became a precious part of what for many was 'the golden age of opera', the decade of the 1890s. In the new century she sang on and on, with performances in almost every London season till 1914. It was also a Melba night that re-opened the house after the war, and she sang her farewell, aged sixty-five, in 1926.

The question remains: 'What was this "Melba"?' The Australian newspaper comes nearest to explaining, with its banal 'one out of ten thousand'. In the first place 'Melba' was the voice. To a casual listener in the present, her recordings may tell of nothing extraordinary in vocal endowment: it might even be difficult to think of the sound as one which would carry in a house the size of the old Metropolitan, La Scala or Covent Garden. But that opinion would probably not last. My own experience is that, to start with, I had no love for the voice, was secretly but deeply disappointed with the first record I bought, as a schoolboy, which was the famous duet with Caruso from *La Bohème*: 'Thank heaven for the top C at the end' was all I could say. 'Depuis le jour' from *Louise* told more, but the 1910 recording of Ophelia's Mad Scene made me laugh, and in everything there was some element of – what to call it? – ungraciousness perhaps. Then versions by other sopranos would appear, and every now and then I would go back to my Melba: always to find myself enlightened and excited at some specific point. Sometimes it was the clean, unhesitating 'take' of a bold interval, sometimes the articulation of a scale or the perfection of a trill. Always it was sufficient to renew the contact, and with the renewal came an extension.

First came a recognition that though Melba was, in the view of many good judges, an exceptionally undramatic, 'cold' singer (Mahler heard her in *La traviata* and said he would have preferred a good clarinettist), nevertheless she brought to her performances something personal, even if it was only energy, which made them live a far more vivid life than most.

The second was that the voice itself was utterly special. Return for a moment to that top C at the end of the *Bohème* duet. There is an oft-quoted appreciation of its effect in the theatre by Mary Garden, Melba's antithesis as an operatic artist but in her time scarcely less famous: 'That note came floating over the auditorium of Covent Garden. It left Melba's throat, it left Melba's body, it left everything and came like a star and passed us in our box and went out into the infinite.' 'Weird' is her adjective, and 'My God, how beautiful it was!' was her less literary but none the less telling exclamation. There is another story, that one night, in Act II of *Bohème*,

Nellie Melba laying the corner stone for the Record Factory, Hayes, 13 May 1907

as the Musetta was about to take one of her high Bs, a different sound appeared in the air, and as though with one accord everyone in the house said to themselves or their neighbour 'Melba!'. No doubt unforgivable, the intrusion must have been unforgettable too, and it illustrates how special and instantly recognisable that voice was. Purity and steadiness, those were two of its attributes. Another was its ability to carry, effortlessly and effectively. In its prime there was another quality: writing after her death, W.J. Henderson, New York's veteran opera critic, sent his memory searching back into the 1890s and retrieved the word 'splendour'. Now this 'splendour' may not be immediately apparent on the records. But try, if you can, to hear (well reproduced) the distance-test she made in 1910 before recording the Mad Scene in Hamlet. She sings a phrase close to the recording horn, and repeats it several times taking a step backwards for each. The first blasts, the third is probably what they settled for: but modern equipment can take the second, and *there* is Melba, and splendour too. Try her again, at the end of her career when electrical recording had come in and you will hear something – not 'brilliant' or perfect, perhaps – but some thing that still makes you sit up. Personally, I find it does much more than that, for I rarely hear her record of 'Swing low, sweet chariot' or of Joseph Szulc's 'Clair de lune' without an unaccountable moistening of the eyes.

She was an extraordinary woman and an extraordinary singer, a mass of paradoxes too, in both respects. She was both coarse and refined (in her life as in her art). She could be mean and generous. She seemed a

34

thoroughly reactionary force in music as it was then developing, and yet a tireless champion of the 'golden-age' standards which she came to embody.

There is a fascinating and supremely well-written short story by Somerset Maugham called *The Voice of the Turtle* (he was a neighbour of Melba's on the Riviera where most of the story takes place). In it he tells of 'La Falterona', an ageing soprano who is vain, brash and in many respects deeply unmusical. Yet, mellowing in mood after supper, she calls out to her female accompanist, 'Shut up, you old cow. Play something, I tell you', and sings first a song by Schumann and then Isolde's *Liebestod*, not part of her public repertoire but sent out into the evening air with a voice which 'even now was exquisite in its quality'. Maugham does not identify the original of his portrait, if it had one; but commenting that everyone has heard of La Falterona, and, giving what surely is a wink and a nod, he says of her reputation that none had a greater, 'not even Melba'.

CHAPTER 8

Maria Ivogün

'If I hear anyone else say that she sings sharp or flat or whatever, I shall … well, I shall hit!' Thus spake a normally mild-mannered and pacific member of the balcony queue at Covent Garden in 1927. His act of gallantry was to be undertaken, should the need arise, in defence of a tiny lady with a fairly tiny voice which was, however, of exquisite quality and used with such skill that on her previous visit three years earlier, she had astonished her listeners and taken all hearts.

'An Ariel of the opera world', one critic had called her: 'an emanation, a woman of fire and air'. She had then sung two rôles: Gilda in *Rigoletto* and Zerbinetta in *Ariadne auf Naxos*. 'The singer's intensity of acting, in which she seems to produce an electric effect quite outside herself' was said to be 'a thing to wonder at'. Her voice was 'pure and fluid in tone' and 'unlike most coloraturas it is capable of great varieties of expression'. After Zerbinetta's solo the ovation that broke from the house appeared to this same critic (A.P. Hatton, *Musical Opinion's* 'Figaro') to show, more than anything else heard there since the end of the war, that great singing could produce such a community of joy in an opera audience that all other forms of entertainment seemed vapid by comparison. After Gilda's 'Caro nome' the most venerable of the resident connoisseurs were seen to be spellbound by this 'spontaneous, ecstatic outpouring of a girl's first love'. That was in 1924. The trouble was that in 1927 her performances were rated 'one of the disappointments of the season'. That was why aspersions had been made in the balcony queue and why the mildest of men felt himself driven almost to fisticuffs.

Maria Ivogün remains a name to conjure with. Its power derives partly from the conviction of a genuine experience conveyed by reports such as those quoted just now. It is strengthened by recordings and there are also the facts of her career which, though it ended early and was largely confined to the three cities of Munich, Vienna and Berlin, nevertheless reached great heights. More than that, she carries with her, in memory and reputation, a sense of quality. The people she impressed were not usually among the most impressionable. When they have talked or written about her it has not been simply as a voice, a technician, an interpreter: there was something special, a refinement in the brilliance, an intensity

36

in the lightness. Whatever its explanation, it was the quality that the great conductor Bruno Walter recognised the instant he heard her, and which Richard Strauss defined as genius.

Walter tells in his *Themes and Variations* (1947) how he sat in for some auditions for the Vienna Opera in 1913, the year when he himself had already been appointed Music Director to the Opera at Munich. In a somewhat forlorn way he listened for talent, knowing that anything really promising would be snapped up by his opposite number, Hans Gregor, for Vienna. A little girl from a good teacher appeared, sang a coloratura aria followed by Mimì's solo in Act I of *La Bohème*, and Walter says he knew immediately that here was a star in the making. He did not allow himself further thought because he was sure she would be accepted. Great was his astonishment, then, when Gregor with his Viennese accent announced: 'Das war nischt!' or 'Nothing to it! Useless!' Walter lost no time, found the shy young woman backstage and so enlisted the services of, as he says, one of the glories of the Munich opera and of the operatic stage in her time.

She was Hungarian by birth, born on 18 November 1891 in Budapest. Her original name was Maria Kempner and the professional name of Ivogün derived from an ingenious contraction of her mother's, Ida von Günter, herself a singer in operetta though not to be confused with the more famous Mizzi Günther who was the first Hanna Glawari in *The Merry Widow*. Maria was educated in Switzerland, trained as a singer in Vienna, and she made her debut with Walter's company in Munich in 1913. Her first rôle was Mimì, her first triumph the Queen of Night in *Die Zauberflöte*. These were the lovely years, as they are to most singers, when all the world is new, as are the rôles, the colleagues, the public. Under sensible guidance, she confined herself mostly to the soprano *leggiero* repertoire: Susanna, Zerlina and Despina in Mozart, Rosina in *Il barbiere di Siviglia*, a special success as Norina in *Don Pasquale* (which she was later to sing at Salzburg), and then accepting some more spectacular challenges such as the Queen in *Les Huguenots* and Violetta in *La traviata*. Her fame spread and before long she was at Vienna, where she sang her first Zerbinetta, chosen for the rôle by Richard Strauss himself.

She stayed at Munich till 1925 and then followed Walter to Berlin. An international career might have opened up with her successes in Chicago and London, but essentially Berlin remained her artistic home for the rest of her active life as singer and teacher. One of her colleagues was the famous Wagnerian soprano Frida Leider, who in her autobiography recalled Ivogün as a singer who 'combined the finest vocal technique, culture and artistic taste'.

The reasons for her retirement at the age of forty-three have always been something of a mystery. The explanation probably requires an acknowledgement that voice and mind are more closely related than is generally realised. Ivogün developed a phenomenally high register in which almost incredible feats could be performed with apparent case.

Hear the record of the aria from Handel's *Il penseroso*. It is a delightful piece of lyrical singing for a start, the tone in perfect focus, the trills and runs all skilfully exact and even; then when the end is in sight a new development begins, and this takes the soprano up for some wondrous fluted notes high above the stave, a brief moonlit enchantment of birdsong beyond the normal compass of the human voice. For years she could do this and all would be well. The main body of the voice never lost its firm centre or its sweetness of tone, and the high notes were obedient to command. But one warning sign that all was *not* well came with the troubles over intonation. For instance, on one of her rare appearances in New York, at a Carnegie Hall concert with Stokowski and the Philadelphia Orchestra, Richard Aldrich in the *New York Times* commented appreciatively on the 'charming quality and delicate colour ... high range and great flexibility ... artistic feeling, spontaneity and brilliance' but added that in her performance of Zerbinetta's aria she was 'not *disastrously* put off pitch' (my italics). That was in 1922, and it is a remark that leads straight to the prospect of a dust-up at Covent Garden in 1927.

Singers are not machines. When the art is under threat, the mind is troubled too; when the private individual is troubled, the art reacts (think

39

of Callas). Ivogün's life was darkened by one great tragedy. A sister or other close relative of her family was drowned at sea and Ivogün could never get over a sense of guilt at having persuaded her to make the voyage. For all the lightness and gaiety on stage and on records, she suffered from severe melancholia, and it was exacerbated by the unhappy outcome of her marriage to the tenor Karl Erb, which ended in divorce in 1932, and by a year of virtual blindness, confined to a darkroom and leaving her with a need to wear spectacles thick as the bottom of a wine bottle.

But again the twists of fortune have a way of taking unexpected turns. Ivogün was always a creative woman (an observer, an acute psychologist and a painter); she was an individualist too (and liked, for instance, to play barefoot when possible). She became a teacher and after a while gained the reputation in Berlin of being the teacher to apply to for a real understanding of a singer's difficulties. Several of her pupils became noted singers in their time, from Alexandra Trianti in the early days to Rita Streich who was with her for a while and then with Erna Berger. The most famous of them was Elisabeth Schwarzkopf, and Ivogün's part in Schwarzkopf's development was probably the greatest creative act of that long second half of her life, which ended in 1987 at the age of ninety-six.

It was the baritone Karl Schmitt-Walter who arranged the introduction. Schwarzkopf had sung Zerbinetta with him, and he had perceived both the potential and the fact that she was floundering. Ivogün agreed to take her on condition that she would start from scratch and rebuild the voice note by note. When Schwarzkopf contracted tuberculosis, Ivogün saw her to a sanatorium. When she started work on Lieder it was Ivogün's second husband, Michael Raucheisen, who helped her to the repertoire and an understanding of it. Through Schwarzkopf's singing, Ivogün's art remained a living force within a new generation; and it is so still, for the pupil is now herself a professor. Schwarzkopf's ultimate reference is still to that legendary 'Ariel of the opera world', the one whose reputation would be defended (in extremis) at the cost of a bloody nose, and who recreated Schwarzkopf's voice giving it this time a firm technical foundation. In the studio discussion ranges far and wide, but there comes a point where debate, for the time being, must rest: a point which is signalled, as often as not, by the two words 'Ivogün said …'.

CHAPTER 9

Fernando De Lucia

In the middle years of this century, Informed Opinion held that nobody could sing Rossini, or at least that nobody could 'really' sing him. Moreover this state of affairs was understood to have prevailed over the last four or five decades.

Informed Opinion then divided on the matter of chicken and egg. Some held that the reason why Rossini's operas were so rarely performed these days was that singers lacked the technique; others that the operas were such poor stuff that neither singers nor their public cared to waste much time on them. Always an exception was made in the case of *Il barbiere di Siviglia*. It sparkled, had celebrated arias and duets, and needed to be kept in the repertoire if only to justify the general knowledge that it was one of those operas which failed on first performance but had been brilliantly successful ever since. When it was due for production, there was generally not too much difficulty in finding a cast: the singers were around after all. But, said the connoisseurs, shaking their heads, it was not the same thing: it was not how Rossini should 'really' be sung. And how should he be sung, you might ask, to which the wise ones would answer: 'Well, now, have you ever heard a record, made in 1904, by a tenor called De Lucia?'

In those days it was highly likely that the record had not been heard by the enquirer after knowledge, since for many years it had been unavailable except as a rarity on the second-hand market. It was of Count Almaviva's first solo, 'Ecco ridente in cielo', though there was also another, of the serenade, 'Se il mio nome', which could more easily be obtained because it kept its place in the HMV Historic Catalogue and was in fact one of the last single-sided discs to survive. This was the record in which I myself first heard De Lucia, and certainly it enlarged the prospects. What one heard may not have been entirely likeable, but there was no difficulty at all in seeing what the old collectors meant when they referred to the technique exhibited here as being beyond anything attained by tenors of a later age. Not that, in the Serenade at least, tenors would subsequently have been allowed much chance of displaying such technique even if they had it, for De Lucia introduced a profusion of ornaments, *fioriture* which were not to be found in the written score and which more modern tenors – such as Tito Schipa, Heddle Nash or, later, Cesare

41

Valletti or Luigi Alva – would have included at their peril. Conductors would have rapped with their batons and critics would have had a field-day. But it could well be that De Lucia's ornamented singing was the more 'historically' correct, and if to any considerable extent it represented the age in which he had been brought up (Rossini died in 1868, and De Lucia was then in his ninth year), this singing becomes historically important as evidence of nineteenth-century practice. It also lent credibility to the belief that a golden age lay just around the corner – not of the future, but of the past.

So what is special about these records? In the Serenade there is an easy grace, an easy familiarity too, almost as though in a personal relationship: the music here is an old friend who understands exactly when you want him to hurry up or slow down, when you feel like letting him say his piece and when you want to do your own little turn, or indeed when the time has come for a modest endearment, a serious protestation, or a joke. The first verse has its incidental embellishments, the second develops with breath-taking boldness. The mechanism of the voice is so well-oiled, its move-ments are so deft and supple that all seems to be done naturally and without any notion of showing-off. In the 'Ecco ridente' the wonder is greater still, for now scales of the utmost rapidity are sung in a scrupulous *legato* style yet the articulation is as precise as that of expert fingers moving over a keyboard instrument.

A big 'but' claims to be admitted at this point, but we will make it wait a while and turn, instead, from the records to the singer himself. He was a Neapolitan through and through. In Naples he was born and in Naples he died; he studied, made his debut and gave his last public performances there. Unlike his fellow Neapolitan, Enrico Caruso, he returned to sing in the city throughout his years of great international fame (Caruso vowed never to sing there again, having met with a disappointing reception – which some attributed to De Lucia's supporters – in 1901); and, though Caruso was thirteen years his junior, it was De Lucia who sang the solo at Caruso's funeral in 1921.

Elsewhere in Italy he appeared in most of the major houses, including some important seasons at La Scala. Abroad he sang frequently in Spain and South America, travelled extensively in Europe (as far as St Peters-burg), and was in the United States for the Metropolitan season 1893/4. In London he became part of what many considered the 'golden age', and from Covent Garden he received the honour of invitations to Buckingham Palace and Windsor Castle. His last appearances in the capital were in a season of Italian opera at the Waldorf Theatre (now the Strand) in 1905, when his operas were four out of the five most closely associated with him: *Il barbiere di Siviglia*, *Cavalleria rusticana*, *Pagliacci*, and *L'amico Fritz*, in which he had sung the title-rôle in the world-premiere at Rome in 1891.

There is one word which might cause some surprise in all of that. What, it might be asked, is *Pagliacci* doing in the repertoire of a lyric tenor whose

fame (to judge from what has been said so far) derives from his singing of Almaviva in *Il barbiere*? Here we come to another of the reasons for the continuing fascination of Fernando De Lucia. Four other tenors were mentioned a while back in connection with the *Barbiere* arias (Schipa, Nash, Valletti, Alva), and the only rôle which any of those would have been likely to take in *Pagliacci* would be that of Beppe, who has Harlequin's Serenade to sing. But De Lucia (though he sometimes appropriated the Serenade too) sang Canio. This is a part for the *tenore robusto*, the Caruso, the Jon Vickers. Reading reviews both from London and elsewhere, one finds no complaints about a lack of power in De Lucia's singing, while on the contrary a great deal is said about the power of his acting. In P.G. Hurst's *The Age of Jean de Reszke* (Johnson, 1958) we read that 'He was so fine an actor that his portrayal of the emotions through which the unfortunate Canio passes were all expressed with complete conviction', and in *The Golden Age Recorded* (Oakwood Press, 1963) Hurst recalls De Lucia's London Canio as 'a masterly study which has never been approached, even by Caruso, for De Lucia had a very personal touch to impart to all his work, and an unfailing artistic sense which forbade even the slightest hint of exaggeration or vulgarity'. He also enjoyed a comparable success in *Carmen*, where 'the picture he gave of the gradual moral deterioration and crumbling away of Don José's character ... was admirably fine, powerful and artistic'.

That comes from a report in the *Boston Evening Transcript* of 1894. It is quoted more extensively in a book about the singer by Michael Henstock (*Fernando De Lucia: Son of Naples*, Duckworth, 1990), and here is a great piece of good fortune to have come De Lucia's way, albeit posthumously, for it is just about the most scholarly study of a singer's life and work ever to have been published. Its author has followed his subject with a thoroughness that testifies to his devotion, but what is more remarkable is that the devotion has not impeded the objectivity. Henstock shows De Lucia in a turbulent domestic life, a contentious professional one (for instance, slapping Mascagni – who may of course have deserved it – at a rehearsal of *Iris*). He is seen to have been a man of superstitions, jealousies, designs and intents: when he came into a room, according to a contemporary, 'it was like a cockerel entering a hen-coop: old or young, widows, married or single, any or all had to be his'. As for his vanity, it was so shameless as to be almost endearing: in Boston, he reported home, 'the entire press praises me to the skies. Here real merit receives just reward.' The character had its sympathetic sides too, just as the art had more to it than I have been able to discuss here. Henstock's book awaits and will reward the interested reader. But (for I mentioned that a big 'but' was impending) there remains one vexed question. Just what did this voice sound like? When I recently asked someone (a tenor, as it happens) about De Lucia, the reply was 'Oh, you mean the bleater'. This man of course had not heard De Lucia in the flesh, but such was the impression he had gained from records. Now the effect of the records depends on the speed, and therefore the pitch, at which they are played. De Lucia transposed extensively, and even did so in music which contained no specially high notes; with downward transposition, the records, and with them the 'bleat', vibrato or tremolo, can be greatly reduced, all but eliminated. Henstock has much to say about this too, and I can offer only a footnote. Once, long ago, I asked the English tenor Tom Burke about De Lucia's vibrato. His reply was very simple: '*What* vibrato?' And he did hear De Lucia, in the flesh.

De Lucia, Mascagni and Calvé at Covent Garden. *Punch*, 1 July 1893

45

CHAPTER 10

Marian Anderson

'Her appearance was not so much as a singer than as a legend, not so much as a Negro contralto than as a regal and majestic celebrity.'

Those were the words of the *New York Times*, for which Marian Anderson's farewell recital at Carnegie Hall on 18 April 1965 was front-page news. On the face of it, the sentence is simple enough, and the tone may be straightforward too: the voice of awed wonder, a reporter's thrilled shiver of excitement in an attempt to convey the consciousness of being present on an historic occasion.

But, willy-nilly, it touches off some questionings. Its construction is based on a series of juxtapositions offered essentially as alternatives: singer/legend, Negro/regal and majestic, contralto/celebrity. Here, on her farewell, she is (in each instance) the one rather than the other. No values are explicitly attached to the terms, and the context would encourage a reader to accept the sentence as conferring praise. By that valuation, 'a legend' is an advance upon 'a singer' and 'a regal and majestic celebrity' is higher than 'a Negro contralto'.

Perhaps because of our distance from the event, or perhaps because times have changed, we are inclined to sense a reserve of independent judgement implicit in the reporter's tone after all. At any rate, we may feel that something is wrong.

Inside the paper, in the music criticism, Harold Schonberg touched very gently on one thing that was wrong ('in recent years she has not been singing well') and for the most part he preferred to write about the great singer Marian Anderson had been as he had known her in the past: 'she is now, after all, 63 years old'. In his discussion of her career he made it abundantly plain that her standing in the world of music needed nothing beyond her merits to explain it. Her voice was 'one of the vocal phenomena of its time', and her art was such that she 'managed to make a great experience of every concert'. But inevitably other matters entered in. With her retirement 'a significant epoch in American culture came to an end'. The critic also made special reference to two events, one in Washington, the other in New York, and he concluded that 'Marian Anderson was the right person in the right place at the right time.' So, effectively, we are back with 'the legend'.

Legends are misty things. Even by 1965, and even in America, there must have been some to whom the name did not mean anything very specific, and now, about thirty years later, the big bold headline news of the 1930s and '50s fades from view or defies the eyesight in the minute print of a footnote or supplementary reference. So the mention of Washington in connection with Marian Anderson may not mean much. But it did then: she was at the centre of a storm which had been blowing up since the abolition of slavery, and which was to break with renewed strength in the long hot summers of the 1960s.

Briefly, the story was this. Anderson, by then a singer honoured throughout Europe as well as the United States, was booked to give a concert, as she regularly did, at the Washington Howard University School of Music. In 1939 their hall was destroyed by fire and they tried to transfer the concert to the Central High School. The school board refused, and when a similar application was made for use of the Constitution Hall, this was refused by the Daughters of the American Revolution (DAR). It was clearly a test case and everybody rallied accordingly. The Parents Association supported the board but Mrs Roosevelt resigned from her membership of the DAR, and Howard Ickes, Minister of the Interior, arranged for an open-air concert in which the banned singer stood on the steps of the Lincoln Memorial and sang (with amplification system installed) to an audience which eventually extended as far as the Washington Monument hill and which numbered 75,000. Of such events are legends made.

There was of course more of the same kind in essence though not as spectacular – hotels and restaurants which denied entrance and so forth. But tolerance – like charity – begins at home, and the musical world spoke on the subject with a cracked voice as long as the stage of the national opera house rejected her obvious fitness for it. Black singers were excluded, and it took all of Rudolf Bing's resolve, when he became Director, to put a stop to this. Again Marian Anderson became a test case and again the cause succeeded. She appeared as Ulrica in *Un ballo in maschera* on 7 January 1955, giving in all eight performances, and again history was made.

These two events – the Metropolitan debut and the Lincoln Memorial concert – flash out like beacons, but the whole latter part of her career was pretty well illuminated. The World's Fair recital and concert for the King and Queen of England on their visit to the White House (these both in 1939); an inter-racial war bond rally with Paul Robeson in 1942; European tours after the war, then South America, Japan, India (Nehru attending); innumerable awards and honorary degrees; and in 1958 her appointment as UN delegate on the Committee of Human Rights in which she spoke independently and strongly on behalf of the Cameroons: all of this stood, personified, before the Carnegie Hall audience at the Farewell in 1965.

MARIAN ANDERSON

AMERICA'S GREAT SINGER

She is the symbol of America. And yet a human being—a great human being with the warmth, depth and simplicity that communicate directly with the hearts of her audiences. In the words of Fannie Hurst—" She has not grown simply great; she has grown great simply."

There was in fact nothing presumptuous about it if she did appear as the celebrity, 'regal and majestic'.

Still, this all deflects attention. It is the nimbus or halo rather than the head itself. In the long run, the singer is more important than the legend (the 'legend' after all owing its existence to the singer); and rather than the celebrity, however regal, what we want to see is the 'Negro contralto'. In some ways the legend has not merely caused a diversion; it has even created doubt. Inevitably the suspicion arises that this singer owed more to being 'the right person in the right place', than to purely musical considerations. I am personally certain that that is untrue: I heard Marian Anderson in concerts when she was still in magnificent form, and for what it is worth can vouch for the general truth of Harold Schonberg's tribute that 'she managed to make a great experience out of every concert' – except that I would have to qualify that 'every' because on the last occasion, which would have been about 1956, the uncertainties of intonation, vibrato and breath-support proved embarrassing.

In fact a decline had probably set in a few years earlier, for in 1954 an article appeared in the American press with the headline ' "Marian Anderson's voice failing" declare top US music critics.' Certainly by 1960 the *Washington Post* 'sorrowfully' felt that she was 'no longer mistress of her voice'. So, along with the 'legend', the performances of later years also need to be put aside in order to reach the singer, the 'Negro contralto', as she should be surviving in the esteem of musicians.

For this we can go back to recordings. Nobody (I should think) could listen to her *Samson and Delilah* arias – those recordings in English, on the old plum labels, that used to be broadcast in every other programme of 'Housewives' Choice' or 'These You Have Loved' – and not feel some tremor or tingle in the presence of sheer vocal glory. Her voice, one would surely have said, was made for opera (in Moscow in 1936, Stanislavski urged her to stay and study Carmen with him, but she had to press on with her engagements and later came to feel that this was one of life's missed opportunities). Or one could turn then to her classical repertoire, to Handel's 'Ch'io mai vi possa', where the sumptuous Delilah-voice sheds its weight as if by magic and covers the ground as nimbly as any light soprano. She always loved and found a natural affinity with Schubert's 'Der Tod und das Mädchen', and her record of that too has the touch of greatness, with its otherworldly stillness in the Death-voice, 'the more insinuating and terrible because it is so soothing', as she herself wrote. Then there are the Sibelius songs, a reminder of an unexpected specialisation in her repertoire. But fine as these and so much else may be, it is the spirituals that remain above all. The deep tone of 'Tramping', the curiously veiled vowels of 'Crucifixion', the rhythmic joy and the triumphant top A at the end of 'My soul's been anchored in the Lord': these are all caught on records, well enough at least for posterity to understand what the legend was really about, and that it was the 'Negro contralto' who mattered.

But her records are far from telling all, and we have to return to the printed word also, and listen to the witnesses: to the tributes paid by Bruno Walter, Sir Henry Wood, Roger Quilter, Toscanini, Sibelius – Sibelius, to whom she sang in his home with the effect that he embraced her and called for champagne instead of coffee. There are also the critics, like Schonberg who so vividly described that 'black velvet' of a voice. And there must be many who remember, above all, a figure on the platform, who changed her voice from the big macho tone appropriate to 'the lyin' man, the gamblin' man, the crapshootin' man' to an infinite tenderness of a lullaby-voice for 'the little bitsa baby'. 'He's got the whole world in His Hand', she used to sing, and when she sang that, you felt that she surely had it in hers too.

CHAPTER 11

Renato Zanelli

When Domingo sang Otello at Covent Garden in 1990 (that was ten years after his first in the house, and fifteen years after his debut in the rôle at Hamburg), one of the regular London critics chanced his arm and spoke his mind. This was Edward Greenfield who, in the *Guardian*, wrote that Domingo was now the supreme Otello of the century. That left an escape-clause for Tamagno, who could retain his supremacy in the previous century, but it also left many others to be ranged mentally and appraised in a summary fashion.

Mr Greenfield is of course an old hand, and he knew perfectly well that people who thought it amusing to do so might pretend to believe that he must be very old indeed ('How did you rate Slezak in 1909?', 'Do tell me, I've always wanted to know, what was Trantoul like at La Scala?') The statement was in fact shorthand for something more complicated, very boring and unnecessary to spell out. And so there it stood: making you think.

It made me think, not of challenging the proposition, but about the question of who, out of the many Otellos mustered in ranks before the mind's eye, might have most resembled Domingo. The name which stuck with me tantalisingly, for one can never really know, was that of Renato Zanelli. So: out of the ranks of assembled Otellos, attention, forward march ...

Zanelli, like Domingo, was tall. 'He is considerably more than six foot high' announced one of the London newspapers in 1928, and 'considerably' may have been assumed by readers to be a typical British understatement, for the headline ran 'GIANT TO SING THE PART OF OTELLO'. He came from Chile, and though that is a fair distance from the Mexico of Domingo's youth, the shared Latin-American background may have some bearing on the similarities of voice and its production.

Domingo also had a closer association, as it happens; the Chilean's brother (who took the name of Carlo Morelli so as not to be confused with Renato) was one of Domingo's teachers. In his memoir, *My First Forty Years*, he recalls Morelli, 'a mystic, a spiritist', and he also remembers that it was in his classes that he reached B flat for the first time. Morelli was a distinguished baritone whose fine voice can be heard in some pirated

51

broadcasts from the old Met. Zanelli began as a baritone too, as indeed – though much more briefly – did Domingo, and it is in the quality of their voices (both of them with signs of their baritonal past) that the more interesting association lies.

Zanelli lived before the years when a famous singer of a great rôle would be sure to record it complete, in all probability more than once. He did, however, record excerpts, and these make a distinct impression. It was not a cleaving voice like that of the first Otello, Francesco Tamagno, and not a sharp-edged one like Tamagno's successor, Giovanni Zenatello. In more recent times a nearer comparison might be with Ramón Vinay, another Chilean and one who not only started as a baritone but reverted to that voice and sang Iago. The recording by Zanelli of the 'Esultate', that most famous and taxing of operatic arrivals, has Otello up front, and it may flatter the sheer size and impact of his voice. Even so, it leaves no doubt that this was an authentic Otello-sound, the voice of command and magniloquence, and Zanelli also has a fine way of making the intense personal conviction of his utterance felt in the words. At the start of the Love Duet, 'Già nella notte densa', the voice comes into its own still more memorably, for here is an ideal beauty of timbre, its richness very comparable to Domingo's in the same passage. One wonders, perhaps, whether this so well-rounded tone is going to have the incisiveness for the angry declamation of Act II, but the recording starting at 'Tu! indietro! fuggi!' shows that this was also at command, and the farewell to arms, 'Ora e per sempre addio', has both a well adjusted, not excessively open, tenorial ring at the top and an exciting baritonal fullness in the final, middle-register phrase, 'è questo il fin'. But the mark of the great Otello is there in subtler ways. In the spaces between bitter anger is an appalling sadness: the two passions alternate in the exclamations, and the phrase which explicitly recalls paradise lost ('che m'innamora') aches with affection. Then from Act III Zanelli has recorded one of the finest of all performances of the monologue 'Dio, mi potevi scagliar tutti mali', originally coupled with Otello's Death Scene, at the end of the opera.*

Perhaps after all Zanelli *was* the 'supreme Otello of the century', the one whom the *Guardian* critic had forgotten. Rather regretfully (for it is always a pleasure to honour the dead, particularly if they have become obscure with the passing of a relatively short span of years) I have to say that I don't think so. There were limitations, which the critics of his own day did not fail to point out; and a greater, brutally factual, limitation upon

---

* The recording of the monologue and Death Scene is a well-known curiosity in the collectors' world, for two different performances were issued with the same catalogue number. The second, with Barbirolli conducting, is a great rarity in its original form, while the first, under Sabajno, is fairly common. The Sabajno version, however, is artistically superior, especially in the opening passage, and at the time of writing has not been transferred to CD: this is now, effectively, the rarity and, for those who can still play 78s, is well worth seeking out.

his work was dictated by the illness from which he died in 1935 at the age of forty-two.

He had a kidney ailment which plagued the last three or four years of his life and was eventually diagnosed as cancer. His career reached its highest point in 1930 or '31, from which time he should, and no doubt normally would, have continued as one of the world's leading singers at least until the outbreak of war. His climb to fame had not been easy. Born of a wealthy and distinguished family, he was expected to go into business or law. The idea of a career in singing aroused strong opposition, and when he persisted after mixed fortunes in the experimental first twelve months, his exasperated wife threatened to leave him. Santiago and Valparaiso, with Uruguay and Argentina for tours in the summer, offered no very glittering prospects: it was clearly necessary to go North or across to Europe.

Eventually he did both. Some concerts in New York led to an engagement at the Metropolitan. This was in 1919, and though he had no more than a modest success in the house, it led to a recording contract which brought his name to a wider public with a best-selling record of a catchy, common little song called 'La spagnola'. Even then, he made small headway against the established baritone favourites at the Met, their ranks being swelled in 1922 with what for Zanelli was the dismaying addition of Titta Ruffo. He sang there for the last time the following year, and then began to think seriously of something Toscanini had said to him: he should be singing tenor. The difficult process of change seems to have been accomplished mostly by private study, and its outcome was that he made a second debut in 1924. With growing confidence he moved from lighter to heavier rôles, then devoted three months to the study of Otello with the conductor Leopoldo Mugnone and sang the part for the first time at Turin in 1925. It is said that the local critic on that occasion wrote that 'Tamagno may sleep in peace', revising his opinion at Zanelli's return two years later when he was hailed as 'Tamagno's true successor'. During this period of the late 1920s his operas, apart from *Otello*, were *Norma*, *Il trovatore*, *La fanciulla del West*, *Pagliacci* and *Carmen*, with *Lohengrin* in 1928 leading to *Tristan und Isolde* in which he scored another of his greatest successes. *Die Walküre* in Rome was followed by the world premiere of Pizzetti's *Lo straniero* in which Zanelli sang the title rôle. And thus began the memorable year of 1930 which also brought him back to Covent Garden (he first sang there in 1928) and, in the December, at last to La Scala. At this time he clearly gave some magnificent performances and had prospects to match. At the same time the chronic disease was taking hold: he sang his last Otello in 1933 at Santiago, gave a few more concerts, and died on 25 March 1935.

Of his Otello in London, the *Gramophone*'s veteran critic Herman Klein gave a warm account. Reminding his readers (as was his wont) that he had heard Tamagno and seen the great actor Salvini in the rôle, he pronounced

ZANELLI, Renato (the late), *Tenor*

This remarkable Chilean singer was one of the most interesting artists of his day. Son of a wealthy merchant, he was born in Valparaiso, and intended to adopt a legal career. Discovery of his exceptional voice led him to abandon his original intention and after four years' study he made his début at the Metropolitan Opera House, New York, in December, 1919, as a baritone. He starred at the Metropolitan for seven years until he found that his remarkable high baritone voice was changing in timbre, and that he had in fact become a tenor. Consequently he retired for a year to adapt his technique and to study tenor rôles. He made his tenor début as Lohengrin, in Italy, early in 1927, and a year later he was heard for the first time at Covent Garden as Otello, where his performance commanded the respect and admiration of both press and public. These triumphs were repeated in 1930, and after that he created a furore in some of the most important Italian cities with his singing of Tristan. He died at Santiago, Chile, on 25th March, 1935.

Exclusive News Agency
ZANELLI

From the 1936 HMV catalogue

Zanelli's performance 'masterly in the extreme': 'he sings the music with a wonderful command of colour and feeling, and he is an actor of the very highest order'. The *Jewish Chronicle* added an interesting detail, pointing out how subtly the audience was made aware from the start that Otello was an epileptic subject. The most eloquent tribute came from Richard Capell of the *Daily Mail*: 'The dramatic vividness of Zanelli's Otello was something rarely seen on the operatic stage. He held the eye, he held one's sympathies. This Otello, one knew, was truly a commander, a man out of the ordinary; his movements spoke of active blood and a proud mind. The greatest heroic ring may not be in Zanelli's voice, yet this true artist made his veiled, compressed, cello-like tone seem characteristic of Otello's nature. Yes, a great Otello, worthy of the wonderful part, the hardest and the grandest in all opera.' This was in 1930. Except for the suggestion of epilepsy, almost all of these comments might have been made about another Otello, in 1980 and again ten years later.

CHAPTER 12

Ezio Pinza

Ezio Pinza's, as I first heard it, seemed the very voice of human dignity. There he stood, summoned by the imagination and the old wind-up gramophone, six-feet tall and upright with the wisdom of the ages, by the side of Rosa Ponselle ('La vergine degli angeli') offering the sanctuary of Holy Church against the worst that Destiny could bring. Later he urged Giovanni Martinelli not to curse ('Non imprecare') but to submit even in the extremity of despair to the Divine Wisdom which he so majestically embodied. Or as a blissfully Italian Sarastro ('Possenti numi') he invoked the aid of other gods to bless other lovers, and on the reverse side of the record in ringing tones, fit indeed to wake the dead, he addressed the nuns in their tombs ('Suore che riposate') assuring such of them as had broken their sacred vows on earth that he, the reincarnated father of Robert le Diable no less, would shortly be joining them in eternal damnation.

It came then as something of a surprise to learn that his most famous role on stage was Don Giovanni, that by repute he was a famous Don Giovanni offstage too, and that he had recently (1949) moved from the Metropolitan Opera House to a theatre not far off on Broadway where he was currently starring in *South Pacific*. A little later on, recordings made in the 1940s and up to 1951 began to circulate in a limited way over here, and though this was still the great Pinza, still that rich voice with its enveloping warmth and magnanimity of character, there was a sadness about it too. The gods do not age, and here was that god-like voice with the mark of mortality upon it.

When Pinza died, on 9 March 1957, he was not yet sixty-five (his birthday fell on the 18th). He had been an exuberantly healthy man in his prime, but in his last years seemed prone to upsets and developed heart trouble which became serious when he was in his second Broadway show, playing César in *Fanny*, a musical based on Pagnol's Marseilles trilogy. The newspapers reported that he had suffered a stroke, and it is notable that at this point even the *New York Times* referred to him as 'star of Broadway musical successes, *South Pacific* and *Fanny*', with no mention of the Metropolitan.

His death was front-page news and the following day he was the subject of a leading article, warm in its recognition of a national figure. One of his

rare qualities, it said, was 'his ability to project himself directly into the life of the persons who heard him and saw him'. He impressed as having a personal concern, and in response 'literally millions of Americans are now mourning the loss of an artist towards whom they have had a feeling of warm and genuinely personal friendship'. At his funeral Eleanor Steber sang the Ave Maria from *Otello*, Rodgers and Hammerstein were among the pall-bearers, and among the tributes from his operatic colleagues was one from Mary Martin, his co-star in *South Pacific*, who described Pinza as 'the most electric human being I have ever appeared with on any stage'.

He was also an essentially humble man, certainly as far as his music was concerned. He never learned to read music at sight, and in his autobiography he recalled the embarrassment at a first *South Pacific* party, when Rodgers played over some of the tunes; Mary Martin could sing them straight off, while he, the great basso of the Metropolitan, could do nothing till he had taken them home and worked on them. Similarly when he appeared in the *Bing Crosby Show* he quite painstakingly prepared a ballad a week in advance. Crosby was shown a copy fifteen minutes before they were to go on, and took a fancy to it, suggesting 'Hey maestro, what if we harmonise?' But it couldn't be: Pinza was not a musician in that sense. Yet this is the man who sang the Missa Solemnis under Toscanini, Mozart under Bruno Walter, some of the great Wagnerian roles at La Scala, and whose roles at the Met included Arkel in *Pelléas et Mélisande* and Boris Godunov.

57

He paid simple and sincere tributes to the conductors who were his mentors. With modesty and good sense he also learned from his colleagues, particularly the basses Journet and Chaliapin. Marcel Journet, though a Frenchman, was senior bass at La Scala in Pinza's time there, and the younger man marvelled at his gifts and skill. With Chaliapin the admiration led him to accept the secondary rôle of Pimen, though by that time he was himself installed as principal bass at the Metropolitan, for the honour of sharing the stage for one scene with the great Boris Godunov.

The other side of this man (or perhaps it was not 'other' but all part of the same thing) was his very evidently emotional love of life. There was a magnetism about his physical presence with his tall, unspoilt figure, his broad smile, his charming manners and gift for adventure. 'O father, there's such a beautiful man at the door!' Bruno Walter's young daughter exclaimed to her father. In late years, Else Mayer-Lismann would recall how Pinza once invited her for a week in Paris, and she added with rather touching shyness that she had been quite pretty then and had always regretted that she had to refuse. His imbroglios could take a tragic turn, or sometimes tragi-comic as in the suit brought by his first wife against the soprano Elisabeth Rethberg. 'They have been frequently seen in the company of each other exclusively,' the Supreme Court was decorously informed. Rethberg, said the wife, was temperamental, 'nothing could be done with her', but £250,000 might improve matters. Mme Rethberg's lawyer replied that there was nothing between his client and Mr Pinza 'but a mutual admiration for each other's voice'. They worked something out in the end, but not before the papers had noted with ill-concealed glee that Rethberg was scheduled to sing Marguerite to Pinza's Méphistophélès the following evening.

He could probably take all of this in his stride, but when a few years later in 1942 he found himself arrested and taken to Ellis Island as an enemy alien, his world seemed to be collapsing in nightmarish fashion. With America's entry into the war there was a tightening-up of security, and earlier that year Pinza had been required to write 88 signatures on documents to cover his forthcoming tour of the States ('The Department of Justice has become an autograph collector of great power and range lately', *The Times* observed). Then in March of that year the FBI were reported as having arrested two Germans and four Italians as yet unnamed but shortly to be revealed as including Pinza. His second wife rallied friends and support, giving evidence of her husband's loyalty to the USA, and eleven weeks later he was freed. But the incident brought him close to despair, facing what seemed a Kafkaesque trial where it was only possible to guess at the charges and where the accused was deemed guilty till proved innocent. He always believed that it was due to the malice of a rival who coveted his rôles, which would seem to narrow the field. Nor was it the first time he had detected a snake in the grass. Of the earlier one he is said to have remarked that if the man had had the talent for singing

ROYAL OPERA
: : COVENT GARDEN : :
Lessees: Royal Opera House Company, Ltd.

THIS EVENING'S PERFORMANCE

Tuesday, June 12th, 1934, at 8.30

PUCCINI'S OPERA
LA BOHÈME
In Italian

Mimi . . . . ELISABETH RETHBERG
Musetta . . . . . RUTH NAYLOR
Rodolfo . . . . ANGELO MINGHETTI
Marcello . . . . JOHN BROWNLEE
Colline . . . . . . EZIO PINZA
Schaunard . . . . ARISTIDE BARACCHI
Benoit } . . . . . OCTAVE DUA
Alcindoro }
Parpignol . . . . . PERCY HARRIS

Conductor . . . GINO MARINUZZI

that he had for intrigue he would have been the greatest singer in the world.

So: it is all part not so much of the Divine Comedy as of the very human. That voice – Padre Guardiano, Sarastro, reincarnated sire of Robert le Diable – it belonged to a man who met with his share of indignities and the other conditions that flesh is heir to. He was also, I imagine, a man of some exceptional radiance, one who moved at ease in a world of wealth, art and fashion, and yet who kept a good deal of the simple countryman about him. He remains now as one of the great basses of the century.

For his surviving art, we do well enough returning to those records that I mentioned at the start, the ones made in the late 1920s when he had recently joined what – rightly or wrongly – people still regarded as the world's greatest opera company. Before then there are those Italian pre-electrical recordings showing the fresh sonority and pliable substance of his tones, ideal in Donizetti and Bellini. Then we have some precious 'pirated' performances, Saturday matinees at the Met, where suddenly a dark lustre will spread over the sound as Ramfis in *Aïda* or Oroveso in *Norma* sings a phrase or two; better still when Fiesco is on stage in *Simon Boccanegra*. Perhaps best are the recordings of Verdi's *Requiem*. There is a line in *Coriolanus* where Volumnia speaks of a heart which is like 'the ripest mulberry that will not hold the handling'. A voice that spills its ripeness is not much use in the opera house, so the simile must not be taken too far. But the mellow fruitfulness of Pinza's tone, the richness of its colouring, the sturdiness of its growth and the strength of its flavour: these enrich his every phrase in the *Requiem*, and they are fine testimony, a homage paid by the world of the senses to the life of the spirit.

CHAPTER 13

Kathleen Ferrier

'By her sublime art and by her loving nature she gave happiness and received happiness, and therefore no dirge shall be intoned to deplore her terrible suffering and early death – I know she herself would prefer to be remembered and spoken of in a major key.' The words of Bruno Walter are sincere, wholesome and sensible, yet something prompts hesitation.

To remember and speak of her in a major key: in one sense that is exactly right, but in another it involves a falsification, certainly as far as many people of my own generation are concerned. There is no use pretending that it is not so: she is inevitably associated with death. In due time it will be different. Already there exists a generation to whom Ferrier is no more than a name, a voice on records that are now classified as 'historical'. 'Yes, I've heard of her of course. My mother used to talk about her. I know she had a lovely voice ... She died, didn't she?' Queries among younger listeners might elicit some such reply. A few more years into the future and even that secondhand personal connection will have been lost. Then 'Ferrier' will simply be her name and her recorded voice, one among many 'great singers of the past'; death, in that sense will be no more. But at present there are still plenty of people alive who heard her and remember her well, and I am not at all sure that for them it is possible to remember her simply 'in a major key'.

Her death, in 1953, was profoundly shocking. It was hardly the less so by virtue of her illness and its nature having been fairly general knowledge for some time before. After all, she was still singing in public late in 1952; there was the Covent Garden *Orfeo ed Euridice* in the new year, and plans had been made for appearances at the Edinburgh Festival. Like many others in the country, I personally can still remember the exact circumstances in which I heard the sad news. But more hideous had been a moment earlier in the previous year that remains vivid and chilling even after this long passage of time. A musician friend who had just arrived from London joined a number of us for tea: this was in Canterbury, and in those days tea at 'The Old Bakery' or some such place was a decorous, comfortable part of the ritual, a time of light talk, with an almost conscious glow of rosy-cheeked good health. Amid the tea-cakes and the chat I heard '... just been in London ... talking to (and he mentioned two well-known

singers) ... They say Kathleen Ferrier has got cancer.' There may have been a second or two of silence, and the chat resumed; but, though it is hard to say how one knew this, it was as though at that moment everyone round that table had felt stricken.

The point was: not the disease ('O word of fear'), not the ineptitude of time, place and manner ('among the cups, the marmalade, the tea'), not simply that it was a singer who had been thus marked out for death (and there is something particularly poignant about the early death of a singer); it was that it should be Kathleen Ferrier.

Now this is something which I think only those who heard her can fully appreciate. We have to go back a few years, from that teashop in Canterbury in 1952 to the Guildhall at Cambridge in 1949. The recital opened with Handel ('Spring' and 'Come to me, soothing sleep'). Ferrier's voice on records had not at all prepared me for this experience of her 'live'; it was not, I suppose, that the voice was essentially different (though reproduction was more 'plummy' in those days), but rather that the combination of voice and presence was a different thing. This was the voice in its prime, with a fresh vibrancy, ample, cleanly defined, a kindly sound beyond doubt but strong too, and, above all expressive of a vitality that was also embodied by this radiant woman in her own prime.

She returned the following year, and this time my seat was up on the platform behind the singer, from where the vitality, the awareness of a living person, was stronger still. I remember the wonder of her back! The breathing, which as far as memory recalls drew no attention to itself from the front, was clearly and impressively visible from the back. There was no raising of the shoulders or anything of that kind, but the back expanded; and again one associated the voice with the body, and the body with its health. So that was why the tale told in a tea-shop chilled our talk, and why the major key does not quite suit. When Bruno Walter wrote that she gave happiness and received happiness 'and therefore no dirge shall be intoned', the logical force of that 'therefore' is perhaps not so compelling as its use might suggest. The cruel and premature cessation of that happiness was as real as the happiness itself, and the key oscillates between major and minor. But, in major key, what songs they were! After Handel's 'Spring', and later in the programme, would come Warlock's ('It was a lover and his lass'), where the grace and ease of her singing, and Gerald Moore's crisp staccatos, disguised all those difficulties which the composer has put in the way of his singer and pianist. In Purcell's 'Hark, the echoing air' all was light of heart and nimble of movement. The Schubert group would probably have ended with 'Der Musensohn' which seemed exhilarating as a ride on Pegasus. In *Frauenliebe und leben* the abiding memories of her performance in the Cambridge concerts were not of the comfortable 'Du Ring an meinem Finger' or of the tragic final song, but of the two fast and joyful numbers, the one to the bridesmaids, the other to the newborn child: they were radiant in expression as in tone.

63

THE CAMBRIDGE ARTS THEATRE TRUST

Founder: LORD KEYNES

•

SUNDAY RECITAL SERIES

1949/1950

•

GUILDHALL

27 NOVEMBER at 2.45

KATHLEEN FERRIER

Accompanist:
GERALD MOORE

•

PROGRAMME   *SIXPENCE*

Best of all (as it seemed to me at that time) were the British songs. In Parry's 'Love is a bable' she could almost persuade us that the song was an improvisation. ' 'Tis like ...' and it seemed certain some inspired image was to be born, but a second's blank ('It's gone! What was it? No, gone. Never mind, on to the next thing') was followed by the unperturbed dismissal: ' 'Tis like ... I cannot tell what.' In Frank Bridge's 'Go not, happy day' the smile was one with the ripple of the accompaniment and the excited contentment of the lyric. Encore-time would bring forth various of the Ferrier favourites we hear on records, and one which (as far as I can recall) we don't have. This was an Irish song, 'The Spanish Lady', set by Herbert Hughes. It seemed the very essence of Ferrier, telling of its pretty adventure with a happy eagerness, varying tone and pace, and, without seeming to exercise any conscious arts of persuasion or cajolery at all, having the audience listen with such attention as they had probably never bestowed on a story-teller since childhood.

This of course is the art of communication, which after all is a highly desirable attribute in opera too. Ferrier's operatic career, as we know, was very limited (Gluck's *Orfeo* at Glyndebourne, the Holland Festival and Covent Garden, Britten's *Rape of Lucretia* in the world premiere at Glyndebourne, and that was practically the sum total of her work on stage). Temperament, time and place all played their part in this, and her background probably had most of all to do with it. 'Sensible' Northern folk of Ferrier's age and that of her parents had a tendency to feel that where opera was concerned you kept your distance. The reasons were partly social (opera was for 'the grand folk'), partly national (not a form that was worked into the musical tradition of the country as were song and oratorio), partly to do with the rationalism and habits of moderation that had their own notion of good taste.

Ferrier found it difficult to 'see' herself on stage. Carmen, a rôle which she was sometimes urged to try, remained with her a comic turn for the amusement of friends, burlesquing the *habanera* with a rose between her teeth and with the slinky movements of the silent-screen vamp. When the florid aria at the end of Act I was introduced into *Orfeo*, she found it slightly incongruous, almost amusing, that she should be singing 'coloratura'. By all accounts she did it supremely well, but it remained somehow foreign to the cultural background. A decade or so later it would probably not have been so. Many things would then have been different. In all probability she would have been encouraged to think and practise 'upwards' in the tone-range, for by that time hardly anybody reckoned to be a contralto; they were all mezzos.

If this had been so, there might have been gains, but losses too. Incalculable, anyway. Incalculable also is the personal loss of her *Orfeo* to enter into the catalogue of a lifetime's memories. I booked for the third performance, which was cancelled and we had Joan Hammond in *Aïda* instead. So my last memory of Ferrier was at a concert in the Royal Festival Hall on 23 November 1952. With Richard Lewis she gave her last performance of 'Das Lied von der Erde'. At the end, the conductor, Josef Krips, visibly moved, turned to her, clicked his heels and bowed in respect. That was forty years ago, and the affection and respect she inspired then are undimmed now; but you can see why the memories refuse to play in the major key only.

65

CHAPTER 14

Giuseppe di Stefano

'Maestro di Stefano' is the programme's term of reference, and 'Well, well' murmur some of the older heads present, smiling gently to themselves and allowing a picture from ages past to form in a corner of the mind's eye.

The man who arrives on the platform, in the wake of half-a-dozen young singers ready to take part in his masterclasses is a well set-up seventy-year-old of professional appearance. His grey suit is of good cut, the collar of his cream shirt is well-behaved, his tie impeccable. The hair, grey but still plentiful, parts in one of the straightest lines ever seen. Though not now using spectacles, he will presently produce them. He is clearly, one would say, a bank-manager, lawyer, or family doctor surviving from the days when such people were expected to look the part. His manner is authoritative without ostentation. His features are regular and, in a man his age, handsome. A slightly severe expression is imparted by the lines which run in prominent verticals defining the cheeks, but the eyes are bright and the voice is friendly.

As he sits to hear the first singer (later he will walk about and listen from further back in the hall), the vision in the eye of the beholder blurs, and as in some cinematic 'dissolve' the eyes of the maestro grow brighter still, the hair turns jet-black and the year is 1946. A rehearsal is in progress and a girl with lustrous dark eyes stands and looks rather doubtfully at the seated figure. He is not (as now) using the chair in the normal way but sits astride it, his arms resting on the chair-back. The girl looks wonderingly, partly because her Spanish countrymen who are also involved in the rehearsal are dressed for the most part in their customary suits of solemn black while this twenty-five-year-old, with his easy manner and unconventional way of sitting, wears a sailor-shirt, sleeveless and with blue and white stripes. She came to find him, as she rather suspected she might, very agreeable company, and the moment he sang all else was forgotten. But for an instant or two, Victoria de los Angeles, looking back to those early days in Barcelona, admits that she was really rather shocked.

From time to time others would be shocked with greater or lesser degrees of cause and seriousness. He himself, even in his rôle of maestro, is quite willing to reminisce about occasions when he was, as he says, 'a

naughty boy'. One such incident arose after he had been cast in *La traviata* at La Scala. He did not, he explained, want the part and, feeling restive, decided not to show up at rehearsal. The consternation this would cause was something of which he would have been of course well aware, and whether feeling contrite or merely curious he went round to the theatre later and found Callas and De Sabata in earnest conversation. As he approached them he felt that the glances turned in his direction were not of the friendliest. But this, he said, was soon changed. He cracked a joke, of which (very luckily I should think) they saw the funny side. When Ghiringhelli walked in, the dressing-room was in uproar. 'Who is laughing here?' demanded the outraged director (who of course had not heard the joke). After that the story grows a little dim, but good humour prevailed and the centre of the operatic universe was at peace again, or as nearly as it ever is. A little joke, a little fun, Di Stefano submits, will do a power of good, restore a sense of proportion, and make everyone remember that opera after all (*even* opera) is for enjoyment.

All of which is no doubt very true, though one reflects that if any of the young singers present at the masterclass were later in life to be so fortunate as to find themselves at La Scala about to sing a leading rôle in *La traviata* it would perhaps not be such a good idea to take the opportunity for testing the local sense of humour in quite the same way.

In such matters as this, and in other senses too, Di Stefano was a summertime singer. He came to us with his great talent, his youth and promise, just as civilisation was beginning to breathe again after the Second World War. In the 1950s when Maria Callas became the sun-goddess of opera, Di Stefano stood very close to her throne. It was also the time of high summer in the record business. With the long-playing disc still a relatively recent invention, the record-buying public could start building its library in earnest. Complete operas, not just short excerpts, were issued regularly, not three or four a year as in the old days but three or four a month. The star-system was supposed to be out of date and out of favour, but in fact the new stars became as potent as the old. In varying permutations, Tebaldi and Schwarzkopf, De los Angeles, Nilsson, Björling and Gedda and Del Monaco, Tucker and Merrill and Warren, Hotter and Christoff, became The Names for that generation. But it is still remembered, in gramophone history, as the age of Callas, and if Tito Gobbi stands to one side of her in the photograph album of that summertime, on the other side is Giuseppe di Stefano.

The trouble with summers is that they do not last. Some singers, knowing this, will lay up store for autumn. The store might be in the mind, which deepens its understanding so that when the voice is gone or going the art will still fascinate and move its hearer. It may be in a judicious adaptation of repertoire, or even be still in the voice itself, the long preservation of which has been ensured by sound technique and wise usage. For Di Stefano, as singer and artist, autumn was not a good season. To some extent his star waned with Callas's; few of the recordings by which he is remembered today date from later than the Callas decade. He had also come to undertake the rôles suitable for a dramatic tenor and at a cost to the lyric freshness which had been so large a condition of his success. Technically he also favoured a very open way with high notes; records show this, and even in the mid-1950s critics began to warn, as did the experienced Rome correspondent of *Opera* magazine (March 1957), remarking of his well-characterised performance in Mascagni's *Iris* that 'Di Stefano's lusty singing has become over-open of late'. By 1959 and 1961 when he came to Covent Garden his voice had hardened into (as I remember it) an instrument of no great beauty, though in *Tosca* it could sound sweet-toned in 'O dolci mani' and ring out excitingly in the cries of 'Vittoria'.

But it is never a very good sign when the best impression is made at the extremes, either in range or volume. When he rejoined Callas for their famous world-tour of 1973, he would sometimes, I believe, sing in a way that would bring tears to the eyes – tears of the right sort. But it was painfully clear that this was a tenor who had seen better days. Essentially he had now to wait for that Indian summer and when this came it brought some warming evidence of fond memories and loyalty on the part of his public, and, for his own part, the authority of the man of history, the

68

LONDON
MASTER
CLASSES

presents

GIUSEPPE DI STEFANO

at the

PURCELL ROOM

Sunday, May 10th 2.30 p.m. and 7.30 p.m.

IN ASSOCIATION WITH   THE SOUTH BANK CENTRE

PROGRAMME   THE
SOUTH
BANK
CENTRE

'maestro'. The remains of a singing voice are still there too: deeper, more baritonal now, with a kind of fullness sufficient to send a thrill around the auditorium where for a moment the past would relay its legend to living ears.

As for the legend, that of course is a matter of record, and records are of three kinds: written, aural and (not to be despised) anecdotal. Let me give examples of each. As a matter of written record, there are seasons in the world's great opera houses to point to, but also an event in 1955 when music critics from all the world over were invited to vote for the best performers in opera during the previous year. The conductor chosen was Toscanini, the soprano Schwarzkopf, mezzo Stignani, baritone Fischer-Dieskau, bass Siepi. The tenor was Di Stefano. For the aural record we can, from the summer of his career, hear the vitality of his singing, making, for example, such a vividly living character out of his Rodolfo with Callas or his Pinkerton with De los Angeles in her earlier recording of *Madama Butterfly*. It is better still to go back to the springtime: to the very

69

first records made in wartime Switzerland through the sponsorship of his Russian admirer, Wala Dauwalder, meltingly beautiful in the freshness of voice and the responsiveness of feeling. As for anecdotal records, well of course there are many tales of temperament, but that is not what I have in mind.

I recall a player in Eric Robinson's orchestra at the BBC, and I should think the year must have been in the very late 1940s. He had played in programmes with so many famous singers – Gigli and so forth – that he could not remember half of them. But this young tenor … 'I don't know how to explain it,' he said. 'It got at me somehow. I could hardly play the notes. It was as though every part of him was voice, and somehow the whole studio was tuned in to this sound. And you felt that if you heard it a little bit longer, well … you'd have energy built up inside you to last a lifetime.' That was the effect the young Giuseppe di Stefano had upon his listeners: it is the special gift of the Italian tenor, and essentially it is the voice of youth.

CHAPTER 15

Luisa Tetrazzini

'What songs the sirens sang, or what name Achilles assumed when he hid himself among women ....' To the time-honoured list of puzzling questions may be added most of the mythology of the opera house.

What is worse, the most cherished tales often turn out to be the ones most untrue, or half-true, or concoctions in which the original droplet of truth may still be found as a glutinous substance at the bottom of the glass. So it occurred to the present writer, who accounts himself among the most credulous of readers, that the oft-told and well-loved story of Tetrazzini's debut might just possibly be a load of bunkum like the rest. After all, whose word have we for it but her own, and this in an auto-biography which must have been pretty substantially ghosted.

Wondering along these lines, I asked Charles Neilson Gattey, whose new and thoroughly researched biography of Tetrazzini was still without a publisher. No, came the answer, it is not really true; or rather, some bits are true, but they are not the best bits. Perhaps we should enjoy the myth while we can.

Once upon a time, or on 21 October 1890, a last-minute crisis at the opera house in Florence compelled the conductor to address the audience. The soprano who was to have sung the rôle of Inez in Meyerbeer's *L'africana* was indisposed, and the performance would have to be can-celled as no substitute was available. At this, from among the audience arose one voice shriller than all the rest, promising salvation. Its owner knew the rôle and was willing to sing it there and then. The audience seemed to support her, and the conductor made further enquiries. The volunteer was, apparently, well-known, of good family, and with an elder sister already well advanced in her profession as an operatic soprano. On the other hand, this was a girl of sixteen, and she had never as yet sung on stage in her life.* Common-sense urged caution but the popular vote clearly inclined towards giving it a go. The maestro made a wise decision: he would accept the kind offer but postpone the performance. In two days'

---

* C.N. Gattey, *Luisa Tetrazzini: The Florentine Nightingale*, Scolar, 1995, pp. 4-5. In this account the substitution was arranged in private, Tetrazzini being then nineteen, not sixteen years of age.

Tetrazzini as Philine in *Mignon*

Gigli (*left*) and Hislop (*right*), both as Cavaradossi in *Tosca*

This comes back to me now not because his height matters much (he was 5'9" or 10", but perhaps by then old age had reduced him somewhat), but because both adjectives – the 'nice' as well as the 'little' – surprised me. Hislop was a man who could inspire admiration, affection, devotion; but 'nice' didn't seem to be quite the word. He could be difficult, downright, and, when he felt like it, pugnacious. Moreover, he quite often did feel like it. Michael Turnbull's new biography of him (*Joseph Hislop: Gran Tenore*, Scolar, 1992) shows a man who probably always had something of the fighter within him, from schooldays when 'he often had to defend his older brother with his fists' to the time when, in his eighties, he was angered by a young man on the London underground and told him that if his nephew had been there he would have knocked his block off, adding 'In fact by the look of you, I could do it myself.'

That, of course, may be all rather endearing. Less amiable is the story of his animosity towards an accompanist who on one of his Australian tours had turned out to be too good: he played his solos brilliantly and won a star's applause. Claude Kingston, the impresario, was told to 'get rid of

77

him'; ' "No bloody good to me, Claude," Hislop said, not caring that Goodman (the accompanist) could hear every word. "You've got to get rid of him." ' On a later occasion Hislop's temper rose to a fury, which the pianist met with silence. Yet the feeling one has is that it was not exactly the man himself who was behaving in this abominable fashion, but rather something which had assumed a life of its own: his career.

Hislop's career was certainly a remarkable one. A Scotsman who went to Sweden as a photoprocess engraver's assistant and became principal tenor of the Royal Opera in Stockholm; that is unusual for a start. Then, at a time when British artists were pointedly excluded from playing any important part in the grand events at Covent Garden, he sang Rodolfo to Melba's Mimì, Alfredo to Selma Kurz's Violetta and Faust to Chaliapin's Méphistophélès. Abroad in a period when British names rarely featured in the international cast-lists, he sang with Galli-Curci in Chicago, Muzio in Buenos Aires, Dal Monte in Milan. He became one of HMV's best-selling celebrities. He undertook vast concert tours, appeared in film and operetta, taught in Stockholm and London, and died back in Scotland, at Berryside in the East Neuk of Fife, on 6 May 1977, aged ninety-three.

Reading his biography, one can hardly fail to be impressed, and moved, simply by the facts, the superstructure, of such a life. There are also frustrations, for the man himself remains elusive. In some ways one is grateful for the occasional flashes of temper and the glimpse of a teacher on whose stairs two pupils (in this instance Sven-Olof Sandberg and Birgit Nilsson) might be found weeping. These are like a telephone-line to the man rather than to the career-man. The fact is that, though Hislop had a 'big' career, there was a time when it must have looked, to him and to those who were closest to him, dizzyingly as though on the verge of what could now be called 'superstardom'.

This was in the early 1920s. Plenty of press critiques from Scandinavia, Italy, North and South America, will bear this out, and can be found in Michael Turnbull's book; but let me take an example from nearer home. One of the best writers on singers in this period was *Musical Opinion*'s opera critic, 'Figaro', or A.P. Hatton. He contributed an article on Hislop in the May issue of 1924, asking in his first sentence 'Have we in Mr Joseph Hislop, the natural successor to Caruso?' In fact as he explains, the question originated not with himself but with one of Covent Garden's most discerning connoisseurs who in the international season of 1920 (Hislop's first) made the suggestion 'with almost lyrical fervour and eloquence'. The writer admits that it came initially as a surprise: Hislop, after all, was very British, and in the British tradition sang a lot of ballads. Yet the more the critic thought about it, the less outlandish did it seem. The voice itself 'ripe and round, mellowed in the school of *bel canto*', was unquestionably special: 'It is a lyric voice so rich, resting on so glorious a foundation of golden chest notes, so effortlessly produced, that it frequently achieves more of "carrying" and even thrilling quality than the voice of the *robusto*

proper.' He recalled a performance of *Tosca* heard from the gallery, in which the softest tones of Destinn and Caruso would be floated, 'pure, round, even and as ravishingly audible as all the most declamatory singing of the second act.' Hislop, he says, has this quality too, and 'I sometimes think that for his *cantabile* singing at any rate he need not fear a comparison even with what we can recall of Caruso's.'

Hislop had more going for him than that, as 'Figaro' did not fail to point out. He was a convincing actor, and in his presence there was something unusual for the operatic stage, an aura of aesthetic refinement. His singing had also that quality so necessary for the real star: an individuality such that (as 'Figaro' said, and as recordings testify) there was 'no possibility of mistaking it'. If this critic thought as much, so did many other listeners; and for a year or two longer Hislop remained on this high level of esteem, which was felt to imply promise quite as much as fulfilment.

Yet the high point was here, here in these few hectic years when every day brought the prospect of a new and exciting development, and when at one time, it must have seemed that the world was at his feet. In the midst of that time came the call to La Scala. For a British tenor it was without precedent and, though I may have forgotten or overlooked some other occasion, I think it probably remains unique in the century – that a British tenor should be called to La Scala to take the lead in an Italian nineteenth-century romantic opera in which their own tenors were generally reckoned supreme. The work was *Lucia di Lammermoor*, in which he took over from Pertile, singing opposite Toti dal Monte with a cast that included Stracciari and Pinza. He sang for four performances, enjoyed a great success, was offered a contract for forty-five further performances ... and turned it down.

'There is a tide in the affairs of men ....'

CHAPTER 17

Geraldine Farrar

'Gerryflapper' is a word unknown to the *Oxford English Dictionary* and, more surprisingly, to *Webster's*. The missing entry, *OED*-style, might have run as follows:

> **Gerryflapper** sb. 1920 U.S. (f. name Geraldine + flapper, slang or colloq. 1903) A demonstrative admirer (esp. young female) of US singer and Film actress, Geraldine Farrar. 'All the little gerryflappers were out last night.' (Henderson)

Henderson (W.J. of the *New York Sun*), who coined the word and disapproved of the hysteria associated with it, went on to offer his own definition: 'What is a gerryflapper? Simply a girl about the flapper age who has created in her own half-baked mind a goddess which she names Geraldine Farrar.'

The goddess was by that time not far off forty years of age, which she considered a suitable one for retirement. As this event approached, in the early months of 1922, the gerryflappers rose amid a mass of flowers, flags and handkerchieves. 'Children, this is no occasion for a funeral,' she told them from the stage of the Metropolitan, where she had just sung her last Marguerite. The last Madame Butterfly was to follow, and this time she took the opportunity to consult the public on the question of her farewell performance. What rôle should she sing? 'Tosca! Tosca!' they all cried. That was one in the eye for Maria Jeritza, whom the management saw as Farrar's successor in the house and whose special preserve this had already become.

Farrar replied that the decision lay elsewhere but she hoped that her present advisers would write to the management and express their desires. They probably did so, but Gatti-Casazza, the manager, was a wily old bird who had had trouble enough with Farrar in his time and did not want more with Jeritza; he also knew that, whatever the opera chosen, there would be a full house, and he settled for Leoncavallo's *Zazà*.

This was on 22 April, a day that was to prove memorable not only in the history of the Metropolitan Opera but also in that of public order in New York City. There had been a steady build-up towards it as, one by one,

Farrar cast off her great rôles – Louise, Manon, Carmen – bestowing keepsakes on the chorus, stage-hands and the more fortunate or favoured of the flappers. At the performance itself – a matinée, with Martinelli and De Luca as her principal associates – Farrar was 'never more eloquent in song and action', but that was nothing to the sequel.

At the end of Act II a banner appeared on stage bearing the legend 'None but you, Gerry! From the Gerryflappers!'. At the end of Act III a crown of pearls and emeralds was presented (and worn), a great American flag that stood amid a basket of American beauty roses was pressed to the goddess's lips, and the crowd surged forward. Farrar gestured for silence and her wish was obeyed. Not so the next one, for when she said, 'I don't want a tear shed in this house today,' a voice from the audience cried dolefully, 'I can't help it'. Outside, according to the *New York Herald Tribune*, 'the crowd which began to gather at 4.30pm had reached mob proportions by six'. When Farrar appeared, waving kisses and dodging flowers, streamers were hurled from rooftops and traffic was held up for five minutes. The stage-hands towed her car up Broadway, and for the rest of the journey four motorcycle policemen acted as escort, while the fans were left to mop up their tears with the confetti and other mementoes of the sad, sweet day.

The cause of all this was not just a voice and a pretty face. Farrar's success gave body to at least one recurrent episode in the American dream of her time. There is a photograph of her on stage making her debut at the Metropolitan in 1906, richly evocative of the period and the occasion. We see the stage with its proscenium arch, the famous gold curtain drawn up, the ornate frame, the boxes on either side, the women splendid in their gowns and in some instances tiaras, the men in uniformed attendance, the stalls full, the orchestra pit contributing to the dignity of the spectacle. The stage, noble in breadth and depth, is graced by what seems to be a very passable, indeed rather handsome, representation of the pillars, balconies and turrets of renaissance Verona.

A large company of singers stands tidily grouped at the back, leaving a respectful space between themselves and the front curve of the stage with footlights and prompt-box, where stands a single figure. She is undoubtedly Juliette, possibly singing her waltz-song, or perhaps receiving her applause after it.

Anyway, it is a dream of a picture. All that is resonant of name, redolent of wealth, suggestive of elegance and culture looks towards that embodiment of youth, beauty and talent. It is as enchanting a prospect as any that could be within the dream-world aspirations of an American girl: of a girl of any nationality, you might say, but here was the special glamour of it, that among this famed international company, inheritors and exponents of an essentially European culture centuries old, should stand Miss Farrar from Melrose, Mass., USA, now the object of all admiration, the star.

It was also the fulfilment of her own dream. By the age of fourteen in 1896, she had formed what she called 'a healthy desire to shine in some

Farrar's debut as Juliette at the Metropolitan Opera House in 1906

romantic world of musical experience'. A little later, the 'romantic world' had gained definition: she had seen her first opera, *Carmen*, and in it her first star, the great Emma Calvé. Soon she discovered the Metropolitan, and 'always in a joyous daze' entered 'the opera wonderland'. About the ultimate objective there was no doubt: 'This wonderful creature (Emma Calvé) was what I hoped – nay, intended – to become', and the Metropolitan was where she hoped, nay intended, to become her.

She was not the only one with that intention: her mother became equally convinced that this was her daughter's rightful place in the world, and between the two of them they made a formidable team. Intelligence and self-discipline played for them too. When the Metropolitan management became aware of this remarkable student and offered her an instant Wunderkind debut, she (or they) declined. It was to be Europe first, experience and study.

From Paris she went to Berlin, thence to what is often seen as the spiritual Prussia of Lilli Lehmann's teaching classes. Farrar was not a docile pupil in this autocratic school, but she realised that Lehmann knew what she was talking about, and long after the ambition of starring at the Metropolitan had been fulfilled she would return annually to Lehmann till the outbreak of war made such refresher-courses impossible. It is a strange connection, this of Farrar the professional coquette on stage and

83

Farrar as Mignon

Lehmann the professional martinet in her studio. In fact the girl had a toughness of character and a compulsive quest for high standards that matched the teacher's. One of the most striking features of Farrar's singing as heard on records is often the cleanness, the assured athletic stride of upward intervals (the precise 'landing' of a high A or B flat, for instance, from a fifth or sixth below), and commenting on this in some fascinating pages in his book *Prima Donna* Rupert Christiansen attributes it to 'the Lehmann aspect of her training'. I am sure he is right, and yet it is also the kind of thing which the autocrat in Farrar herself would have required and respected.

After Lehmann, her career began in earnest, with spectacular triumphs in Berlin, to which the publicised attentions of the Crown Prince did no harm at all. At Monte Carlo she was paired with Caruso, and all was set for the Metropolitan debut in *Roméo et Juliette* and the pretty picture of that event in 1906.

Her success over the next decade was immense, always with an expanding repertoire and with a changing, developing treatment of her established rôles. Not that it was all plain sailing. Parts such as Tosca and the heroine of Dukas' *Ariane et Barbe-bleu* placed a strain upon her voice, and she suffered repeatedly from bronchitis.

It was the resulting need to rest from opera that led her for a while into silent films: there were, I believe, fourteen films in all, including a *Carmen* and a Joan of Arc (*Joan the Woman*), in which she wore an eighty-pound suit of armour, endured the flames with fire-proofed hair and clothing, and was admired for her pains by the cowboy extras. When she saw that her career in films had run its course she retired, just as she did, resolutely, at the age of forty in opera and at fifty in concert-work. After that she lived on, with befitting style and dignity, till 11 March 1967, by which time the lovely girl of the photograph and idol of the gerryflappers had reached the unthinkable age of eighty-five.

CHAPTER 18

Giacomo Lauri-Volpi

'A stra-ange man,' she said, and her beautiful eyes opened wide at the thought of his strangeness. 'Really?' I said. 'Ye-es. He was jealous.' 'Good heavens,' I said. 'Ye-es. He was very jealous. We sing in *La Bohème* and I am young. Nobody know me. But the audience, after the "Mi chiamano Mimì", they clap, they bravo. They like.' 'Oh good,' I said. 'Yes, but he is jealous. In the interval he says "Who is this Tebaldi?" and the next day he send a notice to say he will not sing the next performances. But then, two years later or maybe three we sing again. In *Aïda*. And now he send a letter to say how happy he is to sing with me. He is charming and we get on fine. A stra-ange man.'

This little dialogue is worth recording because it is so typical. To say that Lauri-Volpi could be difficult and that he suffered from no lack of *amour propre* might invite the driest of rejoinders from many who encountered the great tenor professionally. He was a famous exponent of the verbal fisticuff, and sometimes of the physical. Ezio Pinza in his auto-biography recalls how it dismayed him one day, while walking with his father in Bologna, to meet Lauri-Volpi who had not done well the previous evening in *La favorita*, and to hear his father explaining exactly where he had gone wrong: 'What you should do is open your mouth wide and give us your full voice.' And this, as Pinza remarks, was to the man 'who, on one occasion, punched a New York critic on the nose for giving him a bad notice.' But Lauri-Volpi simply bowed politely, said 'Si, signore', took the advice, and the following evening scored a notable triumph singing with full voice and mouth open wide. Afterwards he always referred to Pinza's father as 'my favourite music critic'. So again the story takes a pleasant turn, and in that, too, Tebaldi's reminiscences are typical.

Lauri-Volpi was a man with strong views. He was an individualist, prefacing one of his books (for he also proved himself an accomplished writer) with an aphorism of Leonardo's: 'Chi è solo è tutto suo', or 'The loner is his own man'. Yet he also had powerful allegiances, most especially to the art he served with such passionate fervour, and to those exponents of it whom he esteemed. He was, for instance, an early champion of Maria Callas, and when her performance in *Il trovatore* (and, incidentally, his own) appeared in his judgment to have been grossly

86

Lauri-Volpi as Radamès in *Aïda*

underrated by the prejudiced Neapolitans, he wrote to the Naples press and denounced them. He could indeed be belligerent, and I suppose in some respects rather absurd – there is an amusing account in Harold Rosenthal's *Two Centuries of Opera at Covent Garden* telling of the negotiations on which Geoffrey Toye, as Managing Director, was dispatched to Italy, from where he telegraphed: 'Gigli indignantly refuses, and Volpi will never recover from insult of my offer. Returning London immediately.' Yet he could also be charming (as Tebaldi says), remarkable for his courtesy, having also the manner of an aristocrat and the dignity of a scholar.

Something of the aura appropriate to the university man (he took his degree at Rome in Law) distinguished Lauri-Volpi from the general run of singers, and most notably from his famous rival Beniamino Gigli. To Lauri-Volpi, if there was anything more irritating than Gigli's undeniably beautiful voice, it was his plebeian manner: plebeian, that is, in the absence of reserve, in the willingness to bestow vocal favours upon all and sundry. He would sing from hotel balconies, to gallery queues, to townsfolk in the piazza. In Lauri-Volpi's view it was all very undignified and the popularity itself more than a trifle vulgar. Lauri-Volpi of course could hardly be considered the most impartial of observers, but he did sincerely hold to a belief in the nobility of an opera singer's art and, as a corollary, in the reprehensible nature of any indulgence to cheapen it.

His training and early experience in the opera house also set him apart, in a relatively patrician line of singers. He was one of the last pupils of Antonio Cotogni, a former baritone and a teacher then in his eighties. Among the singers who made the deepest impression on him when he attended his first operas were the great Battistini, the younger baritone Giuseppe de Luca and the tenor Alessandro Bonci, in other words three lyrical singers whose style was that of what even then would have been seen as the old school. The opera of his debut, significantly made under the name of Rubini, was Bellini's *I puritani*. This took place at Viterbo, near Rome, in 1919, and he then appeared in the city itself in *Manon, Rigoletto* and *Il barbiere di Siviglia*. Though he soon added the principal Puccini operas, his repertoire was at this time 'old-fashioned', founded on the older lyric operas, avoiding the modern *verismo*. This in the long term did him good service, for the qualities most commending him to a later generation of critics, such as (in this country) Desmond Shawe-Taylor, were those in which he could be heard as a modern exponent of an old tradition. Shawe-Taylor heard him sing *I puritani* at Florence in 1933 and wrote enthusiastically of a robust voice and ringing high notes, all the more remarkable because they were combined with 'a charm of *mezza voce* and a distinction of phrasing at times reminiscent of De Lucia himself'.

Lauri-Volpi had by then become established as one of Italy's leading singers, with a background of successes in both North and South America. At the Metropolitan, New York, he sang from 1923 to 1933, giving a total

88

Giacomo Lauri ~ Volpi

L'EQUIVOCO

Edizioni BONGIOVANNI Bologna

of just over three hundred performances with the company, including the American premieres of *Luisa Miller* and *Turandot*. At Covent Garden he had only two seasons, 1925 and 1936, on both occasions meeting with a very mixed press. After his debut in *Andrea Chénier*, the management was advised 'in all friendliness' by Ernest Newman to sit down and do some quiet thinking. What was the point, he asked, of bringing to London, at great expense, 'certain artists who are not really first-rate in order to inflict on us certain operas that are not even third-rate'. In 1936, *Musical Opinion*'s excellent critic, 'Figaro', wrote of Lauri-Volpi in *Aïda* as 'singing with all his old ease and lovely quality but with a notable refinement of style', while in *Tosca* his 'E lucevan le stelle' had 'real style as well as glorious quality of voice'. Dyneley Hussey, on the other hand, wanted to know why, in *Aïda*, he needed to 'take his breath so often in the wrong places and so seldom in the right ones'.

As the years went by he added more heroic rôles to his repertoire, including, in 1940, *Otello*. During the early years of the war he sang in Italy until the tide turned, when he withdrew to Spain. But there was no question of retiring, and throughout the 1950s he continued to appear, with declining powers but every now and then securing a genuine personal triumph.

In 1957 *Opera* magazine's correspondent reported on a performance of *La fanciulla del West* with Lauri-Volpi who 'with his unpredictable gesticulation and seraphic, unchanging smile, is guaranteed to give a genial air of musical comedy to any opera'. Yet his high notes proved invincible among the live lions employed in a revival of Donizetti's *Poliuto* at the Caracalla in Rome, and the best was yet to be. At the age of seventy-nine he sang in the Love Duet from *Madama Butterfly* with Montserrat Caballé, and in Barcelona crowned 'Nessun dorma' with a top B that stunned all hearers. At the age of eighty-four he offered the second verse of 'La donna è mobile', cadenza and all, to a wildly cheering crowd, both of these latter events being preserved on record and earning a mightily impressive place among their proud and pitiable kind.

He died in 1979, at Valencia. He lives vividly in reputation, valuably in his best recordings, and perhaps most enduringly in one of his books. His *Voce parallele* takes its title from Plutarch's *Parallel Lives*, and in a fascinating scheme of comparisons places singers of comparable voice-type in pairs. Surprisingly perhaps, this sublime egoist listened to his colleagues both attentively and sympathetically, and in the book he always finds something interesting to say. Eventually he turns to an 'isolated voice', without parallel, the fresh and incorruptible tone of which is 'even today considered the firmest of the lyric theatre', a voice endowed with 'three octaves of vibrations unknown to others'. Its owner: Giacomo Lauri-Volpi. His secret: joy in the soul and joy in the voice.

CHAPTER 19

Carlo Bergonzi

Dolce cosa. The memory of Bergonzi's farewell recital in London, at the age of sixty-eight, refuels not only affectionate regard for the individual at the centre of it but also for opera itself, and more particularly for the tradition of Italian opera, where the heart rejoices in the power of music made manifest, above all, by its singers.

Bergonzi has always been essentially an opera-*singer*. Occasionally it might be reported of a performance that it marked an improvement in his acting, or that he seemed in posture, movement and facial expression to be less indifferent than usual to the calamities supposedly engulfing him and everyone else on stage; but generally it was agreed that you went to hear Bergonzi rather than to see him. His undisputed place of honour in the opera houses of the world has long testified to the primacy of good singing, and his farewell to Covent Garden on 16 October 1992, left no doubt that even in this age of the stage-producer, the conductor and the operatic all-rounder (with thorough musicianship, intelligent study, well-schooled stagecraft), the quality which above all is recognised and cher-ished as the pearl of great price is that of the real singer.

It has also demonstrated that the public is not so naïve or primitive in its recognition of 'the real singer' as is widely supposed. Decibels and top notes are not the inevitable criteria, for Bergonzi's has been a voice of moderate power, and while, in his prime, he never shirked them, the high Cs rarely emerged as a crowning glory. Nor has his tone been remarkable for any very sensuous richness or for the glamour of a specially thrilling vibrancy. His virtues are such as in a well-constituted world of opera would be commonplace. His honoured position in that world simply shows how rare they are.

The first of these virtues is steadiness: the even emission of a firmly focussed sound. In that Covent Garden recital there was not the faintest suspicion of a beat, *tremolo* or wobble.

If the listener had cared to pause and ask just what was different here from the day-in-day-out singing that generally passes readily enough, the answer might have come first as a number of absences: not merely the absence of anything remotely suggesting wobble, but also an absence of syllabic production, the insidious habit of treating each syllable as an entity, of introducing tiny swellings of the tone on the individual notes, of making consonants stand out like so many punctuation-marks in the melodic line. Bergonzi's diction was perfectly clear and the emotional expressiveness of his singing never failed to communicate; but all was achieved within the discipline of the musical line. It is for this kind of thing that the public knows 'the real singer', and, whether analysing it or not, this is what the public has found pre-eminently in Bergonzi.

What, then, of the voice itself? It was not possible that in his sixty-ninth year the tenor should have sung with the resources of his prime. Most evident was the restriction of the upward range, its ceiling set for most if not the whole of the programme at about A flat. Occasionally a 'frog' gave warning, though never too obtrusively, usually in *diminuendo* or on the drop to a low note. More serious were the intimations of age when the style became strenuous, as in the climax of Leoncavallo's 'Mattinata'. At such moments (another occurred towards the end of the *Luisa Miller* aria) you reflected that this would not be a performance you'd greatly want to hear on records. The effect upon the voice was that it gained power at the expense of resonance. Yet this never – at least from my seat which admittedly was on this occasion a privileged one at no great distance from the stage – registered as a dried-out voice, or even as essentially an old one.

The outstanding point to be made about the voice, indeed, is that it had remained, to an exceptional degree, tonally pure. Most readers will recognise (though it is rarely the subject of written comment) the kind of sound that in private notes and personal vocabulary I describe to myself as 'tintop', and which is a kind of overlay, accretion or patina of impure sound heard in many voices, and probably most commonly thought of as 'wear' (yet not infrequently present in singers fresh from college). For the public, I believe, the presence or absence of this impurity is often the governing factor in their perception of a voice as 'beautiful' or not. As far as my experience goes, Bergonzi has always been free of it, and he remained so even in this final recital. That too, in the public estimation, is the mark of a 'real singer'.

As to that experience, the writer's own, it has to be admitted that there are lamentable gaps and limitations; but it does go back to Bergonzi's first appearance in this country, which was at the Stoll Theatre (demolished long ago) in 1953, a full fourteen years before his debut at Covent Garden. I remember it well, and the slight wonderment as to what exactly it was that we were hearing. *La forza del destino* was a puzzle in itself, and to some extent remains so. In this doom-laden opera it proved impossible not to laugh as in the first scene the hero and heroine, caught in the direst emergency, nevertheless found time to come down to the footlights hand in hand to finish their duet so rudely interrupted at the very moment when its passionate final phrases were coming into view.

The tenor no doubt was part of the amusement but he was the real thing

Bergonzi as Don Alvaro in *La forza del destino*

ROYAL ALBERT HALL
General Manager: Frank J. Mundy

Thursday 20th April at 7.30 p.m.

JOHN COAST presents

CARLO BERGONZI

accompanied at the piano by

ENRICO PESSINA

PROGRAMME

Tormento!	*PAOLO TOSTI*
Già il sole dal Gange	*ALESSANDRO SCARLATTI*
Caro mio ben	*GIUSEPPE GIORDANI*
O Primavera!	*PIER ADOLFO TIRINDELLI*
O Paradiso (L'Africana)	*GIACOMO MEYERBEER*
Ah! non credevi tu! (Mignon)	*AMBROISE THOMAS*
Quando le sere al placido (Luisa Miller)	*GIUSEPPE VERDI*

INTERVAL
A warning gong will be sounded for five minutes before the end of the interval

NEAPOLITAN SONGS

'A vucchella	*PAOLO TOSTI*
I te vurria vasà!	*EDUARDO DI CAPUA*
Tu ca' nun chiagne	*ERNESTO DE CURTIS*
Passione	*ERNESTO TAGLIAFERRI*
Piscatore e Pusilleco	*ERNESTO TAGLIAFERRI*
Marechiare	*PAOLO TOSTI*
Voce e notte	*ERNESTO DE CURTIS*
O paese do Sole	*D'ANNIBALE*

all right. We all knew it, though we had never heard of him before, and suspected that our elders and betters would find him beneath their notice. The aria was decidedly impressive, and the duet with Don Carlo (the veteran Tagliabue whom I seem to recall as looking like a cross between Stignani and Parry Jones) resolved into an unforgettable exercise in emulation. But, amid uncertain bearings regarding standards, the conviction remained firm that I had for the first time in my life heard an Italian tenor singing on stage in the way my gramophone records had taught me to listen for and to appreciate.

At that time few of us would have been aware that our tenor for the evening had in fact been a tenor for only two years. He had sung as a baritone for three, and then retrained himself, studying records of Caruso, Gigli, Schipa and Pertile, each of whom taught him something specific. His own earliest recordings (on the Italian Cetra label) show a voice with a rather exciting tightspun *vibrato*, more akin to another of his famous predecessors, Giacomo Lauri-Volpi, to whom Harold Rosenthal noted a resemblance when he first heard Bergonzi, also at the Stoll. By that time he had already sung at La Scala, though without striking roots there. At the Metropolitan in 1956 his 'Ah, si, ben mio' in *Il trovatore* was singled out for praise, and one detail in it, the short trill, made *Opera*'s critic, James Hinton Jnr., enquire in parenthesis 'who else observes the marking?' This was to bear fruit, and Bergonzi remained on the roster for almost every season, totalling 312 performances with the company up to 1985.

In Verona, Desmond Shawe-Taylor found that, despite the lack of a thrilling martial timbre, his singing in *Aïda* was exemplary 'in detail'. It was the polish and elegant finish of his work that attracted the critics. He would, for instance, sing the final note of 'Celeste Aïda' *pianissimo*, which may have offended the locals of the Parma opera in 1959 but 'brought the house down' at the Metropolitan in 1967.

The recurrent adjective was 'impeccable', and sometimes even this was improved upon. In *La Gioconda* at Verona in 1973 'Cielo e mar' was encored each time, and it seems that the arena, as Roger Bramble reported in *Opera* magazine, 'stimulated him to a point where he gave more than in his impeccable performances inside theatres'.

Taken literally, of course, 'impeccable' is negative praise, simply meaning that there were no faults. Sometimes faults were found: vocal faults, that is (his acting, or lack of it, was a regular subject for satire). He would maybe hold on to a high note when the score indicated otherwise. In *Il trovatore* at the end of 'Di quella pira' he would leave the chorus to sing their encouragements and only then add his 'All'armi', with its top C, when they had finished. Later the high notes became increasingly effortful and when he gave his Covent Garden recital of 1984 one noted a careful husbanding of resources. But then, by 1984, he was sixty, and by that age, for one reason or another, most of them have stopped entirely.

Certainly the farewell concert told of something richer and more positive than the merely 'impeccable'. During the course of the evening two memorable voices arose from the audience. One, a resonant bass-baritone in the stalls, cried out: 'Il più grande!' Bergonzi smiled and made a gesture which meant 'Down a bit'. He was right but the acclaim of 'the greatest' made us think. Then the General Director came out to present a token of our esteem, our appreciation and ... 'And our love' urged a *comprimario* in the upper regions. Mr Isaacs added that he was about to say 'our best wishes'. But 'our love' won the day.

CHAPTER 20

Régine Crespin

'Régine Crespin had to build her world career abroad, and she did it, bringing glory to France when French singing and the French repertoire were at their lowest ebb.'

Those words of André Tubeuf, written in 1979 when Crespin's career had entered its final phase, place her accurately in historical context, and carry a warmth of feeling of the kind which this noble singer often inspired. Hers was indeed a genuinely international career. It is also true that for many years Crespin's was the single name known to the general public as representing in the present what they understood to have been at one time a great international operatic school. Gérard Souzay on the concert platform, Crespin in the opera house: this, for many people and for many years, was the sum-total of French singing in modern times. She was applauded at the Metropolitan, La Scala, Covent Garden; her seasons at Bayreuth, Salzburg and Glyndebourne were long remembered; Buenos Aires and Mexico, Naples and Rome, Chicago and San Francisco, Vienna and Berlin, Barcelona, Lisbon, Geneva … the list is a long one and by no means complete.

As for France, it would be wrong to conclude from the summary quoted above that it played no part, or only a small part, in her story. The foundations for the world career were built in the opera houses of Rouen, Nîmes, Marseille and Nice. Though it was a matter of some vexation to her that, having distinguished herself at the Conservatoire, she was dismissed to the provinces, nevertheless her recall to Paris came the following year, and by the end of 1951 she had made her debut at both the Opéra-Comique and the Opéra itself. Her relationship with the Paris Opéra ('ma fausse maison' she called it) nevertheless remained a source of some bitterness, and was to become traumatic. Throughout the mid-1950s, she sang in the provinces more often than in the capital, which seemed to need the reassurance of success abroad before it could fully acknowledge that in her it possessed the greatest asset among the French singers of the time.

In 1958 she caused a sensation at Bayreuth singing Kundry in *Parsifal*. It should not have been entirely a surprise, for she already had Wagnerian rôles such as Elisabeth and Sieglinde in her repertoire; yet Kundry seemed

to reveal a new Crespin, the point being of course that Crespin was still herself but that the realisation of that 'self' needed someone of a kind they did not have in Paris, someone with a certain amount of vision, a touch of genius perhaps: someone such as Wieland Wagner. Her work with Wieland Wagner at Bayreuth was rather like Callas's with Visconti in Italy: it broadened and deepened her, and had the best kind of educative effect, the sense of being drawn upon and of fully realising the resources within. When she returned to Paris it was, in the words of *Opera*'s correspondent, as the *grande dame* of the Opéra. Yet, uncannily, she did not do her best work there. The *Opera* review which acknowledged her position as *prima donna* also reported her to be singing in metallic, shrill and strident tones as Amelia in *Un ballo in maschera*, and later she was 'in bad voice' in her well-tried rôle of Elsa in *Lohengrin*.

In 1962 she made a strong impression ('great and glorious to behold') in *The Trojans*, and in 1965 the popular press made much of her 'svelte silhouette', replacing the well filled-out figure of a hearty eater. By 1972 she had gained what was described as 'a Joan of Arc aura', a prestige comparable to that of the great nineteenth-century divas whom everybody, musical or not, simply had to go and hear. But this was a time of crisis in her life, and it was in the Paris Opéra that the overwrought feelings of a woman who had long been under stress broke out in a way that made an ordeal of any subsequent appearances there.

She was present in the audience at a performance of *Turandot* in which the principal soprano was booed. From the middle of the stalls Crespin stood up and denounced; facing the gallery, she called them cowards: 'Vous êtes des lâches.' The lower part of the house applauded her, and as Charles Pitt, who was in the audience, remarked: 'It certainly had an effect on the booers for the rest of the evening.' But from that time on, she either was, or felt herself to be, a marked woman. She too was booed, and, whether as cause or effect (probably an interaction), her voice failed. At the height of her career, she confronted the prospect of retirement, and then, as one of the most famous singers in the world, decided that she would take herself once again to a teacher, and retrain. The result was a return to the stage in 1975 as Carmen. Her performance, at once human and patrician, impressed deeply, though the vocal resources were clearly limited. She also returned to an opera with which she had a particularly close association: in 1957 she had been chosen by Poulenc to create the rôle of the young Madame Lidoine in the premiere of *Les Dialogues des Carmélites*, and now, twenty years later and singing in English, she joined the cast of the Metropolitan premiere as the dying Madame de Croissy. She retired from the operatic stage in 1988, singing the rôle of the old Countess in *The Queen of Spades* on the huge and inhospitable stage of the Palais de Congrès, at the age of sixty-two.

Five years earlier she had sung for the last time at Covent Garden, also as the dying Prioress, and the occasion as I remember it, appealed more

to a sense of history than to that of hearing, for the voice itself sounded edgy and untamed. But here it has to be confessed that Crespin's voice, as heard in Covent Garden, had never seemed to me a beautiful one, except when she took the edge off, singing softly. This was so from the time of her debut in 1960 when she sang the rôle for which she was most renowned, that of the Marschallin in *Der Rosenkavalier*. She made a most lovely effect in the final phrase of Act I, with the soft, beautifully held high G sharp of 'die silberne Rose' contributing magically to the emotion, which she liked to open out frankly at this point. But for much of the time the purity of her tone was compromised by an upper layer of something metallic or simply of wear (and I was interested to find that this can be heard in 'live' recordings made as early as 1956). It was still more disadvantageous in her *Tosca*, the abiding memory of which is not so much the sound as the character: the impression of magnanimity, of the kind that

99

comes to mind when people repeat the old saying that 'behind every great man there is a great woman'.

It is in fact the impression of a magnificent woman that I retain from what on the whole was the best of occasions on which I heard Crespin in London. She gave a recital with Geoffrey Parsons at the Wigmore Hall in 1982 in which I sat in a row perhaps four or five from the front and so felt very fully the personal magnetism, a grandeur certainly but also tenderness and gaiety. She was superb in the Satie songs, especially *La diva de l'empire*, 'sous le grand chapeau Greenway'. She also sang Debussy most sensitively, and, in the first half, Schumann's *Frauenliebe und Leben*.

As *La vie et l'amour d'une femme*, this becomes the title of her autobiography (Fayard, 1982), which tells with remarkable zest and frankness of a life that might equally well have derived its title from *Tosca*: 'Vissi d'arte, vissi d'amore'. The early chapters trace the development of her art from its probable origins in the care of her beloved grandmother, Mannolini ('she sang out of tune like a soldering-iron at full volume all the time, and she it was who gave me a love of singing'). Then she tells of the decisions, the hard work, the setbacks, the success.

Just as the success begins to glow, so does the heart with the entry into her life of Lou Bruder, whom she married. Then what was delightful as 'one night of love', bringing her to rehearsals at ten o'clock after just two hours' sleep, became alarming when it was one night of love after another. She tells of this as a real and eventually a nightmarish problem leading to separation. Next she found herself in love with a sensitive, cultured and affectionate man who proved impotent and died in distressing circumstances. Another affair which failed to provide the stability she needed, then the trauma of Paris, the crisis of her voice, and the diagnosis of a cancer: all have their place in this 'Liebe und Leben'. It makes one resolve, when thinking of a singer, to spare some thought also for the human being.

CHAPTER 21

Kirsten Flagstad

In the Pantheon of Singers Flagstad is the Bringer of Glory. She brought it twice, in needful times on both occasions. Old W.J. Henderson, most formidable of New York's music critics, had seen the 1930s as 'an age of small things daily growing smaller', but on 22 March 1935 he could report about the new Isolde that she 'proudly takes her place beside the great singers of the rôle who gave glory to the Metropolitan'. Similarly, at Covent Garden in 1936 the opera critic of the *Star*, though not himself a veteran of Henderson's experience, met in the foyer 'a famous music critic who had heard Ternina, Eames and Nordica in their prime' and who pronounced upon Flagstad that 'Hers is the voice of the century'.

On her emergence from retirement after the war, in 1947, Virgil Thomson in the *New York Herald Tribune* greeted 'the dream voice of all time', and in London Philip Hope-Wallace wrote that in the last act of *Die Walküre* 'where she begs Wotan for the protection of fire, her singing could be said to have set the house alight on its own'.

She came above all with a glory of voice; but dignity, humanity and musicianship stood by in attendance. She inspired as a singer transported from the legendary golden age to renew faith and standards in times that had virtually resigned themselves to a belief that greatness of this kind was a thing of the past.

The voice was certainly a noble instrument. It had the power to sail through any orchestral storm and to do so without tacking or furling. There was a fullness in the tone; a good shine on the trumpet-notes, but with roundness and mellowness too. When she first sang in the great international houses her top notes gleamed with healthy resonance. Later they alone were perceived to have lost something of their old ease and freshness, but all else, down to the rich, contralto-like lower register, retained its original qualities of warmth and strength, perfectly firm in production, sure of attack and intonation. The tone also expressed character: this was the voice of largesse, of magnanimity.

What with the heroic rôles she sang on stage and the majesty of utterance associated with them, it is not surprising that her career should acquire a mythology of its own. In that year, 1935, the public was presented suddenly with the complete first lady, a woman of forty, as in one of those miraculous births, a Minerva springing fully-armed from the head of Zeus. The notion that this wonderful creature could have been singing for twenty years in her native Oslo and thereabouts seemed inconceivable. That she should have come to New York via Bayreuth was natural enough, but that the great Isolde and Brünnhilde of the Metropolitan should quite recently have been a mere Third Norn and a more or less anonymous Valkyrie at Bayreuth was preposterous. She had also been on the verge of retirement. She married in 1930 and in the spring of that year had made what was intended to be her farewell to the stage. As a further shock it might have been learned that up to that date she had hardly been a Wagnerian soprano at all.

It was true that the very first rôle she ever learned was that of Elsa in *Lohengrin*, but this had been at the age of ten. She came from a musical family, the father being a violinist and then conductor in an Oslo theatre, while her mother was a pianist with an interest in singing. Flagstad's debut in opera came at the age of eighteen, as the child Nuri in d'Albert's *Tiefland*. She then studied with Gillis Bratt, a celebrated and controversial teacher in Stockholm whose pupils also included Joseph Hislop, Göta Ljungberg and Ivar Andresen.

When she rejoined the Oslo company it was as a light lyric soprano with rôles such as Micaëla, Marguerite and a range of parts in musical comedies wlth titles such as *The Circus Princess* and *The Queen of the Movies*. Even so, she attracted attention as early as 1919 with a Desdemona sung to the Otello of an eminent visitor, the great Leo Slezak, and other rewarding rôles such as Minnie in *La fanciulla del West* began to come her way. A certain stiffness characterised her work on stage, but before the time of her marriage she felt that she had gained a new freedom from inhibitions in her acting with the addition of *Tosca* to her repertoire; and 1929 also brought the first Wagner, with *Lohengrin*, the studies of childhood coming to fruition at last.

The Fates also play a part in this mythology. Just when she might have retired, the bass Alexander Kipnis sang with her and reported on her to Bayreuth: an offer came, the career was extended, and this led to the Metropolitan and the new birth.

Later, when war broke out, she left America to rejoin her husband in Norway. Again, she might have let it end there, but with his death and a number of other external factors at work she was impelled to relaunch her career and a new and still more glorious phase began.

She was then over fifty, but even after her retirement the devotion she had inspired in a younger generation, represented by the Decca company's most enterprising producer, John Culshaw, opened up a new chapter of late recordings and most especially her participation, as Fricka in *Das Rheingold*, in the historic first complete recording of the *Ring* cycle, under Solti. It was just as Culshaw had finished his editing of the third opera, *Siegfried*, on 7 December 1962 that he noticed Solti was 'oddly subdued':

Flagstad as Isolde

'Instead of his usual bounce, and a deluge of questions about whether this, that or the other had come out as we hoped, he said almost nothing except: "I'm very pleased". In the end I asked him if anything was the matter. "I suppose you haven't seen the papers," he said. "Kirsten died last night".'

Such affection and respect derived no doubt from an amalgam of

Flagstad as woman and artist. Her voice alone, now, on records, can inspire it too, but you have to take care over both the choice and the reproduction. Some of her late records were marvellous: her recital of Sibelius songs with orchestra, for instance. In others one is aware of a voice past its prime and of expressive powers that scarcely go quite far enough to compensate. There is also the great *Tristan und Isolde* recording under Furtwängler, subject of a famous scandal when it became known that the two or three highest notes were supplied by Elisabeth Schwarzkopf: none the less a glowing and real performance, and in many ways still supreme.

Pre-war recordings made 'live' show the voice at its freshest, trailing the clouds of glory that recalled to old Henderson in the last years of his life something of the golden age of his youth when the operas themselves were new to New York. But for love of Flagstad and her singing I would recommend the songs: Grieg's *Haugtussa* cycle, for instance, or the *Wesendonck* Lieder to Gerald Moore's accompaniment, or a perfectly simple song of Beethoven's, his 'Ich liebe dich'. This is where you come best to know her, and, as I say, knowledge assuredly brings love.

For myself, I too remember her best in recital. She would be formal in her opening Lieder, taking time to sing 'through' a certain layer of wear on the voice in post-war years; but then in the second half, with the Scandinavian songs that were utterly home-ground to her, and which she perhaps felt as not quite such serious 'high art', a new tenderness, intimacy and happiness would irradiate the voice and her whole presence. She was so much more personal in these things: indeed, I can hear her now in (for example) Grieg's 'With a water-lily', and can both hear and see her catching the simple wholesome enthusiasm of his 'St John's Eve'. It was then, and when she sang Frank Bridge's 'Love went a-riding' in such a way that the last note promised faithfully to ring on in the mind from there to eternity, that one felt most open to the warmth of her genius.

About her ability to portray the real Isolde, and to some extent Brünnhilde too, there was from the start much argument. Many felt that she was too equable, too simply 'nice'. Vincent Sheean, in his memoir *First and Last Love*, takes the phrase from Act I, 'Das wär' ein Schatz, mein Herr und Ohm', as an example of what she could not do: 'The savage mockery, the false sweetness, the snarl: of this nothing was left. It could have been "The Last Rose of Summer".' Ernest Newman, observing very closely, said that he thought it was not a failure of sensibility: 'mentally, she lived the part of Isolde with the utmost intensity'. The trouble lay more in the invariable nobility of timbre.

But that was pre-war. The war years and more particularly, by a sad irony, the first years of peace brought intense suffering. Out of it she herself felt a new Flagstad was born. To Culshaw, the *Götterdämmerung* Act II which he saw first in 1949 presented Brünnhilde as a being of such

intense and terrible command 'that it was impossible to believe that the same tempestuous quality was not part of her own character'.

And indeed perhaps it was: just as the woman who sang with such inner radiance Grieg's song of happiness on the eve of the Norwegian midsummer festival was the same person as the one who that very day a few years earlier had learned of the death of her husband, the culmination of what she saw as a bitter persecution by an enemy who was hers too, and to whom the only answer had to be strength, endurance and renewal through singing.

105

CHAPTER 22

Antonio Scotti

Naples, Italy, Feb. 28. – Antonio Scotti, beloved baritone, who sang for 33 successive seasons at the Metropolitan Opera, New York, died here in poverty on Wednesday and was buried today. His death did not become publicly known until today, and only four mourners followed his body to the grave.

The Associated Press report, printed in the *New York Times* on Saturday 29 February 1936, went on to tell how the singer, aged seventy, had spent his last months almost in isolation. A paid obituary notice had been inserted by friends in the Naples *Mattino* referring to the 'glorious lyrical career which held high the prestige of Italian Art on the stages of the world'; and (they added) the Italian press in general had ignored the event altogether.

New Yorkers especially must have felt a shock, for Scotti had only recently retired, amid honours and deeply affectionate demonstrations from the public and fellow-artists. He had been at the centre of operatic life in the States from the beginning of the century – indeed, from the last month of the nineteenth, for he had made his Metropolitan debut, as Nevers in *Les Huguenots*, on 15 November 1899. He was the Rigoletto of Caruso's house debut four years later, and the two of them, fellow-Neapolitans, were always to be seen together in New York till the tenor's lamentable illness took him back to Italy, to die there in 1921. Subsequently the Caruso era acquired a glamour which scenes-in-being lacked, and Scotti's continued presence with the company for another twelve years, as well as the work he did with his own touring company, provided a living reminder and a link with the grander past.

The *New York Times* certainly did its best to compensate for the neglect in Italy. Tributes flowed in from former colleagues: from Ponselle ('a great friend and a great artist, beloved by all'), Farrar ('his death breaks the link in a golden year of opera'), Bori, Martinelli, the general manager Edward Johnson, the bass Léon Rothier ('I'm heartbroken'). A retired wholesale ice dealer in Jersey City who never missed a performance in twenty-seven years, thus notching up an estimated score of 1,500, wept at the news and pronounced that the world had lost not only a great singer but a noble

106

Scotti as Scarpia in *Tosca*

man. Olin Downes, the paper's senior music critic, contributed a long and warmly appreciative essay on his career and his human qualities. There were also photographs.

One of these showed Scotti in his sixties, a man of modest, dignified bearing with only the very slightest suggestion of an Italian opera singer somewhere about the jaw, and smiling that reserved, reminiscent smile of one who feels that his day has passed. The others were of the three rôles in which he would have been most vividly remembered. 'As the hero of *Falstaff*' is the heading of the first. 'Hero' may not be quite the *mot juste*, but it's a lovely photograph of Falstaff in more than make-up: in gesture and attitude, with a quizzical intelligence that proclaims something other than the red-nosed fatguts. Then, stooping, mean and vindictively suspicious, he is tranformed into the villainous Chim Fen of Leoni's *L'oracolo*, the part which he made his own when the voice had worn thin and the spell had to be sustained by acting. Most famous of all, there is his Scarpia. Here it is a full-face shot, its focal point being the intense eyes, hungry (perhaps) for a love these coldly chiselled features could never inspire, and in default of which the appetite gains its satisfaction from only the most ruthless exercise of power.

There exist other, better photographs of Scotti's Scarpia, formidable in authority, utterly credible. He created the rôle in both London and New York, and for years, in those cities, there was effectively no other. Victor Gollancz tried comparing him with Mario Sammarco, a contemporary of comparable standing: 'But as Scarpia (he writes) I preferred Scotti – preferred him indeed to any Scarpia I have ever seen. His voice was lighter than Sammarco's though never without adequate strength; but what appealed to me most in his Scarpia was its distinction of singing and manner alike, whereas Sammarco was forthright and bourgeois.' For W.J. Henderson, writing in the *New York Sun* at the time of Scotti's retirement in 1933, 'There has never been any other Scarpia. Many have essayed the character, but Scotti's portrait of the scheming police chief has remained the unapproachable model.'

The four photographs are, one would say, of four different people: certainly the three 'character' portraits would never seem to have as their common factor the mild, essentially unhistrionic face of the man himself. He was, by all accounts, a highly distinguished singing-actor. Most commentators seem to be agreed that the voice of itself would not have given him the position he occupied in the operatic world of his time. What may be of interest is the commentary this provides on the common notion that the operatic world of those days was largely indifferent to the dramatic side of the singer's art. Olin Downes, in his *Times* article, put it well. Scotti, he said, was brought up in the old school that asserted the primacy of singing. But then: 'On the basis of good technical schooling, impeccable taste, eclecticism, and the temperament of a born dramatic-interpreter, and without succumbing to its evils, Scotti met the demands of the new

108

A FAREWELL PARTY FOR ANTONIO SCOTTI: QUEENA MARIO, the Hostess, and Her Guests, All of the Opera, at the Party She Gave for the Singer Who Recently Retired After Thirty-three Years With the Metropolitan. Seated, From Rignt to Left, Are: Giuseppe Sturani, Wilfred Pelletier, Queena Mario, Antonio Scotti, Marcella Sembrich and Lucrezia Bori. Standing: Armando Agnini, Rose Bampton, Giovanni Martinelli, Vincenzo Bellezza, Earle Lewis, Tullio Serafin, Giulio Setti, Edward Johnson and Carlo Edwards. *N. Y. Times Jan 29 1933* (Estelle Edwards.)

A cutting from Martinelli's scrapbook, 1933

school.' Puccini put it more bluntly. Writing to his wife from London in the midst of the first *Tosca* rehearsals, he showed where his own priorities lay: 'Scotti, marvellous; bad voice, but talent, and of grand stature in the part.'

That 'bad voice' can be heard on records, and if one is unlucky in the selection (or reproduction) the judgment might seem unflattering but not entirely unjust. An example is the solo from *Tosca*, Scarpia's declaration in Act II telling that venal he may be, but from beautiful women he exacts payment in a different currency. The recording was made in 1908 when Scotti had plenty of good singing-days left. But this, as heard here, is not a Scarpia-voice: there is no juice in it, which you might say is not needful for the character of Scarpia, but it is for his music. The writing lies high in the voice, and in the phrases just before the *cantabile* section ('Già mi struggea l'amor della diva') a downward transposition of a semitone is arranged. That might not matter, if only the rest of Puccini's description had been borne out, but, though the singing is not inexpressive, there is little of the menace, insinuation and indeed passion that we might be expecting.

Disappointments can also arise out of Scotti's part in his duets with Caruso. They recorded five, and it is true that from first (*Bohème* and *Forza*) to last (*Don Carlos*) one can hear how sympathetically they worked together. Moreover, with good reproduction, Scotti's voice is clearly not unworthy of his partner's. Yet in the two excerpts from *Madama Butterfly*, for instance, where it would be so good to feel that here is a convincing memento of their collaboration in the historic British and American premieres, Scotti's tone lacks lustre and his style has something buttoned-up about it.

Far better, for discovering the genuine singer in Scotti, are some of his less likely solos. He sings a first-rate 'Eri tu' (*Un ballo in maschera*): recorded with piano accompaniment in 1905, this catches a brighter tone and has exactly the polish and refinement so reliably attributed to him. The aria from Massenet's *Le Roi de Lahore* is another that is both stylish and beautiful in sheer sound. He was remarkably scrupulous about precise articulation: listen, for example, to the triplets in his duet with Marcella Sembrich from *Don Pasquale* or to the careful detail of his Drinking Song from *Otello*. There are also songs, in some of which he combines an almost French fastidiousness of manner with the Italian gaiety that was native to him.

The elegance that aligns him with the French school of singing, as well as his long association with the opera houses of London and New York, where he was so very much the gentleman among singers, makes it easy to forget his Italian origins. The absence of the more luscious kinds of vibrancy in the voice is not typically Italian either. Yet he was a thorough-bred Neapolitan, seven years older than Caruso, whose career he was able to help through his own seniority. He worked his apprenticeship in Italy, and like many Italians ranged in his early years from Buenos Aires to St Petersburg. He was Italian also in his problems with sight-reading: one of his nightmares, with achievement to match, was learning the rôle of Hans Sachs on a three-week Atlantic crossing, to be sung, under Toscanini, for his debut at La Scala.

He was Italian in temperament too. A great melancholy afflicted him when he returned to England (but not to sing) in 1928. Covent Garden was then, to him, 'a house of ghosts' which he refused to visit for it would mean that he should sit 'alone and cry at the memory of golden voices ... my lost brother Caruso', whose voice, he said, 'still wakes me in my sleep'. But there was an Italian panache and gaiety of spirit too, even when he knew his voice was more than half-gone. Gatti-Casazza, director at the Met, had asked him (he said) if he would sing next season: 'and I answer him "So long I 'ave the arms and legs, I sing!" '

110

CHAPTER 23

Boris Christoff

In the theatre of the mind, like children with their cut-outs, we parade our favourites. From left to right, there stands Callas-Norma, dagger in hand and arm held aloft to slay the kids; then Scarpia-Gobbi darting a look fit to slay the cavorting choirboys of Rome. Towards the centre is Amneris-Cossotto, whose haughty expression tells of a bad smell assailing the fastidious nostrils. Then for the moment we find an empty space, and pass over to the other side of our stage, where poor, tragic Marie Collier contemplates the depths of the River Neva, James McCracken (the whites of his eyes staring through and into the darkness) sees Otello's occupation gone, and feeling her way down the staircase that leads from the gory marriage-chamber to the triumphant scene of madness comes Dame Joan.

Shortly, that space in the middle will be taken. But first the stage itself begins to fill: the chorus move in, the men in fur hats and scarlet robes half-covered by their beards. The trumpets sound, the cries of 'Slava!' peal forth, and slowly he enters (what an entrance it was!), orb and sceptre in hand, there to stand, Tsar of all the Russias, King Boris himself.

In the silence which follows we look upon a face formidable in authority and determination. What he has he will hold. But amid the blazing pomp of the present his eyes look out, unblinking and expressionless, into the double darkness of past and future. When he sings, it is softly. Not a muscle moves, among chorus or audience, during that brief solo. Though it is quiet, there is such concentration of tone that the sound rises with perfect clarity to the furthest reaches of the auditorium. Though the notes themselves are not deep, we are somehow aware of a great depth being drawn upon. When the sombre prayer and meditation are over, and the feast of rejoicing is proclaimed, his voice rises towards the top of its range. That too rings out, clear and secure. The procession moves on, the great moment is over but, again, what a moment it has been.

Referring to another Boris Godunov (the Frenchman, Vanni Marcoux), Victor Gollancz in his memoir, *Journey towards Music* (1964) wrote that anyone who had never heard Chaliapin would have believed Marcoux to be the ideal interpreter. He then added: 'Christoff, too, was superb in his way, but time somehow diminishes a little the impression he made of vocal and dramatic grandeur.'

To those who never heard Chaliapin, Christoff was greatness itself. Comparison of the two singers is in order because Christoff was so clearly performing in the Chaliapin tradition. Certainly he was no mere imitator; in fact it is quite probable that a critically deliberate part of his endeavour was to modify much that he learnt from Chaliapin's recordings. Yet compared, say, with lyricists such as Mark Reizen and, later, Nicolai Ghiaurov, his was a Boris Godunov realised in Chaliapinesque terms. It would be risky to attempt putting them side by side in this 'theatre of the mind', but Christoff's Boris at the very least must be reckoned a worthy companion to Chaliapin's. In one respect it was a greater achievement, for Chaliapin's physical stature gave him, literally, a head-start. He was a very striking looking man in private life too: I think it was Bernard van Dieren who said that the two most beautiful men he had known were Chaliapin and Busoni.

Christoff was not made in this way, and it was interesting to see how much less of an effect he made in a concert performance when he appeared not in costume and make-up but in evening dress. His achievement on the operatic stage is therefore all the greater, for, as with Chaliapin, when Christoff entered, he would – or at any rate always could – become the centre, and, as was said of Chaliapin, when he moved the whole stage moved with him.

This was so in *Don Carlos* too. In our late lamented Visconti production at Covent Garden, King Philip arrived with a pair of magnificent Irish wolfhounds, yet never was there an actor less in need of a boost to the effectiveness of an entry, and even these natural scene-stealers were upstaged. Christoff's Philip II was unforgettable. In the moments of power and authority (that stern entrance and the dismissal of his Queen's attendant, or the confrontation with Carlos in the *auto-da-fè*, or the cry 'Soccorso alla Regina!') he was immense. In the great solo, 'Ella giammai m'amò' the voice was magically indrawn and private, matching the proud public man in his pitiful loneliness. As he faced the Grand Inquisitor, Christoff would always prevail by the perfect continence of his sound whatever the voice opposing his in that battle of wills. When he sang with Tito Gobbi in that long conversation between the King and Posa, it was a wonderful example of the well-matched art of two supreme masters of the operatic stage. But when on one occasion I found myself seated right at the back in one of those low-ceilinged places where the sound comes with perfect clarity but deprived of reverberance, there was quite a striking contrast audible in the production of these voices, Gobbi's emanating unmistakably from the position in which he stood on stage, Christoff's so free of the throat that it might have come from anywhere or from just a few rows away.

His early training no doubt had much to do with that. In Italy his teacher was the baritone Riccardo Stracciari, who, unlike several who pass on their technical knowledge, demonstrated its soundness by the length of

Christoff as Boris Godunov

his own career and the excellence of his singing at an advanced age. No doubt too the natural gifts were exceptional. It was no ordinary voice that arose from the ranks of the famous Gusla Choir, thrilling Toti Dal Monte, an illustrious visitor to Sofia in 1938. Still more remarkable must have been its quality when four years later, by royal command, he sang solo before the King and Queen of Bulgaria and was rewarded with a scholarship to Italy.

The tale is told in Atanas Bozhkoff's biography of Christoff (Robson, 1991), where the second chapter, headed 'The Time before Dawn', sketches what must have been a harrowing development with the Bulgarian in Italy cut off from funds, making his way back through the war-torn lands, returning to find that Stracciari had decided to make a baritone out of him, only to be dissuaded by another baritone, Giuseppe De Luca. When eventually he made his debut (in *Bohème*, with three encores for the Coat Song) he was already over thirty. It was a late beginning, which may have been a blessing in disguise – though at times he may have felt, like Churchill after his defeat in the General Election, that, if so, the disguise was magnificent.

Certainly Fortune's disguises must have seemed impenetrable when arrangements for Christoff's American debut were thwarted by the rigidities of the McCarran Act. This was in 1950, the high noon of McCarthyism, when any Boris was a bogeyman, especially if he came, however indirectly, from Eastern Europe. So Rudolf Bing's opening night was deprived of what might have been its brightest star, and for ever afterwards the Metropolitan would have to add 'except Christoff' when it claimed to have employed all the great singers of the time. He enjoyed a spectacular success later in Chicago and elsewhere, but in New York he appeared only once in the years before 1980. By that time his worldwide achievements needed no further recognition, and the voice, though preserved and used with skill, no longer possessed the magnificent sonority which the audience at his concert would have known well from records.

The recordings are indeed a rich legacy. Already a mature artist at his first sessions, which allowed him full scope for his powers, he performed excerpts from *Boris Godunov* and *Mefistofele* making an immediate impression, not of promise, but of fulfilment. His earliest records, made in the late days of the 78, remain among his best. The complete operas were to follow, including two versions of *Boris Godunov*, the first, under Dobrowen, being unduly neglected nowadays in favour of the less satisfactory Cluytens recording of 1962. But to my mind his greatest contribution to the gramophone is in Russian song. His Mussorgsky album, lovingly prepared and annotated by himself, is a supreme achievement, to which, as in songs by Tchaikovsky and others, he gives his whole imagination, the voice miraculously adapting itself to that of child, nurse, beggar, lover, drunkard: the whole of mankind.

Mankind, of course, is fallible, and so was Christoff. He could be

Christoff at the EMI factory in Hayes, 1957

'difficult': there were highly publicised confrontations with Callas and Corelli; he was said to impose upon management terms such as '*Prince Igor* or nothing', and his curtain-calls were things of wonder. But I remember a night at Covent Garden when an apprehensive audience greeted the arrival of the General Manager on stage with a groan as of worst fears borne out. There was a strike, he explained. The scene-shifters would not shift. He had thought of cancelling *Don Carlos* and sending us home with a refund. Then he had felt a hand on his shoulder, and there was Mr Christoff. 'Why cancel?' he said. 'Why despair? You have no scenery, but you have an orchestra, you have a chorus, and you have me!' And so, thought Sir John, so we did. Everybody lent a hand and lugged such scenery as was luggable, and *Don Carlos* went ahead. We heard Christoff's Philip II then, most of us, for the last time, a little older, a little greyer of timbre, but incomparable as ever.

CHAPTER 24

Adelina Patti

Patti of course is not a 'singer of the century' at all; at least not if the century in question is our own benighted specimen. Of the nineteenth she was probably *the* singer. Certainly to the second half of it and in the field which is our subject, she gave her name. 'The Age of Patti' became the ready phrase, assigning a whole period to an individual in a way which perhaps only Caruso and Callas have inspired in later times. It is a name from the age of crinolines and carriages, from the salons of the Second Empire, the jewels of the Romanovs; a time which for the singer might bring encounters with Rossini, consultations with Verdi, concerts for the Queen in Windsor Castle. So what, it may be asked, is she doing here, among the children of the present century into which, professionally, she barely survived?

Well, supposing her to be on our doorstep and here to join the party, it is hardly to be thought that anyone would suggest she should be treated as a common gate-crasher. Moreover we may see that she has brought her visiting card. It is a round, flat object, in diameter scarcely larger than a saucer, for Adelina Patti is now on compact disc, that miracle unthinkable in any century but the twentieth, which to this extent has adopted her, summoning her voice from the shades and hearing it, in this form, more clearly and truly perhaps than at any time since the far-away years of 1905 and 1906 when it was recorded.

'Ah, non credea mirarti', an exquisite song of loss and of a frail, tenderly sustained hope, was among the arias she sang into the primitive recording apparatus rigged up in her Welsh castle, Craig-y-Nos, during the June of 1906. A ghostly pianist plays the melancholy phrases of introduction and the voice enters, softly, gently, its tone a mellow mezzo-soprano. It too, we think at first, assuredly is spectral, a ghost of its once-brilliant self.

The satin of its mortal dress gleams dimly. The very breath seems to need reassurance as to its existence. 'Ah!' sighs the singer, 'I had not thought to find you dead so soon.' Like the flower she holds, her love has proved shortlived, the blossom of a day: 'passasti al par d'amore, che un giorno solo durò'. The text seems emblematic. Not that the voice and its owner had been short-lived; far from it. But by this time, both (one might think) are faded and almost gone. The record, with its evident flaws, may

116

seem at best to have the fragrance of old lavender, a lingering scent of summers past.

For the moment, then, let it fade, this record, the relic of another age. One thing about records, we can do that with them: turn them down, turn them off, let them lie in the limbo of darkness and silence, and then bring them out for another whirl, as we shall this. But we might also let it serve to lead us back into the true 'Age of Patti', for the singer of this aria, the heroine of Bellini's *La sonnambula*, was one of her most famous rôles. 'Come to Covent Garden tonight and hear *Sonnambula*,' said the manager Frederick Gye to a friend. 'A little girl is to sing Amina, and I shall not be surprised if she makes a big hit.' This was 14 May 1861, the evening of which was to make history and, for Mr Gye particularly, a fair amount of money.

In some ways that date is comparable to another in the history of Covent Garden, to 17 February 1959, when Joan Sutherland sang her first *Lucia di Lammmermoor*. The signal difference between the two occasions is that in 1959 there were few among the audience who would have heard Covent Garden's previous Lucia, Toti Dal Monte, singing in 1925, whereas in 1861, Lucias, Aminas and the rest were two-a-penny. As *The Times* said the following day: 'The musical public has sunk into a sort of cynical incredulity, the result of many sanguine hopes raised, and just as many woefully disappointed.' The triumph of Patti lay in the conquest of this experienced public, sceptical to the point of indifference towards any newcomer in such rôles, particularly if she happened to be, as in this case, a mere girl of eighteen. 'The debutante was at first calmly, then more warmly, then enthusiastically – but always fairly and dispassionately – judged; and she who, to Europe at any rate, was yesterday without a name, before tomorrow will be "town talk".'

The critic's prophecy proved true almost immediately, and sooner even than that the impresario's hunch paid dividends. He had struck a bargain whereby the debutante was to take no payment for the first three performances; moreover, no success was to mean no payment at all. Patti must have been very sure of herself to have accepted; either that or she badly wanted the contract. And, as with many 'either/or's', no doubt both were true.

She went on to make her Paris debut, also in *La sonnambula*, which in addition she sang in Vienna and at La Scala, Milan, every time with resounding success. But of course, though she was new to these European houses, opera and the operatic world in general were far from new to her. At the age of eighteen, in fact, she was already something of a veteran.

La sonnambula, for instance, was the second opera she sang on stage, two years previously in New York. She had learnt the part and other major rôles also another two years before that, and this had been on her return from a concert tour planned to extend throughout the Southern States as far as the West Indies. That in turn had been the culmination of a few

118

Craig-y-nos Castle, Patti's home in Wales

years in which she had sung in every State of the Union, famous for concerts in which honours were shared with the legendary violinist Ole Bull, who in the not so distant past had given recitals with Chopin. The seven-year-old Patti and the forty-year-old Norwegian teamed up first in 1850. And even this was not the beginning. She had already given a concert at the small Tripler's Hall in New York, when one of her solos had been 'Ah, non giunge', the brilliant rondo which follows 'Ah, non credea' in *La sonnambula*. Also at the age of seven she sang 'Casta diva'; and when she was five, teaching by example, she enlightened her elder sisters on the art of the trill.

In Britten's cantata *Saint Nicholas* there is a delightful verse about the Saint's birth, how 'leaping from his mother's womb he cried "God be glorified" '. The childhood of Adelina Patti was such that it would not astonish us to find that her own great leap forward was accomplished while singing a few bars of 'Una voce poco fa'.

There is always something a little unnerving about child prodigies. Patti, with her 'gift from heaven', as she liked to call it, looks in a photograph taken when she was ten the very picture of an old head on young shoulders. It is the composure that is so remarkable. Yet this must have been a condition, if not of her success as a brilliant juvenile, then of her capacity to sustain and survive it. Following her progress through life

119

in the pages of the old biography by Herman Klein (*The Reign of Patti*, 1920), one seems to be witnessing a progress which has a sort of mechanistic, biological inevitability about it: the organism functions by some principle of growth from within, attracting agents that will serve its turn (and their own in the process). There have been other books since then, and a new biography,* which I understand is scheduled, may reveal a less composed and more fully human character. As it is, what we see – to put it another way – is the obverse of Maria Callas. Here are the two prima donnas about whom most has been written, both with a determined inner drive towards success. The mechanism of the one seems to have been well-adjusted so that her allotted three-score and ten (she died in 1919 at the age of seventy-six) flourished in a thoroughly propitious environment, and of course we know about the other.

For us in the present it is probably not the carpets of flowers that so impress, or the sackfulls of dollars or the bounty of monarchs (which was her favourite? 'Oh, the Tsar: he has the best diamonds'). Rather it is the prima donna who also made her contribution to the Handel Festival of 1865, the diva of the Italian opera who, albeit tentatively and late in life, ventured a little Wagner. It is that extraordinary girl of sixteen who in her first season sang fourteen major rôles. Above all it is the maker of that gramophone record which we put aside and to which we now return. Listening again, we hear much more than a middle range of touchingly beautiful quality; there is also a tenderly sympathetic and imaginative art. The trill which the child of five showed off to her sisters is still there for the sixty-three-year-old to spin for centuries to come.

Here, as we said at the start, is not a 'singer of the century', but one who, a little ahead of some others in this series, has proved herself a singer of the centuries.

* J.F. Cone, *Adelina Patti: Queen of Hearts*, Scolar, 1994.

CHAPTER 25

John McCormack

Towards the end of his life McCormack was sitting at home with a friend listening to the wireless and perhaps a little in need of cheering up, when, all in good time, one of his own records was announced. At the end, the presenter used a phrase which would have come easily, almost automatically, to his lips; though doubtless he said it with sincerity, it may not have meant a great deal to him personally. But it meant something to at least one listener. 'That was by the greatly loved Irish tenor, John McCormack,' said the announcer, and the friend could see that McCormack was touched. 'Greatly loved,' he repeated. 'Ah, and I was loved, wasn't I?'

Well, he was and he wasn't. At least, in my part of the world my musical elders would let it be known that they had little time for the praties (or the garden where they grow) and none at all for the rose of Tralee, which were the kind of thing they most associated McCormack with. My young contemporaries were even more dismissive, for, quite apart from what he sang, there was the voice itself, which with the letterbox 'ee's got on their nerves, and to some extent on mine too. 'Beelieve mee eef all those endearing young charms': even now, listening in the mind, I find it hard not to flinch.

Then, though we understood him to be by repute a great stylist, that also seemed far from evident. His recording of Parry's 'Jerusalem' would sometimes be played over the radio. 'And did those feet ...' ('Of course they didn't' snorted one of my mentors): McCormack's way of trying to free the notation so that it could take some of the natural syllabic values of speech was alien to this hymn-like music, where a quaver means a quaver. Or more frequently we would hear him in Handel's 'Where'er you walk', and I can hear it now: that slightly thin, somewhat nasal quality, the habit of taking notes from just a little below, and the tendency to close the vowel prematurely ('cool gales shall fan the glade') depriving the phrase of its true singing quality. All of these were considerations that at the time, as I remember it, made him rather less then greatly loved.

There were other things too. In an early colour film called *Wings of the Morning* he made a personal appearance, as himself, singing to an audience of (at a guess) retired lieutenant-colonels and their wives in an Irish stately home. It was a film remarkable for the beauty of its scenery and of

121

its French star Annabella; but I cannot recall that McCormack's presence, his manner when singing, or his communication with the supposed listeners, had any of those endearing charms that were considered to be so potent. I also remember a broadcast in early wartime when he recounted some of his memories of the operatic past. It was a grave disappointment. He confessed to never having been really happy in opera, but added that it could sometimes be fun in those days, as when after 'Questa o quella' in Act I of *Rigoletto* he would quickly escape into the wings to catch the latest news from the races. It was not what I wanted to hear. Young prig of an aspiring highbrow as I must have been, I scented philistinism, and felt let down.

Fortunately, such experiences were soon counterbalanced by others, and today, as we listen to the best of him on records, we recognise the artist, hear the voice for the lovely instrument it once was, and of course prize the humanity of which his singing was an expression.

The Irishness is an essential part of it, and yet it is a part to come back to rather than to start with. He won much popularity, particularly in America, as an Irishman singing Irish songs, but like all great artists in the field of what we now have to call 'classical music' he had to transcend nationality in the first place. The story of the Athlone boy with the beautiful voice and bad teeth is moving in itself. Born in 1884, the son of a labourer, later foreman, in the woollen mills, he won the Feis Ceoil gold medal at the age of nineteen. Records, judicious backing, Italian training (but only three months of it) and above all pluck and native ability, brought him quickly to the point where he was engaged for Covent Garden, the youngest tenor to have sung there in a principal rôle. This was in 1907, as Turiddu in *Cavalleria rusticana*: 'great promise' was diagnosed in the press and within weeks he was singing with Melba and Tetrazzini. In the States, from 1912 onwards, he came to be idolised, his concerts drawing audiences of five, seven thousand, as many as the halls would hold.

Applying for American citizenship in the First World War, he found himself under criticism from more than one side, but he emerged, outwardly unscathed, and grew in reputation as an honoured international singer. Count of the Roman Empire in 1928, master of Moore Abbey in County Kildare, he became one of the great men of his time. His farewell recitals in 1937 and '38 were crowned, as such things should be, by joy and sadness in almost equal proportion. At the outbreak of the Second World War he sang to the troops, broadcast and made some records; but by then his health was impaired, and in 1945 he died, only sixty-one years old.

His life story is, as I say, a moving one, as befits his art, yet there are anomalies in both. This is always a dangerous line of speculation, but I sometimes wonder whether I would have liked him if we had met. The stories rather suggest the sort of man who, sensitive to criticism himself, was given to what is euphemistically called plain speaking or genial

leg-pull. Knowingly or not, he could be hurtful. At a concert in America for which he was indisposed, he nevertheless recovered sufficiently to attend in the audience and afterwards went behind to congratulate the artists – which he did, with the exception of the tenor who had taken his place. This was Richard Crooks, to whom McCormack was something of a god and who had thought it one of the honours of his career that he should have been asked. He rarely spoke of it afterwards but was in fact deeply hurt. The other side of this was McCormack's capacity to inspire affection (it is something that speaks out in L.A.G. Strong's biography of him), and of course there is the warmth of emotion, as in that brief but intense treatment of a note which swells not in volume but in breadth of tone as the heart swells with the song he is singing.

In turn, this also provokes a query. For a singer who gave so much in character to his listeners he seems to have been an oddly impassive performer. One of the most vivid accounts I know of a McCormack recital

124

was written by Samuel Langford in the *Manchester Guardian* in 1927. Hearing him for the first time, Langford found 'a very genuine, though very small and confined, lyrical gift'. There was much he admired, including the vowels, which were 'absolutely pure and never bleating'. But he found little 'changeful and characteristic colour in his singing', such changes as there were being 'as for a fixed musical instrument'. The other thing that struck him was the physical immobility: if you had taken photographs (he felt), they would all have been the same except for the opening and shutting of the mouth.

Had this been written about his operatic work one would have been less surprised, but of the recitalist it is unexpected. As to his performances on stage, so much has been said about his being simply 'no actor' that it is remarkable how often the press comments, certainly in his later years at Covent Garden, make reference to his 'increased fervour both as a singer and as an actor' (*Traviata*), 'increased vocal power and more freedom of acting' (*Rigoletto*), 'acted as well as he sang' (*Barbiere di Siviglia*), 'improved decidedly in his acting .... His conception of the part of Pinkerton was an individual one and showed that he had thought' (*Madama Butterfly*).

These were all from 1912. As for his singing in those years, that was generally a matter for superlatives: 'He sang like an ideal tenor' said the French press when he appeared with the Boston Opera Company in Paris, and, in England, 'There is no artist at Covent Garden at present who has a finer style and finish of vocalisation than he.'

We, who have his records, know his humanity at first hand. 'Terence's Farewell to Kathleen' and the later recording of 'Kathleen Mavourneen' have it, his Rachmaninov songs too: 'When night descends' with Kreisler and 'To the children' without. We can catch the twinkle in his Irishness: 'Off to Philadelphia in the morning' and 'The Star of the County Down' are delightful examples. Then there is the depth he could convey in a language not his own and perhaps less than fully mastered: Wolf's 'Herr, was trägt der Boden hier' is sung with devoted sincerity and the finest art. We know too his technical mastery and the breath-control exercised in Handel and Mozart. Above all, in his early records, in the Covent Garden years, there is incomparable sweetness of tone and evenness of line: try his *Lucia di Lammermoor* and *Mefistofele* solos, or his duets with Mario Sammarco.

In the November issue of the *Gramophone* in 1945, Compton Mackenzie wrote: 'And now the greatest tenor, since Caruso died, has gone.' I remember reading that, and wondering. But not for long. I went immediately and played two records, 'Una furtiva lagrima' and 'Ah, moon of my delight': 'How oft, hereafter rising, shall she look/Through this same garden after me in vain – in vain!' As that soft high note on the last word fades slowly and gently into silence, the wondering ceases and only the wonder remains.

CHAPTER 26

Victoria de los Angeles

A little rodent sentence that has been gnawing away for about a quarter of a century began with a disparaging comment on some delightful soprano of the past (it may have been Elisabeth Schumann) and added a comparison with Victoria de los Angeles who in our own day, it said, had achieved success 'by smiling at the old gentlemen in the front rows'. I can't catch this by the tail or trace it to its source, despite a search in likely places; but we'll flush it out all the same. The implication is that it was largely a trick of personality: a singer with charming ways and a winning smile can always create an illusion which a more dispassionate assessment of her art would dispel.

The potency of these things lies in the grain of truth. The smile was – and still is – captivating. Old gentlemen sitting in the front rows were no doubt duly captivated. But Victoria de los Angeles's career goes back a long way, far enough for some of us who are by this time at least moderately old gentlemen to have been almost young whipper-snappers then; I can remember that the smile cast its warmth over some very remote parts of the Festival Hall in London, and, for that matter, reached the uppermost slips at Covent Garden. What is more to the point, the voice travelled up there with it, and warmed in like manner.

The 1950s were the golden years. The '60s too, though I seem to recall that we became just a little defensive about her towards the end of them. There were times in her concerts when you basked, or rather, when the soul did its own solo dance of the blessed spirits, blissful as Gluck's, while listening.

For a start, the voice in its prime was so pure and so opulent. To song after song you could listen with uninterrupted pleasure in the sheer sound, with never a scrape or a rattle, never a hint of surface wear or anything mean about the quality. But that of itself gives a poor idea, for it tells of what there was not. What there was was an admixture of mezzo-soprano that used, as I sat there, to recall the records of Rosa Ponselle and in turn has sometimes been recalled when listening during the 1980s to Jessye Norman. Also, as I sat there, I remember identifying the red rose which she wore, with the sound of the voice; it seemed similarly rich-hued, and it told of summer. The smile was certainly part of it. So were the eyebrows.

De los Angeles with Franco Corelli

The eyebrows had a special eloquence: the grief of Granados's *maja dolorosa* was in them. Respighi's sad girl in 'E se un giorno tornasse' too, or the anxiety of Mimì consulting Marcel on what best to do, or 'the pity of it all' as poor old Sharpless used to say of the 'triste madre' who surrenders her child in *Madama Butterfly*. These were also present in the voice of course, but it was the pained upward curve of the eyebrows that expressed them physically, just as the smile at the mouth was all one with the smile in the voice. And how radiant that was.

The Spanish songs would catch it best of all, but if by luck the programme included Fauré's 'Chanson d'amour' or 'Les roses d'Ispahan' it was there too, or in the simple contentment of Schubert's 'An die Musik' or the serenity of Schumann's 'Der Nussbaum'. Of encores there was always a generous provision, but we knew when the evening was coming to an end, signalled in those days not as later by Carmen's Seguedille but by the song of the carnation-seller, 'Clavelitos'. Even then there could be

127

another treat in store, for sometimes instead of bringing Gerald Moore back with her she would return alone, but with a guitar. 'Adiós Granada' she would sing: the bold projected middle voice would fill the hall, the sinuous *melisma* told of dark faces and flickering shadows in a sunny land, and we went out into the chilly night back to the suburbs with an untoward tingling of the blood and with fingers that tapped out a Spanish rhythm on the back of a folded programme.

On opera-nights there was pleasure too, though I can't quite recall the same bliss as in those early concerts. The voice always seemed to me not quite large enough for Butterfly in Covent Garden, but it was a most touching portrayal and I know somebody who went back for every one of the performances (you could always squeeze in in those days and it didn't cost much). Her Mimì was hailed rapturously at her debut in 1950: 'It is rare to discover such maturity of tone in one so young ... a singer of the front rank with plentiful reserves of tone as well as tenderness, and phrasing that was a delight in its effortless shapefulness' (*The Times*). Ten years later those reserves were perhaps a little less plentiful. Philip Hope-Wallace described her then as 'a sonsy little Mimì not overrich at climaxes nowadays, but drawing phrase after phrase with perfect artistry when they lay in the middle of her voice'. It was interesting not long after that to hear her sing Manon, which makes considerable demands upon the upper range. My memory of that is that the top notes were not merely there, but that they came easily, part of a 'thinking-upwards' in the voice. Having lighter orchestration than Puccini's to contend with, she could both lighten the voice and in doing so set the upper register to work with more freedom and soprano-resonance.

She had of course a highly distinguished operatic career, at the Metropolitan and in Chicago as well as Covent Garden and Paris. At La Scala her rôles, from 1950 till '56, were Ariadne, Donna Anna, Agathe and Rosina. In 1962 she sang Elisabeth in *Tannhäuser* at Bayreuth. Throughout the 1960s she was a welcome guest-artist in Buenos Aires; 1969 brought an *Otello* (previously sung at the Met) in Dallas, and 1978 a Carmen, the part she had recorded twenty years earlier with Beecham. Whether she would have been happy working in opera houses during what was becoming evermore 'the age of the producer' is doubtful. She loved her time at Bayreuth, but partly because Wieland Wagner, though so creative a producer, never seemed to impose his ideas: 'In many ways those are the best artistic conditions in which I have ever worked,' she said. Right from her debut she felt herself lucky to be able to work out things for herself ('nobody told me what to do'). Nor were there then, in Barcelona just after the war, any of the star conductors who could so easily dominate a promising young singer: 'You can be destroyed by people who treat you like a puppet.'

She herself is a woman of strong artistic convictions. She has, for instance, a very clear knowledge of what, for one reason or another, is not

128

ROYAL FESTIVAL HALL
General Manager: T. E. Bean, C.B.E.

Wilfrid Van Wyck Ltd announce

SONG RECITAL
by

VICTORIA DE LOS ANGELES
accompanied by

Gerald Moore

Monday, 11th May, 1959, at 8 p.m.

PROGRAMME 1/-

in her. She was always being asked to sing the Marschallin but knew that it was not for her; the rôle she would love to have taken in *Der Rosenkavalier* was Octavian, but nobody asked her. When she sang Ariadne at La Scala, she felt her voice growing, and *Ernani* and *Tosca* were suggested. Instinct and self-knowledge told her that the increased volume was already threatening to interfere with the natural quality of her voice, and again she held to the ancient wisdom of 'to thine own self be true' (Tosca, anyway, went against the grain purely as a character – she could never believe that a woman who has just killed a man, even such a snake as Scarpia, could then go and pick up a crucifix).

To return to the smile: the happiness, and the evident goodness, of her nature perhaps tend to obscure the sheer strength of purpose within her, and also the share of unhappiness that she has known in her life. This has its due place in the biography published in 1982 by Peter Roberts, who quotes her saying: 'Once I had children, I was forced to fight as I had never fought before. In the end it was good that I did, because if you do not fight, you die.'

She, as we know, has been a great survivor. It is, after all, an extraordinary resilience of voice and spirit that has enabled her to fulfil so arduous a concert schedule as she has been doing right into her seventieth year. There was, it is true, a period in which most of us said 'Why does she do it?'. There was a time, frankly, when I myself would not go to a concert in her later years because I feared for the memory of the earlier ones. But marvellously she has come through this. Of course the range is limited, the stamina decreased, and some nights are better than others. Yet in these last four or five years she has held her audiences by the sincerity of her art and the purity and steadiness of her voice. I have never heard the ghost, the faintest intimation, of a wobble. In fact, asked about this on one occasion, she was very definite: 'Ah, when the day comes I hear that ... then I shut up the shop.'

CHAPTER 27

Birgit Nilsson

In the testament of a great singer, masterclasses are a kind of codicil or postscript. Coming usually towards the end of a career, they stand a little apart from it, yet for all that may point more surely to the centre than a whole volume of critical commentary.

This, I think, is true of Birgit Nilsson, whose masterclasses have had the quite unusual distinction of focussing upon technique. She began to give these public singing-lessons a few years after announcing her retirement in 1986 ('the time has come to confine my voice to the bathroom'). In the BOC Covent Garden Festival of May 1993 she conducted a couple of sessions in the Crush Bar at the Royal Opera House, and instructive as they surely were to the young singers concerned, her comments also went far to enlighten the audience on principles that have governed her own singing and endowed it with the qualities for which she has for so long been famous.

'Keep it slender,' she would say; and 'slenderise the voice'. This was gospel, associated always with 'support'. 'Support' by the breath ('breathe deep as though smelling a flower') must increase as the voice goes higher; it needs exercise, making the muscles do hard labour, like riding a bicycle, 'till it begins to hurt and you know it's working'; and, at extreme heights, 'I remember when I had very high notes, like in *Turandot*, I was supporting so much it was hurting in the back, as though cutting in the back with a knife.' To one singer: 'You work too much with your throat. Be very gentle with your vocal cords. Every note should sound in your forehead.'

Later: 'I am against chest voice – the more frequently you use the chest voice the earlier you will get a hole in the middle.' To a soprano: 'Start quietly, you don't need to give so much.' To a mezzo: 'I would hate you having to develop a wobble at your age .... Hum with it, with support, light .... You should work on the voice very soft, below *mezzo forte* think the whole phrase, not bom bom ... *legato.*'

This, it might be objected, could be the advice of any good teacher; it needs no mastersinger of the age come out from retirement to enunciate such very basic truths. But I'm not so sure. We have seen various distinguished singers of the past giving lessons in public, and most have had some special point of focus. With Lehmann it was communication, with

Callas the transmuting of emotion into sound, with Schwarzkopf the exploration of the musical score in relation to the verbal text. But with the basis of a singer's technique they have scarcely concerned themselves on these public occasions, assuming instead that such groundwork had already been done so that they could concentrate on the aspect of the art which interested them most. Nilsson was the first in my experience to focus upon basic techniques of singing. She was also the first to realise that what we the audience, and in all probability the singers too, are hoping for is an answer to the simple, impossibly hard, question: 'How is it done?'

The directness shown here is surely typical. Nilsson's reputation throughout her career as the most downright of divas is well founded. In business arrangements she would come to the point with as little messing about as when attacking a top C. Generally it was simple enough: no goddam dollars, no *Götterdämmerung*. Rudolf Bing's head on a charger was hers for one night when she sang the closing scene from *Salome* in the Director General's farewell at the Met: a joke of course, but still. She was a great one for opening windows, bringing fresh air into the holy of holies (Karajan looking for the incense of oblation would find that all he got from Nilsson was 'Where's Herbie?'). The great pick-axe of a speaking-voice broke into the silky tones of a Domingo-Sievewright interview at a London theatre when Domingo said how he would like to sing Tristan eventually, and sing it with Birgit (who was present). Out from one of the boxes came a cheerful 'Well you'd better hurry up then'. This was the down-to-business realism that she brought to the masterclasses: she could no doubt have held forth on niceties of interpretation and subtleties of character-drawing, but the heart of the matter is singing and how to do it.

No doubt the reflection that she herself never had such guidance prompted her to give it now. At the Covent Garden masterclasses she reiterated the point often made about her own teachers, that they never told her about 'support' ('I just breathed when I wanted air'). In Stockholm, having won first place in the opera auditions of her year, she was sent to Joseph Hislop who, she says, worked on the vocal cords. She gives him credit for wanting to do the right thing – the very thing which she so insisted upon with these singers, to 'slenderise', concentrate the tone, to aim at an equal intensity in each note, 'like a violin'. But as to how these things were to be achieved, she believes it was left to her to work out for herself. She did it first pragmatically by experience in the theatre, and then by thinking about it and working out the principles during a period of indisposition and with the incentive of an imminent performance of Verdi's Requiem.

All of this corresponds very closely with the sound-picture which memory retains of her singing 'in the flesh' (records are slightly different). If I try thinking back, the rôle in which memory captures her voice most successfully is not Brünnhilde or Elektra but Turandot, and the essential term to describe that voice is 'concentrated'. 'Big' is not the word, though

133

it would be for several Turandots from Eva Turner to Eva Marton. Like Turner, Nilsson had a voice that shone brilliantly, without being skinny or shrill ('you've got the stone in the middle of the cherry', she told one of the lighter singers, 'now let the fruit grow round it'). But the effect was not quite of 'bigness' (Gwyneth Jones, for instance, seems 'big' in memory by comparison): much more it was an effect of pure, concentrated, shiny tone. Years ago I remember being surprised when, listening to records of Tetrazzini and wondering who 'in the flesh' had produced anything at all comparable to those high Cs and B flats, the only answer I could come up with was Nilsson. Yet in the same way as with good reproduction of those old records you can hear how Tetrazzini must have projected, almost hurled forth, those top notes of hers, thrilling a packed audience in a large house, so Nilsson's concentrated brilliance and purity was the supreme distinction of her Turandot.

Heard with this in mind, her records tell a similar tale: the weight, never dully ponderous, is 'lifted' by the shining purity of timbre. Yet the 'image' formed by her many records does differ, in my mind at least, from what memory preserves of the very few performances heard 'live'. Because the sound is normally so firm and precise in its focus, the momentary unevenness of line or the fractional deviation from pitch is all the more noticeable. The great *Fidelio* aria was the sort of thing that underlined the limitations: Aïda's 'O patria mia' too, though always there are things that also excite wonder. A certain relentlessness in the bright cold steel of the voice (in 'Or sai chi l'onore' or 'Ocean, thou mighty monster' for example) remains as an overall impression even when at certain points she has conscientiously sought to mitigate it.

Even so, when one goes back to the records, or to the best of them, it is often to find oneself moved afresh by a humanity in them, a degree of warmth and kindliness. A late recording from 1975 of songs by Strauss and Sibelius shows the voice in decline but kindles sympathy and admiration as she softens so tenderly in 'Allerseelen' and the 'Wiegenlied' or as the song we generally know as 'The Tryst' brings out all that is most generous and affectionate in her singing. In the records of her prime there is often a fusion of voice and feeling that warms a listener's response to something well beyond respect for the sheer power, shine and energy of sound. It is touching to sense in Minnie's 'Io non son che una povera fanciulla' something personal and heartfelt. Her Elektra and Salome, magnificent achievements both, are intensely human. The 1966 Isolde from Bayreuth is perhaps most sharply characterised of all.

'Sharply' I wrote, having crossed out 'richly'. That's perhaps unfair, for richness of detail and understanding is there in plenty. Yet the other word suggests more of Nilsson as she is generally perceived: the sharply defined features of face as of voice, the strength of personality as of the highly professional artist. Her toughness and individualism have become legendary: also something comradely about them (John Culshaw writing of her part in the *Ring* recording says 'In all the years, she has never of her own volition wasted as much as a second of our time or money'). We might remember too her part in the grand Gala Concert which took official farewell of the old Metropolitan on 16 April 1966, when in the words of the Met's historian Martin Meyer she 'gave the theatre as overpowering an Immolation Scene from *Götterdämmerung* as it had ever heard'. She wore on that occasion the sash presented to her near namesake, Christine Nilsson (no relation), on the first night in 1883, and by the consent of all was the artist most fit for the honour, being most representative of the traditions which the house at its best had so grandly embodied.

CHAPTER 28

Joan Cross

Not many singers can say, with tell-the-truth-and-shame-the-devil-hand-on-heart certitude, that they have never had a bad review. If anybody can, it is Joan Cross. This was not through indifference on the critics' part or a want of adventurousness on hers. As a singer, she worked in a wide repertoire, and in her other capacities, as administrator, producer and teacher, she was vigorous and outspoken: not the temperamental *prima donna* or anything of that silly sort, but a woman who knew her own mind and was a force to be reckoned with. No: the critical unanimity was based on respect for solid merit. Throughout the 1930s they came to recognise the possession of a beautiful voice and good sense. Most of them at that time seem to have found this to be the exception rather than the rule, and they probably reflected that if there were more singers like Joan Cross they would spend far less of their time grumbling away in the public prints on return from an average evening at the opera.

Anyway, the one major set-back in her career was due to circumstances beyond the control of the music critics, even of Ernest Newman, and that was the outbreak of the Second World War. Joan Cross, as old as the century, was then thirty-nine. When the war ended, her singing days were by no means over, but those six years represented potentially the best of them, and they were crucial. It was hard enough in those days for a British singer to enter the international scene at all. Eva Turner did it by scoring a success abroad first, and of course by having such a spectacular endowment of voice that she could not be ignored. Others, like Florence Easton of Middlesborough, Joseph Hislop of Edinburgh and Alfred Piccaver of Long Sutton, based their careers in foreign capitals and returned comparatively rarely. In 1939 Joan Cross was within sight of achieving the breakthrough in the best way possible, both for herself and for the future of British singing.

She would have done it as a home-trained singer (Dawson Freer – not Peter Dawson as one dictionary has it! – and the Trinity College of Music), then with Lilian Baylis's Old Vic (chorus first, small parts next, then an auspicious Cherubino), then principal lyric soprano at Sadler's Wells with a decade of accomplishment that culminated, that very year, in a highly praised Marschallin in *Der Rosenkavalier*. 'The enchantment of her sing-

Cross as Queen Elizabeth in *Gloriana*

ing, the emotion of her acting, and the beauty of her appearance proved her to be the finest English operatic artist of the day, all the more remarkable when it is remembered that the Marschallin was unforgettably associated with the name of Lotte Lehmann who for many seasons in this country had made the part her own.' The words are those of a writer who celebrated Cross's achievements in the first number of *Opera*, in 1950. As a tribute on her eightieth birthday the magazine reprinted Channell Hardy's article which also made the point that it was the war 'which prevented this opera from being repeated again and again'.

Lehmann, incidentally, was one of the two singers whom Joan Cross had worshipped from afar (in the gallery at Covent Garden) in her own apprentice years – the other was Rosa Ponselle. It was no doubt Lehmann whom Neville Cardus had in his sights when he wrote in the *Manchester Guardian* of the new Sadler's Wells Sieglinde who, though 'she has not yet drawn out all the woman's sweetness ... takes the lovely arches of the melody with ease and fullness of tone', successfully surviving 'comparisons with more famous interpretations of the part given elsewhere'.

Sieglinde was a rôle that stretched her resources of vocal power to their limit, and a watchful adviser (singers could do with more of this kind) recommended against too many repetitions. But the Marschallin certainly was one which, under any intelligent and well-disposed regime at the Royal Opera House, she should have been invited to undertake in the next international season. Only, of course, there was none.

She would not then have been a newcomer to the Covent Garden stage. Her debut there dates back to 1931 when she sang Mimì and Elsa. In 1934 her Desdemona won headlines such as 'Triumph in a Melba rôle' (*News Chronicle*) and 'Miss Joan Cross's great success' (*Morning Post*). *The Times* gave her detailed attention. Noting that her voice was unimpaired in quality, this being her first appearance on stage since a recent illness, the critic found wisdom in her determination not to force her voice in the early acts, with the result that 'by the third act, when the emissary of the Doge arrives, she was dominating the situation without difficulty'. Her Otello was Lauritz Melchior, whom, she says, she liked till she sang with him (he wouldn't rehearse, and then seemed put out when she stood her ground and stayed where she was supposed to be).

Her famous partner did, however, according to the *News Chronicle*, leave her to stand before the curtain and take applause on her own. And, they said, it amounted to a well-deserved personal ovation: she had brought to the rôle 'not only a voice of the loveliest freshness and power, but musical and dramatic skill far in advance of the standard usually cultivated by the *prime donne*'. So it might have been expected that she would be re-engaged – and so she was, for one performance. In 1935 she sang a substitute Micaëla to Conchita Supervia's Carmen. Here too she won distinguished reviews, and, after her aria (as reported in the *Daily Telegraph*), 'applause as generous as that which greets the conclusion of

an act'. All it concluded, in fact, was her career in the international seasons at Covent Garden.

The war saw Covent Garden closed for the duration and Sadler's Wells for long enough to make its future problematic. Concerts, improvised stage performances, hospital work and dodging the bombs became the order of the day; but somewhere along the line, the whole casual comedy of what the newspaper had referred to as the world of the *'prime donne'*, was exchanged for something rather more important.

The first stage came with the recognition of a need for someone to take over at Sadler's Wells. Joan Cross did it. With Tyrone Guthrie as producer, Lawrance Collingwood conducting, and a company of singers and orchestral players with enthusiasm for the work, she organised tours throughout the country. It was round about the end of wartime when they came to my own home-town. The Carl Rosa company was familiar to us, and ever-grateful to them we shall be; but Sadler's Wells was a breath of the future. 'Bliss was it in that dawn to be alive ....' Freshness, taste, efficiency, and a sense of joy in their company: these were features of their *Marriage of Figaro*, *The Bartered Bride* and *La Bohème*. And something of genius was to come.

The acceptance and production of *Peter Grimes* brought excitement, division, and the greatest moment in their history to this little company, which gave the world premiere on 7 June 1945. Joan Cross sang Ellen Orford, and nobody who heard her, then or in subsequent years, will lose the sound of her voice any more than they will that of Pears. She fought for the opera; and, though some Noahs and Methuselahs in the business couldn't recognise it, the triumph was immediate. Her continuing association with Britten's operas is a matter of history. She 'created' Lady Billows in *Albert Herring*, the Female Chorus in *The Rape of Lucretia*, Mrs Grose in *The Turn of the Screw*, and the title-rôle in *Gloriana*.

The unresponsiveness, bewilderment, stuffiness and maybe just honest disappointment of the first-night audience on Coronation Night in 1953 has become so legendary ('the stickiest audience we have ever known' – as some of the singers described it) that the opera's essential triumph has often been overlooked. It was one of the most gorgeous productions I have ever seen, and the score one of the most exciting and moving new works I have ever heard. Joan Cross's part in it was central. Britten had composed it specifically with her diminished power and range in mind, and equally with her strength of character. Unforgettable were her exit in the first scene, carrying Elizabeth's age and her triumph up the stairs with the help of her attendants' halberds, or her emergence in 'my newfangled suit', or her troubled retention of dignity in the scene of Essex's enforced entrance to her private room. 'A melting song, Robin' she sang, with a newly touched affection, and, at the end, the spoken words, with their fragmentary orchestral phrases of punctuation and comment, still prickle the eyes in recollection. It was, as Dyneley Hussey wrote, 'the dramatic performance of her career'.

Though she retired from singing a couple of years later, she did not say goodbye to the stage. Her operatic productions at home and abroad won great praise; she worked devotedly at the Opera School, which she founded with Anne Wood; she wrote translations and gave masterclasses.

Today at ninety-three* she lives in Aldeburgh, keen in mind, resilient in spirit, and still interested in the Festival (this year, for instance, she went to hear Thomas Allen, a favourite among today's singers).

A singer's enduring fame, of course, nowadays depends increasingly on recordings, and of these, in her best years as a singer, she made only a handful. At the time of writing, only one ('They call me Mimì') is currently available on compact disc, but it is a beauty. Better still – some enterprising company will surely bring them out sooner or later – are the Willow Song and Ave Maria from *Otello*. For clear, steady, honest singing, with beauty of tone and sincerity of expression, these are performances hardly to be surpassed. Hearing them, we still need to recall that, though they represent a triumphant last act, they were really, in the 1930s, only part of the prologue.

* Joan Cross died on 12 December 1993.

140

CHAPTER 29

Aureliano Pertile

In the November of 1982, in an interval before the last act of *La fanciulla del West*, Placido Domingo sat in his dressing room at Covent Garden and counted on the fingers of one hand. Or rather, the fingers and the thumb, which was Caruso. For the rest, Chaliapin was the index finger, Ponselle the middle, Titta Ruffo the fourth. And the third? It was Aureliano Pertile, and he was being named in the company of, as Domingo said, 'the great singers, by which I mean the really great'.

An impressive chorus of tenors could be lined up to sing his praises. Think of it: Bergonzi, Corelli, Del Monaco, Di Stefano, Lauri-Volpi, Pavarotti ... all singing a massive 'Gloria a te!' They are among the singers canvassed by the writer Bruno Tosi, whose book on Pertile (*Pertile, una voce, un mito*: Malipiero, 1985) chronicles his life and celebrates his art. Choice praises (freely translated) include: 'Pertile was to be my model, my ideal, throughout all my long career' (Bergonzi); 'Pertile was a singer who influenced all tenors, in my case in a way that was constant and decisive' (Corelli); 'To him goes the gratitude of all tenors who would draw upon the fountain of the purest Italian lyricism' (Del Monaco); 'Caruso, Pertile, Schipa, Gigli ... and then ... who?' (Di Stefano); 'a serious, conscientious and most musical artist ... a technique all his own, inimitable' (Lauri-Volpi); 'the most representative tenor of his time' (Pavarotti).

That last remark is probably the most accurate and thoughtful. The complete sentence reads as follows: 'Ideal interpreter of *verismo* and of the late romantic school (it is sufficient to recall his Otello, confronted to the limits of vocal resource), Pertile is almost certainly the most representative tenor of his time, which was permeated by the culture of *verismo*; and, of the Italian musical *verismo* school, he still represents the most pure and valuable aspects, the most humanly and passionately involved.' This, then, is the specific area of excellence, achieved in an age 'permeated by the culture of *verismo*'.

Perhaps this is the point at which to summon the opposition. At its own 'most passionately involved', hostile reaction to Pertile is expressed by the then-critic of the English periodical, *The New Age*. This was Kaikhosru Sorabji, the composer, a man whose commitment to standards in the art of singing was matched by his outspokenness whenever he found those standards outraged. This was a quite frequent occurrence, yet not many of the offences tried his patience so severely as the performances of *Cavalleria rusticana* and *Pagliacci* he attended at Covent Garden in 1928, when 'the singing of the Italians was utterly execrable'. He was appalled not only by the isolated phenomenon but by what it portended, which in his view was nothing less than the destruction of the great Italian tradition: 'Almost every one of them wobbled abominably, produced sounds of hideous and detestable quality, and had not the notion of a pure vocal line. And these impossible people come from the land that produced Caruso, Bonci, Battistini, Boninsegna and Tetrazzini.'

He arrives eventually at what he considers the prime example: 'Of the Canio of Mr Pertile it is difficult to speak with patience, such an exhibition of vulgar hysteria, mad ranting, and utter lack of anything remotely resembling style or beauty of singing will be (one hopes) difficult to surpass.' Summing up, he writes: 'The generation and type of singers to which belonged the Italians of this performance do not understand – indeed, have no conception of the art of infusing emotional colour into the voice without violating the bounds of pure singing.'

This is the opinion of one man about one performance; but others said similar things (if less vociferously), and other performances at Covent Garden also drew critical comment. It is not that the London critics were hopelessly biased. They greeted Pertile warmly when he first sang there in *Aïda*. For example, 'Figaro' (A.P. Hatton), opera critic of *Musical Opinion* and one who cared about singing as Sorabji did, praised Pertile for his restraint: 'He did not shout, nor was he under the need to turn out all his vocal pockets.' Among the virtues of his Radamès were 'beautifully clear tone', the avoidance of stressing 'points', and the fact that he ' "covered" his head-notes perfectly'. Listeners to his complete recording of *Aïda* made in 1929 will hear what 'Figaro' meant, just as the complete *Trovatore* and many other records of this period make all too clear what it was that Sorabji had in mind.

When he visited Rome in 1929 Sorabji was impressed by the standard of the stage productions he saw there ('a standard that in London is not seen outside a Cochran review') but, listening and giving credit where it was due, he found no great singing and no great singer. He did not hear Pertile then, but: 'I am credibly informed that a certain tenor whose execrable methods I denounced when he sang last season at Covent Garden is an immense favourite here, as well as with La Scala audiences. Such a decline in standards is all the more tragic in that it has come about in what has been the cradle of the art of singing in Europe.'

'An immense favourite' he certainly was. At La Scala he sang in every season from 1922, when the theatre reopened after the war, up to and including 1937. His career dated back to 1911, when he made his debut in *Martha* at Vicenza; and when he retired shortly after the end of the second world war he was just over sixty years old. The golden decade of his fame

Pertile as Cavaradossi in *Tosca*

and fortune was the 1920s, and the great seal of his success lay in his virtual adoption as 'il tenore di Toscanini'.

Under Toscanini he sang in a whole sequence of famous productions: *Trovatore, Ballo in maschera, Aïda*, for example, and, in a more unexpected repertoire, *I maestri cantori (Die Meistersinger)* and *Boris Godunov*. When the prestigious world-premiere of Boito's *Nerone* took place in 1925 Pertile sang the title-rôle, as indeed he did when Mascagni's opera of the same name was introduced ten years later. Here it was partly his ability as an actor that made him the clear choice, and similarly in Wolf-Ferrari's *Sly*, which was first performed at the close of 1927, having as its subject an emotional and tragic treatment of the character of Christopher Sly, the drunkard for whom the play of 'The Taming of the Shrew' is given in Shakespeare's comedy.

Abroad he made less of an impact. There were the Covent Garden seasons, 1927 to 1931, leaving a mixed impression, and his single season at the Metropolitan late in 1921 led to no renewal of contract. In the early years of his career he was a frequent and welcome visitor in South America, and 1929 was the year when, under Toscanini, the Scala company, with Pertile as principal tenor, gave its memorable performances in Berlin and Vienna. Gradually, throughout the 1930s, he came to sing less often and in theatres of a lesser standing; by 1942, when he made his late recordings, the voice appears to have been still powerful and obedient to his needs as an expressive artist but with loosened control over its firmness. His decline in status within Fascist Italy may also have had something to do with his reputation as 'the tenor of Toscanini', the great conductor being then *persona non grata*.

The suggestion is one made by the English authority on Pertile, Paul Morby, who has also done probably more than anyone else for Pertile's memory in this country and has devoted a considerable part of his life and energies to the foundation of a museum in Montagnana designed to celebrate the city's two distinguished tenors, Pertile and Giovanni Martinelli. Unlike most Italians (it seems), he is well aware of the defects that characterise so many of the recordings, made in the late 1920s, by which Pertile is most commonly remembered. What he then insists is that these are not the true Pertile, who is to be found in his earlier series for Fonotopia-Odeon, Pathé and Italian Columbia.

It is not entirely surprising that Italian writers on such subjects should fail to discriminate, for they themselves were the products of that age, the 'age permeated by the culture of *verismo*', of which, as Pavarotti says, Pertile was so typical.

What can be surprising, when you go back to the records, is to find how the beginnings of the disruptive emotionalism and those other qualities of which Sorabji complained are present in the early records, and how much of beauty and unforced lyricism survives in the later ones. In both, you then have to salute a man who is singing with burning sincerity: a tenor

144

who, within his own field and despite his faults, is capable of the most refined, imaginative and memorable art, a voice of unique character, and a communicator whose utterance goes (in Beethoven's phrase) 'from the heart to the heart'.

CHAPTER 30

Antonio Cortis

For the thrill of the singing voice, there's nothing like a tenor. For an aria to contain and convey that thrill there's nothing like 'Nessun dorma'. Inspiration seized whoever it was who first (at a board meeting, perhaps, or a 'wouldn't it be marvellous if' remark at the bar, followed by 'Maybe you've got something there') suggested that Pavarotti should proclaim it to the world. Inspiration seizes the hearing, sets the internal combustion engine ablaze even when it's supposed to be old and fireproof, but particularly when young and inflammable. 'Dilegua, o notte! Tramontate, stelle!' The words themselves have a fine Shelley-like rapture. 'All'alba vincerò!' Expectation gleams like the promise of dawn, and in comes the orchestra *tutta forza* to support the proclamation of that ringing voice.

But in my youth the ringing voice was another's. It did not, admittedly, tell it to the world; and it did not (this too has to be said, by way of warning) let fly the high B natural of 'vincerò' with that prolonged exultancy. What it did suggest, though it too presented the aria as an excerpt, was the context within the opera. 'In the great silence of the night,' reads the stage direction, he, the Unknown Prince, listens to the cries of heralds and distant voices, 'as if no longer living in the real world.' There was a softness about the opening of this 'Nessun dorma' which befitted the night-thoughts of one who repeats words coming to him out of the stirring darkness, and which probably take fire with the conviction of victory. The voice had something of the dream around it, something of pain in its longing, too, and it quietened to a *pianissimo* with the held note of 'splenderà'. The authentic thrill of the tenor voice was there nonetheless; in fact, to my mind, all the more.

The record which still plays so clearly in my ears can, happily, now be had on compact disc. It was made in Milan on 19 September 1929, by the thirty-eight-year-old Spaniard who had sung the rôle of the Prince that spring in Florence. When, in 1931, Antonio Cortis made his debut at Covent Garden, also in *Turandot*, Ernest Newman wrote, 'For once we heard "Nessun dorma" sung without any of the gallery-catching vulgarities of vocal display that generally disfigure it', and in the *Daily Telegraph* Herbert Hughes, describing his voice as 'sweet', resonant and easily

147

produced', added that 'from the first phrase of "o divina bellezza" one knew this to be a tenor *pur sang*'.

Some noted that the voice seemed to be rather less powerful than on records, and others criticised his acting. Yet Newman (not one accustomed to making excuses for faults in the Italian season) found a compensation even here: 'As an actor he is apparently rather unsophisticated, but his very deficiencies in this respect were paradoxically to the good: a Calaf without stage tricks and poses is much more in the picture than the ranting, strutting Calaf of the ordinary tenor.'

Perhaps more significantly still, Cortis won the approval of Kaikhosru Sorabji, so often a devastating critic of new singers. Antonio Cortis, he wrote, 'was a delightful surprise, and he is without question the best tenor we have heard in years. The voice is admirable, excellently poised, and produced with delightful freedom, while the singer's natural and unaffected bearing, coupled with an easy, graceful manner and a very personable stage presence, made of him by far and away the best interpreter of the part I have so far heard. If this delightful young singer (whom by the way one would eagerly welcome the opportunity of hearing in concert work) continues as he bas begun, and does not allow that horrible Latin mania for vocal stunt-mongering to entice him into ruinous singing habits he should in a few years become easily a brilliant artist and the best tenor of the day' (*New English Weekly*, 16 June 1931).

So what happened? Precious little at Covent Garden. Cortis sang the remaining performances of *Turandot*, confirming, as critics reported, the fine impression made at his debut, and then appeared in the world premiere of Romano Romani's *Fedra*, in which all else was eclipsed by Rosa Ponselle and the garish production said by Newman to have brought Hollywood to Bow Street. He surely would have been re-engaged for the Italian season of 1932, except that there was none. 1933 proved a poor, underfunded, shortlived season, and in brief Cortis was heard here no more. At the same time the centre of his career in America collapsed. This was with the Chicago Civic Opera, which was hit, but more severely, by the slump, so that he returned first to Italy and then to his native Spain, shortly to be engulfed in civil war.

The Chicago years lasted from November 1924 till early in 1932. Here he did his best singing and made his fortune. He came to the windy city, as did many at that time, with a reputation gained in South America. He had loved music as long as he could remember, and as a boy played the violin: to be a Sarasate, not a Caruso, was then the height of his ambition, though he had also been mightily impressed to learn of all the dollars the great tenor earned with his famous record of 'Vesti la giubba'. But then after a few youthful visits to the opera and the discovery of a light tenor voice he joined the opera chorus at Barcelona. By 1916 he had learnt ten leading rôles and scored a success as Cavaradossi in *Tosca*, securing engagements the following year at the Colòn in Buenos Aires.

Cortis as Johnson in *La fanciulla del West*

It was here that he sang Beppe to Caruso's Canio, gaining, it was said, the greatest applause of the evening at the end of his off-stage serenade, which he sang so well that the audience apparently believed it must have been Caruso himself. The generous nature of Caruso allowed him to join in the congratulations, and Cortis became a protégé: he was sometimes referred to as a pupil, and, in that period, quite frequently as 'il piccolo Caruso'.

In his heyday at Chicago he was more often 'the new Caruso' and even, by his fans, dubbed 'greater than'. But those times were not foreseen in 1917, when his rôles, at San Paulo for instance, were comprimario parts such as Moralès in *Carmen*, Prunier in *La rondine* and the Steersman in *Tristan*. Back in Europe he sang in Madrid and Naples, then at the Costanzi in Rome, with repertoire, experience and reputation growing steadily, so that on his return to San Paulo in 1921 he had graduated from Beppe to Canio, Moralès to Don José. His voice was essentially a romantic, lyric type, yet Radamès was among his rôles at this time, and, when engaged by the Chicago Opera, his contract required that he should also be ready with dramatic rôles such as Manrico in *Il trovatore*, Andrea Chénier and – a part I believe he never sang – Samson.

It was in these years that he made the recordings by which he is still remembered. His Duke of Mantua in *Rigoletto* is a fine fellow, the laughter spontaneous, his cadenza expert as the flourishing of a courtier's cap. He phrases deliciously, and in the aria 'Parmi veder le lagrime' begins and ends with that sure sign of grace, a well-covered high G flat. Manrico's 'Ah si, ben mio' is one of the few (Martinelli's was another) that capture the melancholy: 'con dolore' says the score at 'ma pur, se nella pagina de' miei destini è scritto'. 'Di quella pira', like Faust's aria and Rodolfo's, is trans-posed down a semitone, but in all of these the top note rings splendidly and suggests that the C would have been no great risk. In French opera (but performed in Italian), he sings Vasco da Gama's ode to the newfound paradise with affection and enthusiasm, while his Don José is as sympa-thetic in duet with Micaëla as he is ardent in the appeal of his Flower Song. Best of all is Des Grieux's 'Ah, fuyez, douce image', almost breathtaking in the softness and security of that 'Ah' and superb in its refinement of nuance and phrasing.

At some point such as this the thought occurs that there really is, in the whole history of the gramophone in this particular tenor repertoire, scarcely a more satisfying sequence of recordings than that of Antonio Cortis. Yet somehow they dropped out of the accepted canon, rather as he himself dropped out of the front line of international singers during the 1930s. He sang on in Spain for many years, making his last appearance at Saragossa in 1951, a year before his death, where there was a sad intimation that Cavaradossi's farewell to his life was the singer's also. He had been a sick man for some years, though he remained active in his local community and as a teacher and even composer (his Serenata 'La Roman-tica' was played by the Symphony Orchestra of Valencia in 1948).

His friend the tenor Giacomo Lauri-Volpi visited him towards the end and found him in a pitiable condition, but (as he reported in his book *Voci parallele*): 'He ended his earthly life nobly, looking into the face of death like a torero fallen in the arena.' For us, there are some two dozen recordings which still bring that irreplaceable thrill of the singing voice, the ring and richness of a true tenor on top form. For him, perhaps, Calaf's 'Vincerò', with its Shelleyan ardour and exultancy, so well heard in the CD transfers, may well be indeed 'the trumpet of a prophecy'.

CHAPTER 31

Christa Ludwig

Christa Ludwig took her farewell of London as a recitalist on 18 October 1993. We in turn bade an affectionate goodbye, with the thought that when her single and exquisite encore (Strauss's 'Morgen') was over, we had heard the last not only of one great singer but of that generation of fine artists from Vienna who in the post-war era did so much to reassure us that there might still be great singing to hear in our time. She was the last of those. Schwarzkopf and Seefried, Gueden and Della Casa, Dermota and later Wunderlich, Kunz and (spreading the net a little) Fischer-Dieskau, were all well-known to us by 1955 when Ludwig made her debut at the Vienna Opera. But it was in their company that she grew up as an international singer, drawn by Walter Legge into that select family of genuinely distinguished artists, last born of them and dearly loved.

Any singer's voice is individual, as is the soul or a face, but through the voice a great singer acquires a special and precious identity. Song is a subtle and powerful infiltrate of the emotions, and songs of parting – or at parting – tend towards tears. They were not far off in Mahler's 'Ich bin der Welt abhanden gekommen'. This, I suppose, is the great retirement-song, but the leave-taker who risks a full share in its tremulous beauty must also exercise iron control. Looking around in the course of a recital one often wonders what is going on in people's heads, the diversity, irrelevance and unaccountability of it; but here, in this song of Mahler's at Ludwig's farewell in the Wigmore Hall, all those heads were as one. There was no doubt: the stillness and the reluctance to break it for applause after the last notes of the piano had trailed into silence, these testified to the spell, to the binding power of music, and to the singer's art. She had sung to perfection. This sixty-five-year-old woman, who had been before the public since 1946, undertaking in her time some of the most arduous of rôles, recaptured for this occasion an unflawed loveliness of tone that would have been exceptional in one half her age. Mahler's song suited her well, because it could be sung smoothly and softly. About the smoothness we noted another distinction of her art, that she could reduce consonants, in the opening lines especially, so that they interfered minimally with the flow of tone, yet all was clear.

About the softness was something rarer still. We can all think of singers

151

who make a special effect of a soft note or phrase, the specialness of which sets it apart from the main body of the voice. With Ludwig the softness still had what Birgit Nilsson in her masterclasses called 'the stone in the middle of the cherry', but the fruit around it was so bountiful that its ripeness seemed to be all. At a full *forte* and particularly in passages that were more turbulent or jocund in movement, the voice, I would say, had for some years been a worn and frayed instrument; but here, in these quiet, sustained lines, we felt it was indeed the identical voice which in the prime years would so effortlessly fill a hall and ride an orchestra.

A few evenings before this she had sung Schubert's *Winterreise*. The greatest of song cycles presents the greatest of challenges. To have the inner capacity for it and then the art to express its mind and heart is the dedicated Lieder singer's ultimate endeavour. It could not be said that the heights and depths were all reached on this occasion, not at least if one was looking for something to match Elena Gerhardt's performances in the inter-war years as described by Desmond Shawe-Taylor (Gerhardt: *Recital*, 1953): 'it seemed as though sorrow and bitterness had etched themselves into the very timbre.' Yet at the same time there were moments when Gerhardt's was the voice that came to mind as Ludwig sang, and there were songs, too, particularly those that have the end of the journey in sight, which achieved a rare sublimity.

In the most robust songs, age caught up with the singer, and they sent the mind back to recordings, which can expose so pitilessly flaws which other factors can partly protect from scrutiny 'in the flesh'. If I try to recall the start of my own misgivings I realize they originated even in the midst of that magnificent vocal prime when the opulence of her tone and the easy extensiveness of her range led her into *Fidelio*. Klemperer's great recording is surely among the classics of the gramophone, with Ludwig's Leonore among its glories. But the firm evenness of her voice here is not impregnable, and comparison with the 'Abscheulicher' aria of earlier singers such as Lehmann, Leider and Flagstad shows that in this particular respect – the matter of steady, even production – not all was well. That was early in 1962. In the same year she sang the rôle at the Vienna State Opera and in Berlin, after which *Opera's* correspondent, Ralf Steyer, concluded that 'the way to the heavy dramatic parts is open to her'.

Although she had made her Vienna debut as Cherubino, and remained closely associated with the mezzo-soprano rôles in Mozart, she had already sung Amneris, Eboli, Brangäne, Ortrud and Fricka at the time when this critic was signalling the way ahead 'to the heavy dramatic parts'. It was, I imagine, all too clear what was being suggested. There are several transition-rôles which a mezzo will undertake on her way into the dramatic soprano repertoire. Ludwig sang Venus in *Tannhäuser*, the Dyer's Wife in *Die Frau ohne Schatten*, and, at Salzburg in 1964, moved from the Composer in *Ariadne auf Naxos* to Ariadne herself. Two years later, reporting for *Opera* from Berlin, a different critic, Peter Katona, wrote:

'she could easily become a true soprano – which would be a pity for her voice might then lose much of its characteristic fascination'. But Lady Macbeth, for the Metropolitan, was another transition-rôle added, and in *Der Rosenkavalier* under Bernstein in triumphant performances at Vienna she sang now not Octavian but the Marschallin. On records the sumptuous quality survived, but unevenness of production could be heard to have increased. In 1969 she was engaged to sing Brünnhilde – and the *Siegfried* Brünnhilde at that – at Salzburg, and an Isolde was announced, under Karajan, for 1970. Happily, wiser counsels prevailed. In 1969 *Opera* magazine informed its readers that Christa Ludwig 'has decided against continuing her career as a dramatic soprano, and will once again confine herself to the mezzo-soprano repertoire'. I fancy that the overwhelming pleasure we had from her Mahler and Strauss at the Farewell concert in 1993 owes much to that decision.

At any rate, more than two decades of solid achievement lay ahead. At about the same time, the non-operatic side of her work began to assume increasing importance. The St Matthew Passion, Missa Solemnis, Alto Rhapsody, the orchestral song-cycles of Mahler: all of these became essentials. Her song recitals also grew in musical range and interpretative depth. She performed her Russian songs in Russian and delved deeper into the French repertoire (always the hardest to present convincingly and idiomatically), bringing a richness of tone and frankness of style quite unlike the French school's own reticence. Even so, German song remained at the heart of her programmes.

At the Farewell concert, especially memorable was the Schumann group just before the interval: a miraculously lightened and broadly phrased 'Nussbaum', a blithe and charming 'Die Stille', and also from the Eichendorff cycle 'Mondnacht', whose rising notes brought no threat of flatness but instead a blissful transcendence of time and place. Her brave, outgoing manner also made Brahms a natural quarry, the quietly reflective 'Feldeinsamkeit' proving over the years as impressive as her way with the 'big' songs such as 'Von ewiger Liebe'. In Wolf she was perhaps not quite the subtle colorist, yet here too she had her own skills and charm, not least in the sense of humour and impulsiveness which in 'In dem Schatten meiner Locken' would leave uncertain to the last moment the decision whether to awaken the sleeping lover, or ... 'Ach, nein'.

It is in such songs that we can most clearly feel the influence of Walter Legge, the man who was so much more than impresario and (in the general understanding of the term) record producer. 'He taught me how to make the word "sun" shine,' she said; 'and how to make the word "flower" bloom.'

The balancing of opera and Lieder can be immensely beneficial to an artist. Ludwig has sometimes been compared with Lotte Lehmann, who was a shining example of this two-way process – operatic experience giving a dramatic quality and vocal amplitude to the Lieder, and the study of

song encouraging an attention to words and to a more intimate, detailed kind of communication in the opera singer. We felt it in the fun and tenderness of her Dorabella and Octavian, and even amid the grandeur and refulgence of her most dramatic rôles. She was, as I say, essentially a member of that school, the school of those who were only a decade or so her senior in the postwar years at Vienna: the school which, with her farewell, seems to have closed its doors at last.

CHAPTER 32

Dietrich Fischer-Dieskau

After ringing the old year out and the new one in, the next thing is to open the desk-diary and transfer birthdays and anniversaries. This means turning over the pages of the previous year, and thus in the course of surveying 1993 I came upon certain arrangements for Sunday 28 March, and there for a moment stopped.

It is the sight of two concerts entered in that day's diary which brings about the pause. One of the concerts was scheduled for four o'clock, one for seven. The second has a tick by it, and it was duly given, at the Wigmore Hall, with radiant success by the young mezzo-soprano Jennifer Larmore. 'Ring in the new.' The other, which has a cross, was to have been by Dietrich Fischer-Dieskau: only, a week or so earlier, he had announced his retirement, and this concert, a *Winterreise* at the Barbican, was not to be.

There is always a sadness when a great artist who has come on the scene in one's own lifetime, almost as part of one's youth, passes out of it. Not indeed that this man has 'passed', for his retirement from singing does not mean retirement from music, let alone from life. Nevertheless, it is as a singer that we think of him first and foremost, his wider self seen also in the light of his position among the singers of our century. It is the special quality of this that we shall miss.

A singer of course is essentially a voice, but in the case of a singer with whom one has, in a manner of speaking, been brought up, and whose appearances have been annual entries in the diary, there is almost insepara-bly a sense of the physical presence. Fischer-Dieskau has always been one of those blessed examples, none too common, of singers who look as they sound.

Hearing his voice, one pictured a man of dignified bearing and whole-some features, a man who in his appearance might be said to embody the best of his nation's culture. Looking at him, one could also, in imagination, hear a voice that was not cast in any extreme form, a baritone with reserves of range and power that could be drawn upon as required but not for show, a voice which would be put to the service of the music and the words, with emotion, intellect and technical skill uniting in a controlled and devoted pursuit. The tall, well-kept figure, the fine head, the deport-ment which suggested a decent, and not very modern reticence, to which

156

Fischer-Dieskau as Sachs in *Die Meistersinger*

the cult of personality would be inherently distasteful, this also is what we shall miss. Part of his being as a singer was as a force for the preservation of standards. He never gave countenance to the idea that there is no real difference between the culture which he represented and that which is prevalent now. He did not sing pop songs or what we are now coming to rank as pop-classics; he was not to be found in musicals, films or television chat-shows. He rarely gave interviews. He concentrated upon what within his culture he respected, and he worked to be worthy of it.

His wider contributions have included conducting and writing. Eight books by him have been published and a ninth, a study of Debussy and his circle, is due shortly. These are not the usual easy-going volumes of singer's reminiscences, though he has written an autobiography, *Echoes of a Lifetime* (1987, English edition, Macmillan 1989). Among the earliest echoes, as so often, is music in the home. His father, a doctor, was also an amateur composer, who arranged concerts in Berlin where Emmy Destinn and Claire Dux were among the singers. At the age of four he heard his first opera, *Lohengrin*, on the radio, and 'for days I ran around feverishly'.

Then another fever entered German life. In 1933 Fischer-Dieskau was eight, and as the 1930s took their dreadful course he found that for youth 'in the no-man's land between school and home' no one had control of his own life. He stood and listened to Goebbels proclaim that, 'Where there is an argument between young and old, youth is always in the right.' Political arguments were endless; he in his adolescence retreated to philosophy. At the age of nine or ten, he says, he had become convinced of his own ugliness, and, though he himself does not apply pat amateur psychology, perhaps it was this that also prompted him to look for beauty in art. Brahms's *Four Serious Songs* came into his life when he was sixteen. Then came the army, drafting to Russia and Italy and then a period as prisoner-of-war. It did not look hopeful, but by 1943 he had already sung his first *Winterreise* (interrupted by an air-raid and resumed after the all-clear), and in 1947, as a substitute soloist in Brahms's Requiem, his career began.

That career, which took him to the great opera houses and concert halls of the world and made his name pre-eminent in the history of Lieder singing, has not been uncontroversial. There was much antipathy among 'connoisseurs'. Older and retired singers too: it became predictable that if asked to localise their general moan about the younger generation then the chosen example of all that was wrong would be Fischer-Dieskau.

Part of the explanation, I'm convinced, is that they found it hard to accept that this young man could bring out of his music so much more than they had ever known was there (not all had the humility, or whatever it was, of Toti Dal Monte who went to Callas's dressing room in tears at the realisation that she had sung Lucia di Lammermoor for so many years missing so much that was in it). But the reasons given were usually of two kinds. One was that his singing was 'too studied', too self-conscious and analytical; others had to do with voice-production, style and technique.

158

Resentment flared most vehemently when he sang Italian opera. Essentially this means Verdi ('I was privileged to begin my life on the stage with Verdi,' he says in his autobiography, recalling his debut in *Don Carlos*, 1948). *Un ballo in maschera, I vespri siciliani, La forza del destino* were other Verdi operas sung early on; *Rigoletto*, he decided, was not for him (there are some rôles for which it is a disadvantage to be 6'3"), but he recorded it; *Macbeth* (in a blond wig) at Salzburg in 1964 and '65; *Falstaff* in many houses including La Scala, Iago on records: there has been no shortage of experience. The voice itself was not Italianate, that's true: its resonance was not vibrant in the way of Italian dramatic baritones from Amato to Gobbi, nor had it the roundness of a lyric baritone such as De Luca or in more recent times Bruson.

His style was often felt to be too emphatic, disruptive of the smooth vocal line. The interesting thing then is to test this on specific examples and have the score in hand to follow. It will generally be found that there is good reason for whatever he does and that he is a greater respecter of Verdi's scores than are the Italians themselves.

But then comes the objection: 'Ah yes, but it's all so studied.' This is a peculiarly irritating cry from the bandwagon, partly because it can hardly mean what it says (its users can hardly be suggesting that the rôle or the song should not be studied, or be studied but not thoroughly). The intended meaning, I suppose, is that the singer *shows* that he has been studying, whereas he should somehow give us the results of his study and not show the working. It usually goes with such remarks as 'Fischer-Dieskau dots every "i" and crosses every "t", and it means absolutely nothing.' But, of course, we're not talking about dots and crosses. We're talking, for instance, about Iago singing a trill where the score tells him to and where Italians and others usually assumed that Verdi didn't mean it. When Fischer-Dieskau supplies the trills, he also makes you see the reason for their being there (Evil relishing its sardonic energy). Fischer-Dieskau should *not* have studied and found this: is that what we are supposed to gather? Or that having found it he should somehow present it in a way that doesn't make us think about it? The whole thing is bunkum.

As for the singing as 'pure' singing (using the voice to make beautiful sounds), as the years go by, and speaking personally, I am usually amazed afresh, on returning to Fischer-Dieskau's records, to find just how beautiful his tone could be, how far his resources extended (so that the deep-voiced songs of Schubert, for example, will be sung almost with the depth of a bass), and how smooth a line he could draw when that was wanted.

I think I can also say that I have never heard Fischer-Dieskau sing without being able to learn something from it. With learning comes feeling. There is no dichotomy here. Intellect and emotion are fused; that is the distinctive mark of the civilised European culture which Fischer-Dieskau throughout his long career has represented so well.

CHAPTER 33

Titta Ruffo

The time has gone now, but not so long ago it was still possible to hear of and even meet people who had heard Caruso. One reminiscence would lead to another, and soon it would be Melba, Destinn and Tetrazzini, Chaliapin and ... But here silence betokened genuine memory, one that almost surprised the teller, who left off reciting the roll-call and grew wide-eyed, as at the arrival of Hamlet's ghost. Into the shivery quiet would then fall the word 'Ruffo'.

'In my lifetime there have been three miracles – Caruso, Ponselle and Ruffo. Apart from these have been several wonderful singers.' Tullio Serafin's summation is often quoted, as is the rival baritone Giuseppe De Luca's 'Non era una voce, era un miracolo.' Ponselle herself located the miracle of Ruffo in subtlety of colouration as much as in sheer magnificence of volume. Victor Maurel, to whom, as the original Iago and Falstaff and a pillar of the so-called Golden Age, Ruffo might have been a highly suspect whipper-snapper and noisy representative of modern youth, affirmed that his upper notes (D flat to A flat, though reputedly he had a top C available for private display) were the most glorious he had ever heard from a fellow baritone. Even Caruso was said to be nervous about the prospect of singing with him. In 1922, the sixteen-year-old Walter Legge heard him at a concert in London, and came away so overwhelmed by the sound of that voice that for the rest of his life he went around in quest of another like it, but answer came there none. It was, as Lauri-Volpi wrote in his *Voci parallele*, a 'lion-voice', one which in phrases such as the 'Ring up the curtain' ('Incominciate') at the end of the Prologue to *Pagliacci* could create such excitement that 'the theatre would boil over and the audience go crazy'. He was unique: a baritone whose personal following matched that of the most famous of tenors.

Perhaps Battistini in Warsaw or St Petersburg, Lassalle in Paris, Tibbett at the time of his first furore in New York: but no, Ruffo's triumphs appear to have been more elemental and popular, more productive of the boiling-over, the encores, curtain calls and carpets of flowers. 'Then [a Buenos Aires newspaper reported in 1910] the stage itself was gradually filled with servants carrying innumerable gifts to be presented, and among them we will only mention a huge engraved golden chalice, a pin

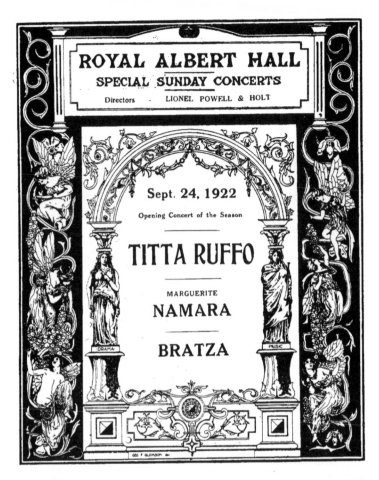

ROYAL ALBERT HALL
SPECIAL SUNDAY CONCERTS
Directors - LIONEL POWELL & HOLT

Sept. 24, 1922

Opening Concert of the Season

TITTA RUFFO

MARGUERITE
NAMARA

BRATZA

with a priceless pearl the size of a large pea, and an oil painting.' The Colón in that city had become very much Ruffo's artistic home, as is well illustrated by Eduardo Arnosi's contribution to the anthology edited by Andrew Farkas (*Titta Ruffo*, Greenwood Press, 1984). But wherever he went in his heyday he brought excitement. 'When Titta Ruffo sings, there is bedlam,' reported *Musical America* in 1920. In Bucharest he was carried shoulder-high from the theatre to his hotel. In Madrid the leading *torero* killed a bull in his honour. Even London permitted itself a demonstration unusual in the history of Covent Garden, for when he sang full-voice at his rehearsal for *Rigoletto* in 1903 the chorus and orchestra broke into spontaneous applause and Melba herself was alarmed.

This is the start of the famous (by now infamous) story which Ruffo tells in his autobiography. He was hardly able to sleep that night, he says, for thoughts of the performance the following day. 'A nasty surprise awaited

me. Arriving at the theatre, I saw my name erased from the programme and that of Antonio Scotti substituted. Angered by this unjustifiable affront I accosted the director. I was received by Maestro Messager, who, in reply to my energetic remonstrations, declared that he did not know the reason but believed that it had probably happened at the request of Melba by arrangement with the theatre's director. I became furious. The half-hour or more in which I awaited their arrival seemed like a century. Then at last I could express my indignation ... to which the director, who was English, replied with typical British *sang froid* that Madame Melba did not intend to sing with me because I was still too young to sustain such a rôle and she had herself begged (the indisposed) Scotti to make an effort and sing as well as he could, and that Scotti, making a great sacrifice so as to please her, had agreed.' The pay-off came years later in Naples, when Melba attended a performance of Ruffo's and sent round a request that she might sing Ophelia to his Hamlet. 'Assuming the coldness which the Anglo-Saxon director had shown me in his London office, I replied: "Tell Melba that she is too old to sing with me."' He adds, perhaps a little defensively, that he would normally dislike spite or reprisals but that on this occasion it seemed just about right.

The autobiography, *La mia parabola*, first published in 1937, finishes its account in 1924. The downward curve of Ruffo's career had begun, but he was still an active singer, only forty-seven, and he had a regular contract with the Metropolitan Opera, New York. The success of his debut as the Herald in *Lohengrin* at Rome had launched him brilliantly in 1898. On tour abroad from Santiago to Odessa he gained in experience and reputation, so that his debut at La Scala with a series of sixteen *Rigoletto* performances in 1904 came when his voice was in its first full bloom, with his artistry starting to blossom too. At Monte Carlo he sang in some of those mouth-watering casts that were assembled there in those days (*Il barbiere di Siviglia*, for instance, with Storchio, De Lucia, Pini-Corsi and Chaliapin), and his great seasons at the Colón in Buenos Aires began in 1908. He made a sensational North American debut at Philadelphia in 1912, and then centred his career on Chicago, rejoining the company after the war in 1920. It is said that plans were afoot for him to sing Iago to Caruso's Otello at the Metropolitan in 1922, but the tenor died in the previous year and when Ruffo came to the Met it was as Rossini's Figaro followed by an all-star but unfavourably reviewed *Ernani*.

Ruffo appears not to have been in the best of health, but the leading New York critic, Olin Downes, was unsparing: 'Mr Ruffo sang with a roughness, a shakiness as regarded the entrances, and a general crudity of manner, in the earlier part of the performance, which would have condemned better music. At the end of the third act the naturally remarkable qualities of his voice and an instinct that replaced in considerable measure the apparent lack of musicianship made his greatest moment and won him frantic applause.' In that same year, 1922, he returned to London

164

for three concerts (he never sang again at Covent Garden). Critics remarked on the colossal chest from which 'he poured out tone with cheerful abandon', but found the voice-production 'cloudy at times' (one described his quality as that of a bass-baritone), swallowing up the words, and his manner 'playing into the hands of his noisy admirers'. These were the concerts that so thrilled the young Walter Legge. In the *Gramophone* magazine the following year, a reviewer of Ruffo's newly released recording of 'Quand'ero paggio' remarked that he had heard it said that 'he sings like a butcher', adding 'I wish my butcher sang like that.'

Throughout the 1920s the downward movement of the *parabola* continued fairly inexorably. He gave his last performances at the Metropolitan in 1929, bade farewell to Buenos Aires in 1931 and to opera with scenes from Thomas's *Hamlet* (probably his greatest rôle, a triumph of acting as of singing) at Nice in 1934. He refused to teach. He said that he had never really known how to sing and would not seek to pass on to others what he had imperfectly understood himself.

That, in its sad way, is a noble utterance; and it came from a noble man. There is no doubt that a contributory factor in the decline of his fortunes was his opposition to the Fascist regime in Italy. This was temperamental and intellectual, for he loved liberty, but an extra twist had been given by his sister's marriage to the rich and respected Socialist deputy Giacomo Matteotti, whose body was discovered dumped outside Rome in the June of 1924, shortly after Mussolini had come to power. Ruffo himself was the victim of thugs, had his passport confiscated and was even at one point jailed on Mussolini's orders. At the Metropolitan the Italian contingent had strong pro-Fascist sympathies, and no doubt this also played a part in Ruffo's exclusion from ever performing there some of his best rôles, such as Rigoletto. Throughout the war he lived in difficult and dangerous conditions. But his voice was heard once more in public. In July 1943 the news spread that the dictator had been arrested at the Villa Savoia, and in Florence the sixty-six-year-old Titta Ruffo opened his window and sang the *Marseillaise*.

165

CHAPTER 34

Maria Cebotari

Walter Legge used to say that if he were asked to found an opera company, the first singer invited to join him would be Cebotari. It was not merely that she could, and would, 'sing anything', but that she was so utterly reliable, never missing a rehearsal or an entry, the one by so much as a minute, the other by a semiquaver.

An infant prodigy, a beauty, a film star, she was in several ways the kind of opera singer who might have been held in deep suspicion by serious musicians, conductors included. But they loved her. She would never come along half-knowing her music, she could be entrusted with something new and it would be learnt, and learnt intelligently. She could act, and in a natural, unstylised way that would make the character credible in an age which was acquiring its ideas of dramatic truth from the flicker of a film actor's eyebrow rather than the movement of a stage actor's arm.

'Sing anything' was of course a nonsense. But she was extraordinarily versatile. Salome and Turandot were in the repertoire of this Sophie and Mimì. Micaëla and Carmen, all three soprano rôles in *Hoffmann*, Violetta and Gilda in Verdi, Tatyana, Lisa and Iolanta in Tchaikovsky: all of these were at her disposal, and so at the disposal of the impresario. The Gretel of one evening's performance could become the Arabella of the next. The resident Cio-Cio-San could turn her hand and her voice to Handel's Cleopatra, Gluck's Euridice or Massenet's Manon. A 'modern' composer looking for an attractive premiere could safely recruit her, as, first of all, did Strauss for his *Die schweigsame Frau*, then Sutermeister for his Julia in *Romeo and Julia*, and von Einem for Lucile Desmoulins in *Dantons Tod*. Her oratorio and concert repertoire ranged from the St Matthew Passion to *Gurrelieder*. And she was a delicious asset to any operetta production, particularly in *Fledermaus* and *Zigeunerbaron*.

Cebotari was also a human being, unique, prized and loved. Her life was such as dreams, and films, are made of. As a girl brought up in Bessarabia, while Europe and much else of the world were at war and Russia was in revolution, she discovered a singing voice at the age of four, and with her elder sister would sing in churches, with solos ready for baptisms, weddings and funerals.

It does not seem to be quite true, as is sometimes said, that she lived

Cebotari as Violetta in *La traviata*

more or less as a gypsy (she was a teacher's daughter, and the family had its home in Kishinov); but certainly the second phase of her life took her on a wandering and adventurous course, leading across Europe to Paris. In her hometown, a troupe of Russians, emigré actors from Moscow, performed their Tolstoy, Gorky and Chekhov. As it happened, they needed a young actress who could also sing in Russian, and enquiries led to the fifteen- or sixteen-year-old Maria Cebotari who was bilingual and already had a local reputation for her beautiful voice and charming appearance. In fact, both of these attractions proved so powerful that the actor-manager of the company, Alexander Virubov, fell in love first with the voice and then with its owner. She appeared with the company, caught the infection of stage, grease-paint and lights, and (like Manon) heard mention of the alluring word 'Paris'. She left home, married Virubov, and reached the city of *La Bohème* where up to a point there was a public for Russian drama played in Russian, but where the income of a singer had to be supplemented by popular arias and the café songs of the moment.

Eventually the Parisian appetite for Chekhov began to wane, and the Virubovs set off once more, this time eastward, making for Berlin where Alexander hoped to make a film. It was here that the next and most decisive turning-point came in Cebotari's career. She was heard by a professor of the Berlin Music School, who gave her three months' intensive training. Then Fritz Busch heard her and signed her up for the Dresden Opera where in turn Bruno Walter engaged her for Salzburg. She made her debut at Dresden in April 1931, and the opera was *La Bohème*.

Meanwhile Virubov's film proved to be a blind alley, and his career was at a stand-still just as hers took off. She rapidly built up an operatic repertoire, showing herself to be a first-class musician in mastering the fearsome challenges of Strauss's writing for the heroine of his new *Die schweigsame Frau*, and then scoring a huge personal and popular success later in 1935 when she sang *Bohème* in Italian with Gigli at the Berlin Staatsoper. Her circle of friends and professional acquaintances now extended far beyond Virubov's group of emigrés. She also began to make films, and found herself playing opposite Gustav Diessl, an actor with strikingly good looks and strong personality. They fell in love and after Cebotari's separation from Virubov were married in 1938. Through all the stresses of those years (Diessl was a pacifist and an active opponent of the régime) and then in the early post-war period, they remained a devoted couple, combining ever-busier careers with a stable family life, till Diessl suffered a stroke and died early in 1948. Cebotari, who had earlier told friends that life without Diessl was something she could not contemplate, had herself little more than a year to live, and in her fortieth year, in June 1949, succumbed to cancer.

Brilliantly gifted, she had been the favourite of Fortune who then, it might seem, deserted her. But in fact part of the curse was laid in the year of her birth. She would spend the best part of a singer's life under the

Cebotari and Beniamino Gigli in *Mutterlied*

shadow of war. Her success with Gigli had led to an extension of her career in Italy, and the visit of the Dresden company to Covent Garden in 1936 introduced her to audiences in England. Films and recordings had also spread her fame throughout Europe and beyond. Almost certainly she would have made an American debut in 1940, and the following years would then have seen her at the height of her powers. Instead, when international opera revived after the war and Cebotari returned to London as a member of the Vienna State Opera, she was overshadowed by other singers who were greeted eagerly by a new generation and who, being just a few, vital years younger, had the shine of freshness on their voices. In particular there was Ljuba Welitsch, whose Salome created such excitement that Cebotari's, which followed, seemed beautifully studied but smaller-voiced.

Another of the new singers in those years was Lisa della Casa, who later recalled Cebotari warmly, speaking of her gypsy-sounding voice that was nevertheless highly cultivated and possessed of a timbre that 'once heard was never forgotten'. That timbre can be heard now on a large number of recordings, some of which are still coming to light. There exists, for instance, a recording of the premiere at Salzburg of *Dantons Tod*, conducted by Fricsay and with Paul Schoeffler in the title-rôle. The Ariadne

169

which she sang in excerpts under Beecham on Strauss's return to London in 1947 was also recorded and, with a fine studio performance of 'Es gibt ein Reich', represents her well. Safi's aria from *Zigeunerbaron* shows the more exotic 'gypsy' sound, while the verve and spontaneity of her *Merry Wives of Windsor* solo contrasts with the eager recklessness of her Salome. An example of the freshness of voice and charm of style which she brought to her music in early years is the Love Duet from *Madama Butterfly* recorded in 1932 with Marcel Wittrisch.

Her sound recordings need to be supplemented by the films: alone, they reveal an occasional unevenness of production, and account only in part for the effect she had upon her audiences. Not that they are great films. Her first, *Mädchen in weiss* (1936), tells a Cinderella-like story. *Mutterlied* (1938), the first of her films with Gigli, only very narrowly misses the sentimentality threatened in the title, but at least we see the famous tenor in action (including a glimpse of his celebrated female impersonation), and it is good to find Michael Bohnen, 'the German Chaliapin', as the villain waiting to be shot in a dressing-room in mid-*Ballo in maschera*. Best is probably *Première der Butterfly*, which works on a parallel between the opera and the film prima donna's real life. Cebotari here gives a touching performance, 'doubling' the fictional singer and Butterfly herself. She was a 'natural': a beauty who acted as well as she sang, and practised a style which had scarcely anything of the conventionally histrionic about it.

She also made a film about the tragic Maria Malibran (1942), and this was recalled, fatefully, by many at the time of her own untoward death in 1949. She had inspired great affection, and in Vienna some ten thousand filed past her coffin. Friends who were with Richard Strauss on what was to be his last birthday saw tears spring to the old man's eyes as he read a greeting from Cebotari. The date was June 11, and she had died on the 9th.

CHAPTER 35

Rosa Ponselle

For some years after her death in 1981 Ponselle's home in Maryland was kept as it had been in her lifetime. Visitors were admitted by arrangement and were shown the cobalt blue barrel-vaulted foyer with its staircase and balustrade where Rosa would make her appearance at grand parties waving to the guests below. Then there was the music room, with its lifesize portrait and the piano on which she would accompany herself when the time came for singing. The dining room, sombrely sumptuous with high-backed chairs and a panelled ceiling; the library, rather denuded of books since the fire of Christmas Eve, 1979; the bedroom with its crystal and silver crucifix and ample bed; the costumes, for *L'amore dei tre re* and others, magnificent indeed and so famous through photographs that one had to rub the eyes and confirm reality, yet (as is always the case) somehow diminished and unmagicked by being deprived of the lights, the space and the body that gave them valid life. Outside, there awaited the swimming pool where Rosa completed her statutory underwater lengths well into her seventies. All around were the green acres, and the busy world seemed far away.

It was a moving experience to go there as a guest, which I did in 1982 when with Graham Sheffield, then of Radio 3, preparing a programme (or as it turned out two programmes) for the BBC. It was also one of the most complicated of experiences, having crossed the Atlantic and been driven in deep-seated opulent ease to the legendary place, to have the front door opened to the living sound of a dead voice familiar to me since childhood. Rosa, as though in person, sang *Auld lang syne*. For a moment it was hard to believe she was not there. I never heard such good reproduction in the house again, but this was as to the life. It forbade a normal exchange of greetings and introductions. As we were about to speak there came a phrase in the legendary *pianissimo*, and a moment later another in that incomparable low register, so that words again failed and the heart fairly turned over.

Yet it was not all delight. The contrivance, the assault upon the emotions, even the weird, slightly ghoulish sense of the dead summoned as by some illusionist mechanism, brought other instincts into play. This was a

Ponselle as Norma

shrine, and shrines, especially when new, are so charged with emotion that a mild demur seems like apostasy.

But of course reservations do arise. They did so even while standing there outside the open door in a trance of wonder at the sound of that voice. Why, one objected, did she so insist that it was a 'coop' of kindness we were to take? She must have thought it authentic. Then the eyes, even in the process of watering, would wander to the welcoming 'Pace'. The house, of course, was 'Villa Pace', named partly in reference to the aria from *La forza del destino*, the first two notes of which were formed in metal work, with a treble clef and key-signature. But the watery globules that wobbled so perilously with the 'coop of kindness' could not hide from view the fact that they'd put the E flat in the wrong place.

Within, the loving care over every detail in the house preserved the spirit of its dead mistress as faithfully and touchingly as the recording had preserved her voice. In the living personal care of its present occupants all was generous hospitality, consideration and warmth. Yet little veins of cold water would runnel through the system even then.

Part of the shivery thrill of the place was induced by the survival, beyond death, of The Voice as it had been heard singing within these walls by people who were still around to tell of it. Ponselle had appeared for the last time at the Met in 1937, and, although she never formally retired, that was the end of her career, aged forty. But she had not lost her voice, and its preservation was awesome news that reached the outside world, partly attested by recordings made in the house. All who spoke of her voice even in advanced years would say that the quality was still pure and rich like no other. Moreover, in sheer volume, as one of the house-guests at that time put it: 'I've heard plenty of powerful voices, but with Rosa it was as though if she really opened up the walls would come tumbling down.'

All this I truly believe. Yet there was also talk about the visit of Pavarotti, the mingling of the two great voices and so forth, and of this event, alas, there was a tape recording. It struck me as a sad memento. The voices 'mingled', as I remember, in a four-note phrase, with the tenor gently humouring his hostess by taking it up and repeating in duo throughout a number of embarrassing sequences. He was then persuaded to sing something and she struck up with 'A vucchella' which he sang in an intimately informal way while she apologised about not being able to see the notes very well and improvised a still more informal accompaniment. It was, quite probably, a lovely evening. But heard as part of the legend, the failure of what should have been valuable evidence was chilling.

The photographs of Rosa almost always showed her gleaming with 'having-a-great-time' happiness. She spent hours by the pool. She was devoted to her large family of (I think) French poodles, with operatic names ('Oh, Fedra, stop it' she calls out in one of the recorded interviews). It was all very nice, but the artist wasn't made out of this. There was, in

173

fact, within Ponselle and her life a whole lot that all of this never touched upon. I found it in some ways a great relief to hear her biographer, James Drake, who had worked closely with her on the book, say: 'I do believe that Rosa Ponselle was in Shakespearean terms a classical tragic figure.'

Perhaps that was over-dramatic, and questionable in 'Shakespearean terms' (as if Hamlet, surviving the duel, evaded abdication but retired to a quiet turret in Elsinore with a pack of Great Danes still to be heard soliloquising at seventy). It nevertheless comes closer to the crux. Ponselle's, after all, was no ordinary life, just as her art was that of no ordinary talent. Her debut at the Metropolitan opposite Caruso in the house-premiere of *La forza del destino* at the age of twenty-one, when she had never in her life sung or acted on stage, was a kind of madness. Divine, inspired madness maybe; but it should never have been allowed to happen. Gatti-Casazza, Caruso and others having discovered this prodigious gift should not have treated it this way.

'She isn't a bit afraid,' Gatti is said to have reported. But she became terrified: 'You call this slow death of mine a break?' 'Vaudeville singer dies at Met debut': she foresaw such headlines. Of course it was a triumph, but such an ordeal leaves its mark. The tensions stayed with her. Pre-performance fright remained endemic. Years later she told an interviewer how she would stand in the wings envying the mezzo in *Aïda* or *Trovatore* with no high notes to worry about. She also, in the height of desperate depression after her 'retirement', would (according to Dr Drake) cry out things like 'It is my career that has done this to me.'

From *Forza*, she went on (via a *Cavalleria rusticana* in Philadelphia) to Weber's *Oberon*, also a Metropolitan premiere. Extraordinary procedure. Later in the season came a world premiere, an opera by Joseph Breil called *The Legend*, a lamentable affair Ponselle thought it and a poor reward for the flurry of learning the rôle of Giorgetta for a far more prestigious event, the world premiere of Puccini's *Trittico*. The part was taken by the soprano originally intended for it, Claudia Muzio, to Ponselle's disappointment; and again this was no way to treat a young girl in her first season.

Later came the triumph of her Norma, the Covent Garden Violetta, the Vestale in Florence, and the Donna Anna which W.J. Henderson regarded as her greatest achievement of all. During this time she became widely considered the world's greatest soprano, and I daresay that if some (absurd) nomination were proposed for 'Soprano of the Century', Ponselle would vie for the title with Callas. Yet her career petered out with a Carmen that was at best controversial and probably disastrous, with proposals, counter-proposals, disagreements, marriage and withdrawal to Maryland.

There, in the house of peace, there followed much that was not peaceful. The marriage broke up, though by good management her personal fortune survived the financial crash. There were bleak times and eventual re-emergence, with life and voice renewed. Her work as coach with the

LA GIOCONDA

OPERA IN FOUR ACTS (FIVE SCENES)

(IN ITALIAN)

BOOK BY TOBIA GORRIO (ARRIGO BOITO)

MUSIC BY AMILCARE PONCHIELLI

LA GIOCONDA	ROSA PONSELLE
LAURA ADORNO	CARMELA PONSELLE
ALVISE BADOERO	VIRGILIO LAZZARI
LA CIECA	GLADYS SWARTHOUT
ENZO GRIMALDO	GIOVANNI MARTINELLI
BARNABA	ARMANDO BORGIOLI
ZUANE, FIRST SINGER	ALFREDO GANDOLFI
SECOND SINGER, ISEPO	GIORDANO PALTRINIERI
A MONK	LOUIS D'ANGELO
A STEERSMAN	ARNOLD GABOR

Act I. Dance. "La Furlana"
Act III. "Dance of the Hours"
By CORPS DE BALLET
Arranged by ROSINA GALLI

CONDUCTOR..TULLIO SERAFIN

CHORUS MASTER..GIULIO SETTI

STAGE DIRECTOR..ARMANDO AGNINI

POSITIVELY NO ENCORES ALLOWED
PROGRAM CONTINUED ON NEXT PAGE
CORRECT LIBRETTOS FOR SALE IN THE LOBBY
KNABE PIANO USED EXCLUSIVELY

One of the few performances in which Rosa Ponselle appeared
with her sister Carmela, 2 March 1934

Baltimore Company Opera was also no doubt therapeutic as well as valuable to the company.

For the visitor standing on the threshold of Villa Pace and hearing the fabled voice sing from the machine within, there were in fact better grounds for emotion than the opulence, the welcoming smiles and the 'coop of kindness' could suggest.

175

CHAPTER 36

Florence Austral

Arthur Hammond, principal conductor and music director of the now defunct but affectionately recalled Carl Rosa Company, was a man of many memories. They came up bright as a button and were as obedient to his call as the genie of the lamp. I once mentioned Florence Austral. 'Ah!' he said promisingly, and his mind went back to the 1920s when he was a young man who had been in the opera business for a few years and thought he knew it all. His stories of course became other men's and were retold more than once, as I fear this has been. Here it comes again even so.

A piano rehearsal of *Die Walküre* was about to start, and the people involved were sitting around in chairs, he himself chatting away with the nice rather motherly woman next to him. The music commenced and looking round he remarked inwardly that there seemed to be no Brünnhilde. You can't get far in Act II without her, and already Wotan had begun to sing commands to his daughter apparently *in absentia*. Then, said Arthur Hammond, as the pianist introduced Brünnhilde's Battle Cry he was never so surprised in his life as to hear a mighty 'Hojotoho' from beside him. His nice rather motherly neighbour was still sitting and as far as he was aware had not even troubled to draw a preliminary breath.

But it was a voice such as he had never heard. Solid, exact, effortless: the octave leaps, the trill, the full-voiced easy high B natural, everything was in place, and it had all been done in a way that made falling off a log seem difficult. This, he learnt, was Florence Austral, and the voice remained for ever after in his ears. And not only the voice. The cool professionalism was equally impressive, and in later years he found this to be typical of her. He once met her leaving the theatre, after she had sung superbly as ever, on her way home where earlier she had come back to find that she had been pretty extensively burgled. Everything of value had been taken, but she had a job to do and that came first.

The poor woman was to need all the fortitude and forbearance she could muster. As early as 1930, when she was no more than thirty-six, signs had begun to show of the arterio-sclerosis which shortened her career and crippled her severely in later life. She went back to her native Australia at the beginning of the Second World War and, after teaching for some

years at the Newcastle Conservatory, retired to face a condition of near poverty right up to her death in 1965.

Among those who wrote of her, Harold Simpson, author of *Singers to Remember* (Oakwood Press 1973), referred to a letter in which she told him how well she was sustained by happy memories; and Don White, who contributed a valuable article and discography to *The Record Collector* (Vol. XIV nos. 1 and 2) visited her in 1960, when he found a woman of clear, energetic mind and 'of overwhelming charm' though almost totally paralysed.

If, in those darkened years memories of the illustrious past did indeed rise to cheer her, then perhaps she must have paused to wonder 'what if?' After her first decisive success, in a scholarship at Ballarat, in which she won both the soprano and mezzo-soprano prizes, she made a modest studio-opera debut and then left Australia for the United States. Her studies in New York prospered so well that in 1920 she was offered a contract with the Metropolitan. Like Geraldine Farrar before her, she thought it premature.

Hard to say: she might have been taken on and dropped after a season or two, as happened with several good singers in the period, or perhaps have shared rôles with another Florence, Easton of that name, from Middlesborough, England, one of the most useful and not least celebrated members of the company, in those starry, prestigious years. As it was, she sailed for England, and the scene of her first triumphs was not the Metropolitan but Covent Garden.

Her debut there – and, as far as I know, anywhere – was as Brünnhilde in *Die Walküre* (her adjudicator in Ballarat had said that she was 'a Brünnhilde' which at that time was something she had never heard of). This was with the British National Opera Company in 1922, and she was put on stage, for the first time and in this fearsome rôle, as a last-minute substitute (some say for her compatriot Elsa Stralia, but more probably for Beatrice Miranda, who with Agnes Nicholls was the company's resident heroic soprano). Agnes Nicholls was the Sieglinde of that performance, Edna Thornton, Walter Hyde, Clarence Whitehill and Robert Radford were the other principals; Albert Coates conducted. So the newcomer was in good company, and in it she proved outstanding.

Two nights later, in *Siegfried*, she 'greeted the light without any effort, and sang with richness and depth'. In the second cycle she added *Götterdämmerung* to her repertoire and thus became established; it was generally agreed that here was the finest new talent to be heard at the house since the war.

What was then hoped was that the magnificent voice would remain and the acting be improved. In the following season she repeated her success in the same operas, and the excellent 'Figaro' (A.P. Hatton), opera critic of *Musical Opinion*, reported that while Hyde and Nicholls were artistically the most satisfying singers, 'Florence Austral, the Brünnhilde, is a voice,

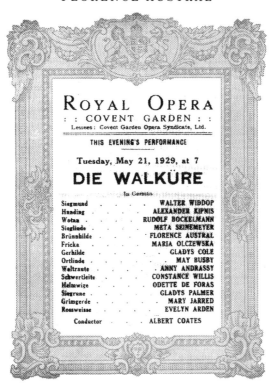

ROYAL OPERA
: : COVENT GARDEN : :
Lessees: Covent Garden Opera Syndicate, Ltd.

THIS EVENING'S PERFORMANCE

Tuesday, May 21, 1929, at 7

DIE WALKÜRE

In German

Siegmund	WALTER WIDDOP
Hunding	ALEXANDER KIPNIS
Wotan	RUDOLF BOCKELMANN
Sieglinde	META SEINEMEYER
Brünnhilde	FLORENCE AUSTRAL
Fricka	MARIA OLCZEWSKA
Gerhilde	GLADYS COLE
Ortlinde	MAY BUSBY
Waltraute	ANNY ANDRASSY
Schwertleite	CONSTANCE WILLIS
Helmwige	ODETTE DE FORAS
Siegrune	GLADYS PALMER
Grimgerde	MARY JARRED
Rossweisse	EVELYN ARDEN
Conductor	ALBERT COATES

a great one, vibrant and warm – though not yet an actress. Vocally, she fits so perfectly into the Wagnerian scheme, like a superb solo orchestral instrument, that one feels almost resentful that she should be required to fit into stage pictures and dramatic actions as well.' (Note, incidentally, that that *was* a requirement in those days.) The deficiency was more inescapable when she offered her first Isolde. In 1924, her Aïda, though 'rather modelled on Wagnerian lines', still provided some lovely singing; 'in acting and gesture, of course, she has still something to learn'. Later that year, from Manchester, came the news that 'her acting has improved very considerably and the voice seemed to have taken on a still finer shade of bloom'.

1924 was the year when the Germans came. Covent Garden that year was full of talk about the brilliant new generation: Lotte Lehmann, Elisabeth Schumann, Maria Olczewska, Lauritz Melchior, Friedrich Schorr, all arrived that year, and with them the singer who for Londoners was to be the adored and incomparable heroic soprano of the age, Frida Leider. Austral returned for the international seasons of 1929 and 1933, but her place had been taken by an artist whose stage presence was so compelling that, a generation later, not even Kirsten Flagstad could shake

179

the loyalty of those for whom Leider was the unique Isolde and the unapproachable *Götterdämmerung* Brünnhilde.

Shortly afterwards, the BNOC dissolved, and Austral, without a company-base, turned to concert work, where she developed a surprisingly varied repertoire and sang innumerable Love-Deaths and Immolations. Beethoven's Ninth (under Weingartner), Verdi's Requiem, *Messiah*, Bach's Mass in B minor, and many recording sessions, were worked in with tours of Canada and the USA.

In 1930 came an early intimation of the crippling disease, for having almost completed her first Brünnhilde in Berlin she was unable to stand after kneeling for Brünnhilde's plea. The great Friedrich Schorr was her Wotan in this performance and, understanding her plight, placed himself in front of her so that the audience could not see as she held to the back of his cloak and hoisted herself up. In spite of her disability she sang in opera throughout the 1930s, in her native Australia and in the States where she was warmly acclaimed. No second offer from the Metropolitan came her way, but in Philadelphia, Chicago, San Francisco and Boston she was hailed as one of the great singers of her time. 'Hers was an amazing voice,' wrote one of the American critics, 'a marvellous instrument that stands supreme among the dramatic sopranos of the present generation.'

Records preserve this. The pity is that the records themselves have not been preserved to better effect in this her centenary year. She recorded exclusively for HMV (now EMI): 'In the early twenties Florence Austral was the most important recording soprano we had, thanks to the beauty, power and compass of her voice,' wrote Fred Gaisberg. Of her 1928 Immolation Scene, Neville Cardus wrote in the *Manchester Guardian*: 'The waters of the Rhine seem to mount high, and over all rides the triumphant voice of Austral as Brünnhilde. Her singing can justly be called queenly. Even after hearing the glorious singing of Frida Leider on other records, Austral's triumphant voice remains in the mind.' Another Manchester critic (in the *Musical Times*) writing of a live performance of the *Ring* in 1926 reached further back for an even more resounding comparison: 'Not even Ternina at her best in the late 1890s sang with more supreme nobility.'

Let us hope that in her last afflicted years she was able to recall these praises (and there were plenty more). Let us hope also that some record company will at last devote a disc to her (and it could include famous duets with Chaliapin and Miguel Fleta, and still better ones with Walter Widdop and Tudor Davies).* Meanwhile all honour to Florence Austral, baptised Florence Wilson, later known as Florence Fawaz (the surname of her stepfather), born Melbourne, 26 April 1894.

* See p. 252 (Dates, Books and Records).

CHAPTER 37

Arleen Auger

In a shady nook in the land of Might-Have-Been, there sits a group of people with a woman in their midst, a soprano evidently, her voice raised in some phrases from an aria that might be by Handel. Her listeners concentrate, and we observe that most are violinists, all of them holding a bow in one hand and a stringed instrument in the other. Having listened, they play. She then repeats their phrases, and we hear that her singing now flows with a still finer freedom and evenness. Again they listen and again they play, their tone acquiring a lovelier quality, a more expressive warmth: closer, indeed, to that of the singing voice.

In a rehearsal (I believe with Simon Rattle's City of Birmingham Orchestra) some of the players noticed that as Arleen Auger sang, the fingers of her left hand moved as though 'stopping' an imaginary fiddle. Afterwards they questioned her about this, and she, herself originally trained as a violinist, explained that she found it helpful when singing to 'think instrumentally'. 'Well,' they said, 'there's a funny thing, because when we're playing we're really trying to sing.' They agreed that perhaps one day she should instruct them in singing, while they in return would give her some tips on how to 'play'.

But of course 'one day' has a way of never coming. Arleen Auger, at the age of fifty-three, died on 10 June 1993 after a year in which she underwent three operations for brain cancer. Her loss was one of the most grievous to strike the musical world, and those who were close to her were for long inconsolable. All speak of their feeling for her not only as an artist but as a person who brought with her and spread around her a sense of value, and that the love of a Handel aria, or a newly found song, was part of that same process which might go under the general heading of a love of life.

A sense of both what was achieved and what was left behind incomplete is quickened by a posthumously issued record, called 'The Art of Arleen Auger' (Koch). Like most compilations with that kind of title, it is really 'Part of the Art of Arleen Auger', but of course you can't call a record that. Along with songs by Purcell, Mozart and Schumann, she sings a song-cycle which she had commissioned and of which she hoped to have given the first official performance. The settings are of six of Elizabeth Barrett Browning's *Sonnets from the Portuguese*, Auger's own choice and her favourite poems.

The composer, Libby Larsen, writes of her as 'a superbly graceful, intelligent, spiritual and deeply talented human being', and she quotes from the last letter which the singer wrote to her. The warmth of appreciation, and the sense of a real communication with her correspondent, make particularly moving the restrained acknowledgment that she herself 'will not be able to premiere it and that someone else will have that pleasure and honour because it will and must be performed!' The recording was made as a kind of trial-run in November 1991, and it is wonderfully good to have. The composer has written with unerring sympathy, particularly in some rapturous phrases in the second song, 'as if God's future thundered on my past'; Auger's voice can rarely have been been better suited, and she sings with that strong commitment which was regularly so striking a feature of her work.

The voice itself had a flute-like quality, and was often at its most beautiful in music that called for a soft, well-rounded tone of the kind Germany used to produce so well in sopranos such as Tiana Lemnitz and Emmy Bettendorf. And like these singers she had also an often unsuspected capacity for fullness. When she first sang in the London Spitalfields Festival the sheer amplitude of her voice in that church astonished her hearers. This was in the title rôle of Handel's *Alcina* in 1985, and so strong was the impression of combined beauty and power that plans began to be laid for her to sing there in Bellini's *Norma*. This never happened and her other rôle at Spitalfields was Poppea in Monteverdi's *L'incoronazione*. By this time she had settled so naturally into the lyric soprano repertoire that it came with something of a jolt to recall that she had first been known principally as a light coloratura.

Her operatic debut had been made as long ago as 1967, at the Vienna State Opera, and her rôle on that occasion had been the Queen of Night in *Die Zauberflöte*. She went on to sing Konstanze in *Die Entführung aus dem Serail*, also formidable in its demands upon the upper register and for a virtuoso's facility in florid music. She had less to do with Italian opera, though here too her early rôles were of the coloratura type: Donizetti's daughter of the regiment and Verdi's tragic daughter of the jester Rigoletto. The reputation of a light soprano was no doubt fostered also by appearances in operetta, such as *The Merry Widow*, in which she sang Valencienne, and (netted by Elizabeth Forbes in her obituary notice for the *Independent*) by her Mabel in *The Pirates of Penzance*, given in German on Cologne Radio.

Throughout her life she seems to have resisted categorisation. Certainly she did not intend to be docketed as a coloratura or soprano leggiero. When there was a danger of her being typecast as a singer of eighteenth-century music (from Bach and Handel to Haydn and Mozart) she determined to enlarge her confines here too. More decisively, as far as the

182

outline of her career was concerned, she turned her back upon what she perceived to be some highly uncongenial features of a life in opera. At Vienna she hated the politics, the pushing and intriguing, the rivalry and egotism. Her career took her (though briefly) to the Metropolitan and La Scala, but so often in opera it seemed there would be an irritant, a frustration – a cast put together piecemeal, an autocratic producer, a conductor with only part of his mind on the job. Increasingly she felt that there was no sense in doing something simply for the sake of a career, and while she would never let down anyone with whom she was engaged (even at the expense of losing a longed-for opportunity to sing the Marschallin in *Der Rosenkavalier*, which was offered at Zürich and had to be declined), she guarded very carefully her independence and worked where colleagues and conditions would be to her liking.

There had always been an unpredictability about her life. Singing had been part of it from the first, yet nothing in her upbringing pointed towards a career in music. Her Californian hometown and a family life which was centred on the evangelical church provided her with only a very limited musical knowledge. A piano album of classical highlights was her first intimation that the great composers existed. There must have been something special about her even then, for she was given the Mary Martin rôle in a local production of *South Pacific* when only fourteen; but it seemed sensible to look for a steady job and so she qualified as a teacher. Again the voice called, and she left the school to study singing full time. When the money was gone she was on the point of a return to teaching but in the nick of time won a competition that sent her to Vienna. There she gained a powerful supporter in Karl Böhm and was given some of the plum rôles, inaugurating a career which might have gone on wheels had she let it. But wheels on tracks were not her idea of progress. She declined as premature Böhm's offer of the rôle of Countess Almaviva in *Le nozze di Figaro*, and striking out on a freelance career breathed the fresher air of independence.

One valued association remained with her from the Vienna days. As an American girl, with hardly any knowledge of the German language, she was delighted to find living there the American pianist Irwin Gage. In him she encountered the fully committed type of musician she was most wanting to meet and for many years he played for her in recitals. Another source of fulfilment lay in teaching, which remained somehow 'in the blood'. She served as professor of singing at Frankfurt and her master-classes were remarkable for the way she had of drawing out her students to comment and discuss, always in what onlookers felt to be a genuine one-to-one relationship. This was the same human warmth which had so greatly endeared her to those who mourned ber death. It is good to know that in her last years, despite the great suffering during her illness, she found understanding and happiness, a richly deserved return for all that she had given to so many, through her voice, her art and her humanity.

CHAPTER 38

Giovanni Zenatello

Sitting outside a bar or restaurant this summer in Verona, within sight and perhaps sound of the Arena, there must surely have been at some time a group, of which one member, idly and hardly expecting an answer, will have remarked: 'I wonder what made them turn this place over to opera' (it could, after all, have been a racetrack with a really great Wall of Death). The *genius loci*, looking over their shoulders, would then have replied as follows: 'Fare forth, oh voyagers, but ere ye go, turn back your head and look upon this very place where even now ye sat. The mist of one-and-eighty years has fall'n upon't, but soon will clear and ye shall see ...'

Well, enough of that. But in fact, if the account in Zenatello's biography is to be believed, it was a group of five who sat together on a warm day in June 1913 in the Piazza Brà and discussed this very proposition. There were two conductors, two singers and a friend. 'There,' said one of them, looking towards the Arena, 'is the great theatre which I have so been hoping to find and which, I believe, could be adapted to put on fantastic performances of opera. Only it would need to have good acoustics, that's all. I see it already. Why don't we go straight away and try out our voices?'

The speaker was the tenor in their midst and sure enough over into the Arena they went. 'Celeste Aïda, forma divina,' he sang. 'Mistico serto di luce e fior.' 'Bravo, bravissimo,' shouted the others (though how they could be sure without an orchestra to complicate the issue I do not quite know). The thing was as good as settled on the spot. Maestro Serafin was to conduct, Maestro Cusinati would see to the chorus, the friend became impresario. *Aïda* was the chosen opera, and they would open on 10 August. Maria Gay, the other singer present, would be their Amneris, and Giovanni Zenatello their Radamès. He, having proposed the idea, was also to find the money.

So, when the Pearl record company, issuing their virtually complete Zenatello Edition in 1994, decided to adorn their booklet with a fine coloured photograph not of the tenor himself but of the Verona Arena in operatic action, they were not (as might have been thought) drawing attention to the scene of his triumphs. This *was* his triumph, and it remains his most richly endowed living monument.

Or perhaps that huge Arena must share its monumental function with

186

Zenatello as Otello

the two tiny boxes that contain his records. Compressed within them lie something like nine hours of singing. Some of the recordings are of duets (with artists such as Ester Mazzoleni, Emmy Destinn, Pasquale Amato and Maria Gay), but most is solo-work, and that is a good stretch of time in which to hear a singer of those early years. He sang, with clattering piano accompaniment, into the primitive recording horn set up in Milan, for the first time in February 1903. His final studio recordings were made at Camden, New Jersey, in March 1930. He was then in his fifty-fifth year and had been singing in public since the age of twenty-two.

Though Zenatello began as a baritone, there was little of the baritonal in his bright, cleaving tenor. He made the change more or less overnight. Having sung both baritone rôles in *Pagliacci*, he also knew enough about the rôle of Canio to assure the distracted manager that though they had lost their principal tenor and the tenorino substitute from Milan had not turned up, all was not lost. 'I have studied the part. I know it, and if you want the truth, you had better know that I had to pretend to be a baritone because I couldn't find anything otherwise.' *Pagliacci* was his first success, *Andrea Chénier* his second, and before long Toscanini, no less, was inviting him to La Scala for the Italian premiere of Berlioz's *Damnation of Faust*. This was late in 1902, and ahead by little more than a year lay the premiere which places Zenatello most securely in the history books, though at the time that seemed an unlikely outcome.

On 17 February 1904, the curtain rose for the first time on Lt. Benjamin Franklin Pinkerton's Japanese love-nest on its 999-year lease. At the end of the first act, Puccini, already widely acknowledged as Italy's leading composer, appeared on stage leaning on a cane after his motor accident, and 'with long and dolorous face' acknowledged the general public indifference. Later came the shrieks of laughter, the shouts, the cat-calls. The curtain fell on the premiere of *Madama Butterfly* (according to La Scala's manager, Gatti-Casazza) amid 'an absolutely glacial silence. Not one shout of applause! Not one shush-shush-shush! Not one shout! Nothing! It seemed that the opera was dead and buried.'

As we know, resurrection was to follow, for changes were made and on 28 May the opera triumphed in Brescia. Zenatello was the Pinkerton of both performances (Rosina Storchio the Milan Butterfly, Salomea Krusceniska at Brescia). Later he recalled Puccini's tears on that first night, and then three months later, when his aria, 'Addio, fioritore asil!' added to the score in its revision, had been twice encored, the pride and happiness he felt in leading the composer out on to the stage, there to leave him to take the applause that was now doubly his.

In those years Zenatello was the leading robust tenor in his own country (Caruso, his senior by only three years, left Italy in 1903 and returned rarely to sing there). He became internationally famous, in Buenos Aires, London, St Petersburg, and in 1907 signed a five-year contract with Oscar Hammerstein who saw in him the best prospect his Manhattan Company

188

Royal Opera Covent Garden

Proprietors, THE GRAND OPERA SYNDICATE, LTD.
General Manager ... Mr. NEIL FORSYTH
Musical Director ... Mr. PERCY PITT

THIS EVENING'S PERFORMANCE

Thursday, July 16th, at 8

VERDI's Opera

OTELLO
(IN ITALIAN)

Otello	...	... Signor ZENATELLO
Desdemona	...	Mme. MELBA
Iago	...	... Signor SCOTTI
Emilia	...	... Mme. EDNA THORNTON
Cassio	...	... Mr. JOHN McCORMACK
Lodovico	...	... Signor NAVARRINI
Roderigo	...	... Signor ZUCCHI
Montano	...	... M. CRABBÉ

The Bellew and Stock Choir

Conductor ... Signor CAMPANINI

Stage Manager ... ... M. ALMANZ

had of finding an answer to the Metropolitan's Caruso. His debut in *La Gioconda* on the opening night of the second season brought immediate admiration for the finish of his singing as for the brilliance of his voice. He became Hammerstein's most highly paid male singer – Melba heading the female roster – and when the two sang together in *Otello* as they did on Chistmas Day 1908, a thrill which ran through the house was caught even by the critics: 'a fervid seep of passionate intensity [wrote Reginald De Koven in the *New York World*] ... made the atmosphere seem overcharged with a vibrant force that was electrical.' Over the years *Otello* became Zenatello's greatest rôle, and it has been estimated that he sang it more than five hundred times.

His last performances in that opera were given in London on a surprise return in 1926. Not everybody was impressed. Ernest Newman wrote: 'I had never, so far as I remember, heard Zenatello before. All my friends seemed to be listening to him with their memories of long ago. I, having nothing but my ears to guide me, frankly found his tone for the most part unpleasant.' Basil Maine, in the *Spectator*, thought the sound 'hard and laborious', the acting 'curiously congested'. Kaikhosru Sorabji (*New English Weekly*) found him 'very nearly the Italian tenor of caricature, a bad singer and actor, he hardly ever once moved his eyes from the front of the house, into which everything was shouted in the worst Italian manner'. Against this, at least in part, can be put the recordings, made 'live' in the opera house on the night of 17 June, when he was reportedly in much better voice, and in which 'Crescendo' of the *Star* said, 'He sang the scene of the oath with thrilling effect.'

Those recordings from the stage are indeed a precious memento, though they tell a mixed tale. A first impression, at the start of Act II, is that, at fifty, he sounds surprisingly young. When a more lyrical style is required and a more complex state of mind to be expressed, however, there is a stiffness of manner, and, with other singers in mind, a notable want of subtlety. The Iago, Giuseppe Noto, is a kind of vocal jellyfish (the Desdemona, Lotte Lehmann, was said by all to have been exquisite, but contractual difficulties prevented her from being recorded). In flashes, Zenatello can be thrilling: his outburst 'Miseria mia', with its high B, suddenly comes through, tense and shining, almost as it must have done in his prime. But for a man who has given over five hundred performances, he often sounds in need of a fresh look at the score: note-values are loose in 'Ora e per sempre' and later he hurries. The Oath Duet catches again that knife-edge tone, but he is hard-pressed to sustain the 'Dio, vendicator'. The Monologue hurries and again wants subtlety, yet he still commands the resources for a fine climax. The Death Scene, also partly hurried, preserves a memorably concentrated tone in 'Pria d'ucciderti'. It is, as I said, a mixed tale (there is a record made near the end of his life, in 1947, of the Death Scene with piano, still firm and showing what exceptional material this voice was made of). He rarely satisfies completely; yet he haunts the memory.

There is a fascination in Zenatello's singing even in this late period. Going back then to the golden time, which I take to be around 1905, you hear a voice of marvellously distinctive character, with some pain at its centre. Emotionally he is primitive, yet at his best in those years there ran the ennobling discipline of his country's vocal tradition. Hear him, for instance, in excerpts from *Un ballo in maschera* (the opera in which he sang so well one night at La Scala that the audience demanded an encore and Toscanini left in a huff). There the line is true, firm yet supple, and, as with most of these early singers who are still remembered today, there is something intensely personal about it. The compact-disc collection on Pearl itself testifies to that. As a boy of sixteen, its editor, Keith Hardwick, found his first Zenatello in a schoolfriend's waste-paper basket. He played it, and was hooked for life.

190

CHAPTER 39

Galina Vishnevskaya

It would be impossible, I should think, to read Vishnevskaya's autobiography dispassionately. But then, there was difficulty enough in trying to maintain a normal degree of critical detachment at her recitals, so intense were the gloom and radiance of her performances. Opera was different. In the West at any rate, reactions contrasted quite markedly, and, though well aware of those who, like Harold Rosenthal, could say 'she belongs to the small handful of present-day singers to whom the adjective "great" can be applied' (*Opera*, July 1962), I myself at that time rather belonged to the opposition. There remain the memories of concert appearances, certain recordings, the book, and, most essentially, the interaction of all three.

Galina (Hodder and Stoughton, 1984) is a book fired by the need to fight. At one moment, in the first sentence, life offers 'bright sunshine and emerald meadows'. In the next, as a child of four, she is literally in deep water: 'murky green. I stand on the bottom and thrust my hands towards the surface, clenching and unclenching my fists.' She was rescued from drowning, given what is still called 'a good hiding' (never a 'bad' one) and left to ponder on life's injustices. But already she was a veteran in the hard school of experience. At the age of six weeks, she had been dumped by her mother and taken in by her grandparents. The grandfather would get drunk and announce his return, like some hopeless character in Dostoievsky, striking a majestic pose in the doorway and declaiming 'So it is I ... Andrei Andreyevich Ivanov!' He came to a horrible end, but not much worse than a lot of others. Grandma in the meantime gave this wild, scowling little girl some love – but never, as Vishnevskaya recalled years later, a kiss.

She grew up in the terrible decade of Stalin's purges. Children then had two heroes: Stalin, who 'unmasked the Trotskyite enemies', and Pavlik Morozov, a twelve-year-old who informed on his father and grandfather. Then came the war, and, at the age of fourteen, the end of childhood. Life depended on 'four ounces of flour waste products that fell apart in your hands'.

Kronstadt, where Vishnevskaya lived, was starved and bombed and disease-ridden and frozen. The grandmother died of burns; cousins died of dysentery; at one time, in 1942, Galya fell asleep and would certainly have died of cold had she not been disturbed by women collecting corpses. The lifting of the Leningrad siege and a first love affair brought sudden, almost unbearable glimpses of happiness. But her young man was a sailor, and one day a wretched woman, fellow-worker in the 'blue division' of women doing menial jobs, shouted to her over the patch of land they were weeding that his ship had been sunk.

Out of all this affliction came the singer. At school she was called 'Galka the Artistka'. She had never had training but had always sung. As a girl, she would sing her rheumaticky grandmother to sleep with a song about Marusya, a girl of seventeen who found work in a brick factory and shortly afterwards died. At school the songs were about Stalin and Voroshilov. But for her tenth birthday, her mother (who lived in Leningrad and occasionally had money to spare) bought her records of *Eugene Onegin*. The excitement was profound, and from this first encounter she decided on the form her future would take. Fifteen years later, as she says, she 'would stand on the stage of the Bolshoi and sing Tatyana'; but it must have seemed a distant vision indeed as the frozen corpses were thrown on to carts or as the jeering woman shouted her news across the weeding-patch.

Most pitiful of all these episodes is the death of her baby, born in desperate conditions and buried with an infinity of grieving tenderness. We are still only in the introductory chapters, and I will not summarize further, simply say that it is not one of those life-stories which (within the span of the book itself) emerge from the valley of the shadow into the sunny uplands. That would be to reckon without Comrades Bulganin, Brezhnev, Krennikov, Furtseva and the rest; moreover, without the abomination of a system in which opera-house intrigue was intensified to read like an unwritten chapter of *Nineteen Eighty-Four* – which, accidentally or otherwise, was the year of *Galina*'s publication.

The lesson I would wish to draw, for myself at any rate, is that when one sits in comfort at the opera house, appraising this felicity of interpretation or that momentary failure of technique, one should perhaps not dismiss, as irrelevant or sentimental, thoughts of the bread-queues and the frozen bodies, the artist thwarted by institutionalised pettiness and surrounded by potential spies. It is not irrelevant, because it has all worked together to form the singer into the artist she is, and knowledge illuminates the special nature of her artistic contribution, most particularly the intensity of expression and large-scale radiance of personality which I think everyone felt at her recitals.

Assuredly, if I had known more of the background in the late 1950s when her first records appeared over here, and then in 1961 when she first sang at Covent Garden, I would have been readier to learn and less prompt to criticise. Harold Rosenthal's eulogy in *Opera* rights the balance: 'an utterly captivating Aïda, revealing a vibrant and lustrous voice that easily cuts through the orchestral and choral fabric of the ensemble and tapered

192

down to a shimmering *pianissimo* in the hushed moments of her arias and duets. A certain tentativeness here and there (most noticeable in a nervous 'O patria mia') and an unfamiliar Slavonic quality of diction and vocal production scarcely dimmed the excitement of her interpretation. A beautiful woman and a natural actress, she was breathtaking, vocally and visually, during the Nile Scene duets' (*Opera*, January 1962).

Of her voice in those performances I remember the disembodied floating quality of some soft high notes and then a thickened quality ('gum-boots', I used to call it) in the low register but it was not a unified voice, and the quality of middle notes at a *forte* or *mezzo forte* I can recall as not intrinsically beautiful (neither quite pure nor quite steady). The acting made a strong impression but not predominantly a favourable one. Its method, in this rôle, was deliberate and is explained in the book, but it involved a striking of poses, the kind associated with the Delsartian 'plastique' school of stage production, which may work in Gluck's *Orpheus*, and might even do so in *Aïda* if the rest of the company were conforming. Whether it was a more 'integrated' part of the Bolshoi production she does not say, but at Covent Garden, strong, vivid and individual as it was, it belonged to another world and after a while became simply too much. *Tosca*, as I remember, was better dramatically, though by then (1977) the voice had become worn. Her visual appearance, in those costumes made for Callas, was rather tremendous (but hers was a tremendous Tosca-personality); and then there was that moment which everyone remembered, when in Act II, tried beyond endurance, she answered as though by reflex the question about Angelotti's hiding-place, and only then, clapping her hand to her mouth, realised what she had done.

By this time, Vishnevskaya and her husband, the great cellist Rostropovich, had become well-established figures in the West. The Soviet Government, no doubt finding them a thorn in the flesh, came to a working agreement on leave of absence, and they were able to return every so often to Russia, where in their *dacha* they had given protection and a home to the writer Solzhenitsyn. Knowing well that the authorities were capable of anything, they were nevertheless outraged to learn, by hearing it on the French television news, that on 15 March 1978 they had been stripped of their citizenship by decree of the Praesidium of the Supreme Soviet. The affair became an international scandal, *The Times* taking 'West's gain: Russia's loss' as its headline for the first leader. Interestingly, their names were coupled with that of Vaclav Havel, 'now scandalously imprisoned'. One indignity which they might not have expected to meet with at this time was an article in *The Times* by Bernard Levin (19 April) who criticised them for having made an implicit bargain with their monstrous government instead of denouncing it. The Master of Corpus Christi, Cambridge, in a letter to the paper, came to their defence, finding Levin's attack 'very distasteful', but if readers were looking forward to the un-

leashing of Vishnevskaya's well-known fury in reply they were disappointed.

To some extent, the story does have a happy ending, in that the new Russia has welcomed them back; the book, *Galina*, exposes frankly and fiercely the iniquities of the past, and has now (1991) been published over there; and her name lives in history. This is so partly on account of her distinguished career (twenty-two years as principal soprano at the Bolshoi, guest appearances at La Scala and the Metropolitan, and recently work as a producer), but also because of close artistic associations with the two greatest composers of the age, Shostakovich and Britten.

The soprano part of Britten's *War Requiem*, written with her voice and character vividly in mind, constitutes a portrait in music such as few singers have inspired. Likewise there can be few singers who at the end of their days can know that they have enriched the lives of four men of supreme genius, effectively embodying the struggles of artists and oppressed people the world over.

CHAPTER 40

Giuseppe De Luca

It must be a comfort to a singer, must it not, if (say) lying in hospital at the age of seventy-three and facing an operation from which, naturally, he hopes to recover (but then who knows?), he can reflect that, wherever his kind of voice is thought of, his name will be remembered. I have no knowledge of whether this was so with De Luca, but it could well have been. He died in 1950, and up until the very last year he could still be heard from time to time singing in public, his voice still musical, his use of it even more so, always warmly applauded with that special kind of enthusiasm that rewards an artist from the past who has done something splendid in the present. So he must have felt an assurance of honour in his lifetime. What he could not have known is that, as the century nears its own end, this honour has in no way dimmed, but wherever the Italian lyric baritone and its repertoire come to mind so do the name and voice of Giuseppe De Luca.

His career dated back indeed to the final years of the previous century, and early in its long progress it took on board some notable events such as the premiere of *Adriana Lecouvreur* (1902) in which he 'created' the rôle of Michonnet and that of *Madama Butterfly* (1904) in which he was the original Sharpless. The niches of operatic history had another and yet more prestigious vacancy for him to fill, as he did in 1918 when at the Metropolitan, New York, in the premiere of Puccini's *Trittico* he was the world's first Gianni Schicchi. All the same, it was probably not these illustrious events that stirred first in the public memory as news was read of his death: rather, it was the voice as 'learnt' through the medium of the gramophone record, and the memory or hearsay recollection of his St Martin's Summer, a period of mellow fruitfulness with his reappearance at the Metropolitan in 1940 and Golden Jubilee recital seven years later.

His return to the Met was to have taken place a year before it did, but with nine other leading opera singers in the fraught October of 1939 De Luca was detained in Italy, unable to get a passport. The opera planned was *Don Pasquale*, in which he had been heard during his last previous season, early in 1935. The postponement made the gap in time that much greater (it must have seemed very probable at this age – he was now over sixty – and with Europe at war, that his American career would be over),

196

and when he eventually returned it was in his classic rôle of Germont in *La traviata*. He came on stage, in the second act, to such thunderous applause that the emotion visibly affected him. 'When he did open his mouth to sing [Olin Downes reported in the *New York Times*] the first five notes made the pulses beat because of the art and the beauty of the song.' The first notes, of course, are simply those with which Alfredo's father accosts (as he thinks) his son's seductress: 'Madamigella Valery?' They are not exactly 'song', but it is interesting that that is how they sounded when De Luca sang them. They are also unaccompanied and lie in the fine upper-middle part of the voice, so that one can well imagine how the recognition of those once familiar tones, echoes of the age of Caruso, in the wake of that tumultuous reception would, as the critic puts it, set the pulses beating. 'The quality of the *legato* [he continued], the perfection of the style, the sentiment which ennobled the melodic phrase, struck the whole audience.' Violetta was sung in that performance by the admired soprano from Czechoslovakia, Jarmila Novotna, then in her first season at the Met, and Olin Downes summed up: 'Thus, a young singing actress of radiant beauty and interpretative resource, and a veteran of many years of mastery, gave the whole opera of *Traviata* an ordinarily unsuspected measure of meaning.'

That last phrase is very much of its time. A critic would be unlikely to write exactly those words nowadays, for the musical world seems now to be agreed that *La traviata* is a masterpiece and so full of 'meaning' that little of it could be thought of as 'ordinarily unsuspected'. In 1940 such operas were still 'old-fashioned' (though a little less so, perhaps, than they had been twenty years earlier). The type of singing called *bel canto*, of which De Luca had the acknowledged mastery, was also widely thought of as belonging to an earlier age, the age, in fact, of those 'old-fashioned' operas. De Luca was something exceptional in his rôle as the guardian of *bel canto*. Vividly recalled, for instance, was the way in which he gracefully rounded off the first verse of the aria 'Di Provenza' in that performance. It spoke of another age, not one of dramatic clamour but of vocal refinement. And so it was when he sang this same aria at the close of the official programme in his 'farewell' concert at the New York Town Hall in 1947. 'The packed house, including many who had to sit on the stage, listened breathlessly to this performance and cheered when he finished. Nor could such a tribute have been better deserved. For this was the performance of a man with the soul of a true artist, a devoted servant of his art, and a master of singing' (*New York Times*, 8 November).

In that concert he sang arias by Monteverdi, Handel and lesser known seventeenth- and eighteenth-century composers; there were the three principal solos of Méphistophélès in *La Damnation de Faust*; some modern Italian songs, and then a generous selection of encores. The occasion was privately recorded, and it is at encore-time that today's listener can most readily share the mood of those who were present. Most captivating of all

198

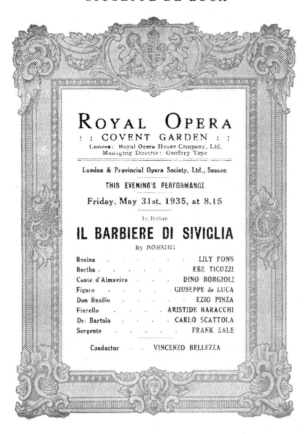

De Luca returned unexpectedly to Covent Garden in 1935,
his first appearance there since 1910

is his regular encore-song in very Italian English, 'Marietta' ('Won't you
fly away with me'), and the voice of this septuagenarian singing there, fifty
years after his operatic debut, is not so very different from the voice we
hear on a delightful recording of the song made in the early 1920s. That,
after all, is some tribute to the schooling and to a lifetime's practice. As his
friend and colleague, the soprano Frances Alda, said in her speech of
tribute at the concert, there had certainly been bigger voices among the
great baritones of those last fifty years, 'but no one of them was more
consummately the master of *bel canto*'.

So what was this famous *bel canto* as understood in those times? De
Luca's favourite rôle was Rigoletto, which he sang at the Met in 96
performances. But is that what we think of as a *bel canto* rôle? Looking
down the list of his rôles in the house, we see Amonasro, Gérard (in *Andrea*

Chénier), Escamillo, Alfio, Barnaba in *La Gioconda*, Tonio, Scarpia. There are, to be sure, three Rossini operas, four by Donizetti and one by Bellini. But this is certainly not the repertoire of a specialist in *bel canto* operas as expounded in his book by Rodolfo Celletti (*A History of Bel Canto*, Oxford, 1991). It has nothing, for instance, which puts to any very severe test the agility of the singer: nothing in common with the type of vocal music represented in the recording which was occupying my attention the day before writing this, a recital called 'The Heroic Bel Canto Tenor' whose music apparently required the range of three voices and the speed of the legendary Gonzales.

The answer of course is that in one sense De Luca was born into the wrong period of operatic history. In Italy it was the age of *verismo*. In the world generally Wagner was paramount (and at La Scala, De Luca found himself cast as Alberich and Beckmesser!). Even with Verdi, only the later operas were taken seriously by 'serious' musicians. Gatti-Casazza, manager of the Met, described De Luca proudly as 'our admirable singer of *bel canto*', like a Headmaster displaying the school's specialist in ancient Hebrew; but he didn't give him much to do that fully exercised that speciality. *I puritani* was the prime instance, and of De Luca's 928 performances with the Met this accounted for seven.

No: with De Luca, *bel canto* means quite literally what it says. The voice was beautiful in timbre; the phrases were beautiful in their evenness; the words and feelings were beautiful in that they became part of the music. For a demonstration, hear De Luca singing on records two phrases of Rigoletto's, 'Piangi, piangi, fanciulla' and 'Miei signori, perdono, pietate'. Hearing those, we know in what sense Rigoletto is indeed a *bel canto* rôle, and if his Alberich and Beckmesser were on record we would probably be able to say the same of them! We also know why, at the end of this century, when a lyric baritone voice and repertoire are in view, this man who died half-way through it should still be the one who first comes to mind.

CHAPTER 41

Lucia Popp

Drop the name of almost any singer into a conversation of opera-goers, and the faces will express reverence or disgust, interest or indifference, and probably a mixture of all. Make the name Lucia Popp, and the faces as with one accord will brighten. It was so on stage. At a dismal *Der Freischütz*, with a production devoid of magic, Agathe a wobbler and Max a boor, the Aennchen entered like a breath of spring. When she was on stage the whole house smiled. 'And do you remember,' a fellow enthusiast said to me years later, 'how they laughed when she said, "Das Bild dort fiel herunter"? They didn't know what it meant, or most of them probably didn't. That was the charm … they would eat out of her hand.'

Indeed we would. Aennchen's remark isn't very funny anyway. Max has arrived for his tryst with Agathe but seems moody and is concerned to see that she has a scratch or bruise on her forehead. Aennchen, her pretty cousin, explains that the picture over there fell down. It isn't even meant to be funny, but it lightens the atmosphere, breaks the tension between the lovers; and if I shut my eyes I do believe I can 'see' that adorable Aennchen intervening as she did all those years ago, with wide innocent eyes, standing slightly a-tiptoe, bending slightly from the waist, hands behind her back. Perhaps I am making it up, but the audience loved it, even though (in her own words) she was 'dressed like a dustbin'.

Popp's voice then was a light, bright-edged soubrette; later it filled out, and the last time I heard her in the opera house was as the Marschallin in *Der Rosenkavalier*. The figure had filled out too, and one was aware of a strong back and sturdy swimmer's shoulders beneath the gowns. Her face on stage you always watched. In repose it had an aristocratic cast of feature, with high cheek-bones and heavy eyelids. In its habitual mobility, a thousand shades of merriment and anxiety would cross it, and one came to know a woman of enchanting vitality and innate dignity. When she stood at the doorway in Act III her presence had immediate command: the character we know as the Marschallin is after all the Princess of Werdenberg and a very great lady indeed. She made us more aware of nobility than I can recall in any other performance, and it was done without pompous assertion of rank but with the high bearing of one whom we had previously known so intimately in the privacy (albeit shared and invaded) of her bedroom.

From Aennchen to the Marschallin is a long jump, and if taken as a jump is then asking for calamity. In fact Popp covered the ground in a much more sensible way. The development of her career, from the lightest and highest of rôles to what is generally thought of as the 'central' lyric repertoire, was accomplished step-by-step. The twenty-three-year-old who made her debut at the Theater an der Wien as Barbarina in *Le nozze di Figaro* went on to sing Susanna all the world over, and it was very natural that she should eventually turn to the Countess. Internationally she was first known as the Queen of the Night, chosen in 1963 by Walter Legge for the famous Klemperer recording which also introduced Gundula Janowitz. The *staccati* and *altissimi* of that rôle remained her concern until as late as 1971 after which she became her own daughter, and a more lovely and touching Pamina can rarely have been seen or heard. Similarly, from Sophie she graduated to the Marschallin and from Zdenka to Arabella.

She became also one of the most delightful of concert artists. Her programmes had a special flavour, perhaps through the inclusion of something unexpected, a Schoenberg group for instance, or the introduction of the Moravian folk-songs she had known from childhood. From Schubert she might choose a group of Italian settings, and *The Times* would report (as of a concert in 1982): 'one was forced to wonder whether earlier commentators might have revised their opinion of these songs if they had had the benefit of Miss Popp's exquisite rendering.' If she took something familiar she would make it new: Schumann's *Frauenliebe und Leben* had a freshness of tone and utterance that let the sunlight in on what can often be an airless and overheated atmosphere. At encore-time she would be generous and instinctively right in her selection: a recital might end with a favourite such as 'An Silvia', or, as she sent her audience out into the chill of the London January night, 'Schlechtes Wetter'.

Always she was the true professional. One of her concerts at the Wigmore Hall was sung in pain after a hip operation, but nobody would have guessed. When she sang as Vitellia in *La clemenza di Tito* at Zürich nobody would have guessed either that this was to be her last appearance in opera. She herself knew it well enough. In 1985 when she was briefly in hospital her place in a London recital was taken by Brigitte Fassbaender, and it was Fassbaender who in that same hall in November 1993 announced her death. The music that evening was Mahler's *Das Lied von der Erde*, and the final song, 'Das Abschied', was dedicated 'to Lucia Popp, a dear friend and a very great artist'. As Fassbaender's strong voice rang out with grief unmistakably in its tone few could have been unmoved by the aptness of the words: 'The sun departs behind the hills; into the valleys descends the evening with its shadows full of freshness.'

Freshness is the essential quality one still associates with Popp. It is

there in all her many records. At her death EMI reissued several recitals and it is moving now to sample each of them in turn, going back first to 1967 when a collection of arias by Handel and Mozart came out, conducted by her first husband György Fischer. The *allegro* Handel arias, from *Serse*, *Ottone* and *Joshua*, are deliciously spry, the scales well-oiled, every phrase alert and rhythmical. Most characteristic in its tone-quality is the slow movement, 'Tu virginum corona', of Mozart's *Exsultate, jubilate*: an oboe-soprano of fine concentration and unusual sweetness. When she returns to Mozart in this series the year is 1983, and much is included that would never have been attempted in the previous recital. Arias of Donna Elvira and Donna Anna, for instance, show how her voice had warmed and her expressiveness deepened. She is perhaps at her peak here, the high notes taken with complete ease, and the long difficult run of Anna's 'Non mi dir' sung not as an exercise but as a way of conveying the woman's exhilaration. A Schubert recital from the same year includes 'Gretchen am Spinnrade' and 'Die junge Nonne', big songs, which she would probably have left alone earlier – though it is still to the lilt of 'Seligkeit' and such songs that we turn for the singer we know.

Probably best of all these is her 'Slavonic arias' record, which opens with Popp singing Dvořák, Janáček and Smetana in her native Czech, and ends with Tchaikovsky in Russian. The operetta disc also has some tasty singing, though in it we notice (as in the others) the habit of what might be called (for short) the 'squeeze' technique, or the 'hairpin legato'. That was one of the features which, to my mind, limited enjoyment, the other being the presence of a light metallic patina, a tinkly upper layer that would compromise the purity of tone at any rate when she sang loudly. In the generally adorable recital of songs by Richard Strauss this is noticeable from time to time, though nothing interferes with the delights of her gentleness in 'Die Nacht' and the 'Wiegenlied'.

These and many other records (including a version of Strauss's *Four Last Songs* just released on the Sony label) remain to perpetuate her memory. For the personal memory, it remains a vivid and precious one shared by all who heard her in performance. Beyond that, one is aware too of an unusually lovable woman, and not, it must be said, in any arch, simpering or merely pretty way. She was a crisp and sophisticated business-woman, not a person in any sense to be taken for granted.

She was also a reader and a thinker. Dostoievsky, Tolstoy and Mann (in the original languages) were her passion, and another passion was to *know* things. 'Tell me, what exactly is the manifesto of the Ulster Unionists?' she asked Graham Johnson during the course of their work together on Schubert. She was also a marvellous cook and a great mimic. She could charm her way past customs officials and major-domos. She was loved by her colleagues, and in Vienna was adored: at the end of each performance she sang at the State Opera, a member of the orchestra would hand her a posy, token of affection. In an interview with Hilary Finch for *Gramophone*

magazine she spoke of her future. 'I am learning to bring something of my
own struggles, pain and life into my singing ... going back to the funda-
mentals, to try to achieve the apparently artless simplicity of a Chinese
painting.' Alas, she had not long to do it. The article was published in June
1993, and only five months later a saddened world learnt of her death from
cancer, at the age of fifty-four.

205

CHAPTER 42

Ernestine Schumann-Heink

Some kind friend, sounding like Noël Coward, said of Dame Sybil Thorn-dyke: 'I don't think I could love *anybody* quite as much as Sybil loves *everybody*.' Schumann-Heink's love may have been slightly less inclusive than that (for one thing, a number of fairly strenuous animosities would also flare from time to time). Nevertheless she was known essentially as a woman of heart, and that organ was deemed capacious and expansive enough to offer more or less universal accommodation.

She was then, in her lifetime, and in the United States at least, a great public figure, a personality who happened to be a singer, a name and a character known from the White House to the 'one-horse backwash out West'. She was a German who became Mother to America and its armed forces. She was the opera star of the Home, the Diva of Domesticity. Associated with her were smiles and tears and a song called 'Taps', popular in the First World War. That and 'The Rosary', 'Danny Boy' and 'Silent Night' were Schumann-Heink's songs for the people, who had a perfect right to the music that gave them pleasure. And so forth. Today, she is a connoisseur's singer, known and respected by a (relatively) select few.

Through a small number of gramophone records made during the years of her prime, and at least one from some time later, we can still hear very clearly the singing voice which was the foundation of this superstructure of stardom and personality-cult. It is rich and warm as befits a contralto voice, but also wonderfully light and multi-coloured. The power is impres-sive, doubly so because its effect is heightened by contrast. In songs and arias which exploit it, the range can be heard to extend well beyond two octaves (a member of the family who was close to her in her last years once told me that she would practise her scales up to high C and that the ceiling was the F above that). Still more notable is the flexibility: trills and scales, all the apparatus of *coloratura* singers, are at her command.

But that is only the beginning. With this admittedly exceptional mate-rial, she achieves a style that concentrates attention as only the greatest of artists can do. No phrase is inert, no moment can be taken for granted, and each item has its own character. The Brindisi from *Lucrezia Borgia* is almost weirdly tremendous in its panache; the plaintive solo in *Le Pro-*

phète has such intensity as to be almost tangible, like the tenderness of a physical hurt. The harrowing narration of Schubert's *Erlkönig* becomes real beyond the normal limits of the concert platform. The pulse of Wagner's 'Träume' is controlled with uncanny sensitivity. The yodelling cries of a Swiss folk song called 'I und mei bua' know nothing about inhibitions. The lilt of 'The Kerry Dance' is charmingly caught, and in 'Still wie die Nacht' (the song Einstein asked her to sing before the six thousand who welcomed him to the States in 1934) she mixes an unforgettable blend of strength and repose.

The recording referred to earlier as not belonging to this remarkable woman's vocal prime was made in 1929 at the age of 68. This is a sizeable portion of Waltraute's Monologue in *Götterdämmerung*, a rôle in which Schumann-Heink was considered incomparable. The authority of the opening line – 'Höre mit Sinn' – is regal; but it is the humanity of the latter half that makes so special and characteristic an appeal. The voice shows vulnerable areas, but its steadiness and surviving opulence are most movingly preserved. At such an advanced age, in 1926, then in 1928 and finally, as Erda, in 1932, Schumann-Heink reappeared after long years of absence at the Metropolitan, New York. One of those performances, of *Das Rheingold*, was attended by the Lieder singer Elena Gerhardt who had not seen a copy of the programme and did not know who the singers were to be: 'I suddenly sat up [she writes in her autobiography], thrilled when Erda came up and sang the first lines, "Weiche, Wotan, weiche". This could only be Schumann-Heink! Never have I heard Erda sung so wonderfully.' Another who was present at her last *Götterdämmerung* was the soprano and teacher Blanche Marchesi who found one line, the sentence about Holda's apples, strike so to the heart that she left her box, overcome with emotion.

A few years later, Schumann-Heink learned that she had leukaemia. On her death, in 1936, the veteran New York critic W.J. Henderson recalled those last operatic appearances and wrote: 'The magisterial authority of her reading of the vocal lines and the profundity of the feeling she put into them were things for all young singers to remember.' He also reminded his readers of her history: the authority of style and the dramatic significance of her performances had been learnt as far back as 1897 in Bayreuth. Actually, Henderson, not infallible, had written 1878, which was the year of her debut. She appeared, as Ernestine Rössler, in *Il trovatore* at the Royal Court Opera in Dresden: an Azucena of seventeen! It was a blazing talent that was thus rewarded with such a star rôle, and Dresden was no operatic backwater. But over the next ten years, there and at Hamburg, she had to learn the trade in a succession of small parts, many of them comic, with a tendency to type-cast. One great occasion was a performance of the Alto Rhapsody for which she had been selected by the conductor Von Bülow and at which Brahms was present. She later wrote that no subsequent triumph elated her quite so much. The next break-

through came in 1889 when a series of indispositions brought Schumann-Heink forward to fill the vacancies, with three great rôles in succession – Carmen, Fidès (in *Le Prophète*) and Ortrud – all triumphant.

From then onwards, Berlin, Bayreuth, Paris, London, Chicago, New York ... one led to another, and by the turn of the century she had a secure place among the acknowledged great singers of the world. So it was a surprise, to put it mildly, when in 1904 she took to musical comedy, heading the cast of *Love's Lottery* on Broadway.

Her defence against the inevitable criticisms (for 'crossover' was not so much in vogue in those days) enlisted the usual arguments: it would bring good singing to the masses, and so forth. But the show seems to have been feeble, and her part in it (a German laundress, making great play with cries of 'Mine English iss goot, ja?') sounds embarrassing. Money, publicity and fun were the rewards, and there was a lot of this kind of thing (though not taking the same form) from that time onwards. Moreover, the most important extension of her operatic experience was hardly an encouraging one, for at Strauss's request she took the rôle of Clytemnestra in the world premiere of *Elektra*, and hated it. 'It was frightful ... we were a lot of

209

mad-women.' Her own life, if not quite Aeschylean, had its quota of tragedy. Her first marriage presented her after a very short time with four children and an absentee husband. Work was refused her, the bailiffs stripped her living-room bare of everything save the stove on which she had nothing to cook, and one miserable day in winter she took the whole brood, the baby in her arms, down to the railway line. The cries of the eldest child broke the nightmare and they huddled together in a pitiful group as the train rushed past, but such had been the desperation. Further distresses lay ahead with the outbreak of world war where Schumann-Heink, by now an American citizen, had sons fighting on both sides. One, the captain of a German submarine, was lost at sea: 'My sympathies were with the American cause,' she said, 'but my heart went out to my son on the other side.' Shortly afterwards another son died of typhoid, and disaster of a different kind struck in 1929 when the Wall Street crash deprived her of the security which should have enabled her to retire. The family fortunes were also tied to hers in a most unfortunate way so that the pressures upon her, now a grandmother, were intense. She even joined a travelling vaudeville company, 'Roxy and his Gang'. There were plans for film appearances (Marie Dressler had recently died, and Schumann-Heink was a possible successor). In *Here's to Romance* she appeared with the young tenor Nino Martini, but the experience was not an easy one.

It was a turbulent, courageous life, and in a unique way took the popular imagination. The newspapers and magazines of those days thrived on stories about opera stars, but if they were women they were usually creatures of fashion and beauty, and invariably sopranos, the heroines of romance and high tragedy on stage. In youth and again in old age Schumann-Heink had beauty of a kind, one that had more to do with character than with features. She was also quite short of stature, so that her command of the stage could not have been easily achieved. Her character was a strange one too, an odd mixture of impulsiveness and calculation. Dilemmas confronted her at all stages. Her first marriage, with Ernst Heink, presented the common problem of family and career; the second, a more stable one with an actor-producer Paul Schumann, brought differences over the upbringing of the children and the drift away from Germany; the third, with her business manager William Rapp, ended in a rancorous law-suit. Now, all that has melted away, and we are left with the recordings. Those and the words of two American women will be legacy and testimonial enough. In her autobiography Rosa Ponselle spoke of 'an understated elegance' about Schumann-Heink, 'a rich, lovely quality that shimmered like a Latin voice: and she was *involved* in what she was singing ... a communicator, a disciplined medium between the composer and the audience.' Another was the wife of W.J. Henderson, who put it as simply as this: 'She was the most beloved of all singers.'

Jon Vickers

Of course, Samson (it suddenly struck me) was blind: at least he was so by the third act of Saint-Saëns's opera.

'And why [says another inner voice] should that so "strike" you?'

Well, I was thinking of Vickers and what rôle it was I last heard him sing.

'And?'

And, you see, I had been thinking it must have been Otello or Grimes, but now I rather think it was Samson.

'And?'

And, well, I was rather …

'Pleased?'

Of course he was a very distinguished Otello and a very memorable Grimes …

'But there's a "but" in all this, isn't there? Come along, speak out. We're all friends here. What's this "but"? You didn't really like him, did you?'

I couldn't stand all that pacing.

'Pacing?'

All that striding. All that slow, weighty walking up and down, up and down.

'And what have the eyes got to do with it? I mean, why is it revelatory, in some way, to recall that Samson was blind?'

Ah, now that's harder to explain. You see, in memory I see his Otello and Grimes as blind too. They strode slowly up and down in a world from which they were apart. Perhaps this was Jon Vickers's vision: how he saw, or felt them. But it went against the music, less stubbornly perhaps in *Peter Grimes* than in *Otello*, but gradually over the years in his portrayals it became common to both, and I found it weakened sympathy and (in *Otello*) to some extent credibility. The point was made, more sympathetically, by David Cairns reporting on *Otello* in the *Sunday Times* (9 November 1980): 'He now moves across the stage in somnambulistic slow motion, like a being apart, abstracted, hardly connecting with those around him, as though in an invisible sea of misery.' The critic went on to say that, although on this occasion it was 'exaggerated and extreme', the interpretation nevertheless had hypnotic power and might still 'work' if the 'chemistry' were right in its relationship with the production as a whole.

To my mind, the ingredient with which that slow stride and apartness could not combine (as chemistry) was the music; and so as the seasons went by and the manner became more fixed my own antipathy must have grown. Samson at least was physically blind, 'eyeless in Gaza at the mill with slaves', a man apart if ever there was one. And in the scene of the mill, Vickers was at his inspired and unforgettable best: hence pleasure in the thought that this was probably the rôle in which I saw him for the last time on stage.

Back now, from the last time to the first. This was in (and as) Verdi's *Don Carlos*. We had all heard by then of this young Canadian who had been cabled by Covent Garden just as he was thinking of giving up professional singing altogether. Those who heard him at his British debut, which was with Covent Garden on tour in Cardiff, experienced that rare and envied thrill: the recognition of an artist in whom flamed the promise of greatness. 'A great acquisition,' was Harold Rosenthal's unequivocal phrase in *Opera*, June 1957. 'He possesses a true dramatic tenor voice, not inherently beautiful, but of exciting timbre .... One sincerely hopes that his stay with the company will be long and successful and that he will neither be overworked nor given rôles to which he is not suited. If he is sensibly used he should go far, and in the distant future (not the near one, please) should make an Otello and Siegmund.' The estimate and prospectus proved remarkably well-judged, and for once all went according to plan.

The King in *Un ballo in maschera* (sung at that time in English), Don José in *Carmen*, Aeneas in *The Trojans* and Radamès in *Aïda* were the rôles of his first year at the Royal Opera House, which then moved into its centenary year, 1958, celebrated in a production which lives in the memory of all who saw it, as among the great operatic events of a lifetime. *Don Carlos*, conducted by Giulini, produced by Visconti, effectively introduced the work to a new generation. The cast was headed by Gré Brouwenstijn, Fedora Barbieri, Jon Vickers, Tito Gobbi and Boris Christoff. Of these, Barbieri may have been surpassed by other artists in later performances; the others were not. Of Vickers I can truly say that (in a way I associate only with Martinelli on records) his timbre and expression were so deeply etched upon the music that to this day I hear, mentally, the great anguished phrases of the rôle in his voice and his alone.

He had, among the tenors of our time, an incomparable intensity. A sense, not exactly of strain, but of high notes that were not easily won, was part of it – not an invariable feature of his singing but part of the grieving, troubled soul of these characters. Radamès in the agony of choice and betrayal, José in his surrender and confession, Riccardo (or Gustavus) in his moment of irrevocable decision – 'Ah, l'ho segnato' – these were passages into which Vickers put all the intensity of his being. He knew (or

Vickers as Peter Grimes

practised) nothing of the familiar vocal sign-language (the sob being merely the most obvious); and if there had not been working from within a genuine spiritual refinement the sheer size of his voice, breadth as well as power, would surely have bludgeoned the listener into insensibility. Later, I believe, there did come a sort of thickening in the lines of his art; phrases lost their shape in his quest for expressiveness, and in his softer singing the voice would slip (albeit easily, pleasantly and sometimes movingly) into something which may not have been a croon yet which had a way of calling that word to mind. On the whole, the Vickers of my own most prized memories is that of the first ten to fifteen years.

But of course this was a massive career. It included a wide range of rôles that are not readily associated with him – Andrea Chénier for example, Laca in *Jenufa*, Sergei in *Katerina Ismailova*, even the stuttering Vasek in *The Bartered Bride*, sung at the Met in 1978, when Patrick J. Smith reported in *The Times* (14 November) that 'Vickers easily walked off with the show'. As Jason in *Medea* he showed himself to be one of the very few singers who could match Maria Callas in the magnetism of performance. Another of his finest rôles was that of Handel's Samson: William Mann wrote of his first performance, with Covent Garden at Leeds, that it was 'dramatically and vocally and both together, the finest that he has given in this country, noble and moving from his first pitiful appearance to his last exit' (*Opera*, June 1959). His Bayreuth debut in *Die Walküre* was deemed the greatest personal success of the season; in Vienna the audience applauded his Siegmund and the Sieglinde of Birgit Nilsson throughout the first interval. At Salzburg and at La Scala, in Buenos Aires and all the main cities of America he was felt to be (as in this country) one who conferred a certain greatness upon the age.

With the great go their foibles. With Vickers, 'foible' ('failing or moral weakness' – *OED*) is hardly the word, for moral and religious conviction was at the heart of it. To a distraught record-producer he would explain that he would not, after all, be recording Gerontius, as Newman's words were not such as he could now conscientiously sing. To a diplomatic General Manager he would point to Tannhäuser's last words as prohibitive ('Heilige Elisabeth, bitte für mich' makes a saint of Elisabeth who therefore comes between the man and his God). When as Tristan he arose from his sick-bed to admonish a fidgeting audience, it was not just through personal irritation but the sense that a noble, serious art was being impeded and dishonoured. For allied reasons he rejected an offer to star in *Camelot* on Broadway: it would have netted a great deal more than all those *Tristans* and *Parsifals*, but to him the opera singer's was a high calling or it was nothing.

Out of that – an essentially religious conviction that these characters on stage are human realities through whom, by the divine power of music, others may come closer to the divine themselves – there arises the special power which Jon Vickers's singing has had. The voice was indeed an

214

exceptionally powerful one, but that was not it. Though of no more than average height, he had a natural stage-presence which would always command attention, but that did not account for him either. Better to summon the memory of that voice and let it cry, as it did so often, out of the darkness of Florestan's dungeon: 'Gott! welch Dunkel hier!' To invoke it is to hear it, and with the inward hearing comes the sure recognition of music that *matters* profoundly. Theoretically, we know this perfectly well already: in practice, we depend on artists like Vickers to give it flesh and blood and voice.

CHAPTER 44

Elisabeth Rethberg

'First I fell in love with her voice,' said George, 'and then I fell in love with her.' George was ninety. His eyes were as bright as his mind, and only that morning he had been rehearsing the Metropolitan Opera House chorus in their Russian for *Boris Godunov*. In this place he was practically the oldest inhabitant, having joined the company in 1926. George Cehanovsky had left Russia as a young man, had a full-scale odyssey to relate concerning his journey across Europe, and arrived in the States in time for Christmas 1923. He did not say that, but so it must have been, for he auditioned at the Met on a day when *Ernani* was being rehearsed. On stage were Ponselle,. Martinelli and Ruffo, and the performance itself was on Christmas Day. What happened then I don't know: presumably they told him to go away, gain some experience and try again. Eventually he made his debut there as Köthner in *Die Meistersinger*, with Elisabeth Rethberg as Eva. But he had heard her a while before as Pamina, and that was when he fell in love with the voice.

Rethberg, he quite understood, could not obligingly fall in love in return: her heart was soon to become heavily and often painfully engaged to the young bass Ezio Pinza. Cehanovsky told Rethberg that if she ever needed someone who would love and devote himself to her he would always be there. He waited and eventually was rewarded. Rethberg became Mrs Cehanovsky and they enjoyed years of happiness till she suffered a stroke after which she could deal only in German, her native language. A German-speaking nurse was engaged and tended with devotion till Elisabeth's death on 6 June 1976. George, in his narrative of these events, then paused, though something in the corner of his eye suggested that this was not a story with an unhappy ending. 'That nurse,' he said, and paused again with the expert timing of one who has trodden the boards and counted the bars for the best part of a long life, 'is now the second Mrs Cehanovsky.'

Cehanovsky (who died in 1986) was not the only one to love the Rethberg voice. Toscanini, after a performance of Brahms's Requiem (and what one would give to have heard her sing that solo in her prime) had compared it to a finely played Stradivarius. The Guild of Singing Teachers of America had voted hers the most perfect voice in the world. That was in

216

1928, the year when in Dresden, the city of her apprenticeship and first triumphs, she 'created' the title rôle of Strauss's *Die Aegyptische Helena*. It was also a time when review after review spoke of the loveliness of her art, as did the critic of the *Chicago Herald*, who declared: 'Rethberg is to this generation what Schumann-Heink was to my youth, a superb German singer who proves that vocal art is no Latin monopoly.' 'You might easily be reminded, by her phrasing,' wrote the New York critic Lawrence Gilman, 'of the art of a master of bowed instruments, so just is her sense of the shape and balance and musical designs, her delicate instinct for line and cadences and proportion.'

America, and the Metropolitan in particular, were at the centre of her career from 1922 onwards. Her early years in Germany had developed an innate musicality, nurtured by a musical family, with plenty of classics for study at the piano and, so it is said, the songs of Schubert (including *Winterreise*, tried out at home at the age of seven). A sound training at the conservatory, where she enrolled in 1912, and then good grounding in a variety of rôles at the Dresden Opera prepared her for recognition as one of the most promising singers of the new postwar generation. She came to England first in 1925, when she sang an Aïda that immediately won high praise: 'a perfectly produced voice, very beautiful in tone and absolutely true in pitch,' reported the *Morning Post*. And 'Figaro' (A.P. Hatton) of *Musical Opinion* is worth quoting at length:

> Eclectic opera lovers will almost certainly single out Elisabeth Rethberg as the most distinguished of the new singers in the Italian season so far. Her voice is of exceptional beauty, vibrant with colour; she controls it like an artiste and her *cantabile* is a joy. As yet she does not always make the voice subserve the mood of the drama as she will probably do later: its lack of power and 'ring' was also notable in the pageant scene, and there is often a steely quality on a high *forte*. It has, however, all the rich promise of a really fine voice, and one can have no hesitation in saying that her Aïda will be something to remember when the essential body of her voice and the dramatic vesture of her acting are one and indivisible .... She remains an unforgettable artist, and the luscious beauty of much of her singing in the Nile scene was of a type not heard at Covent Garden for many a moon.

It was to be many a moon also before it was heard at Covent Garden again, a full decade in fact and then only by accident. The story is told in Josephine O'Donnell's book *Among the Covent Garden Stars* (London 1936). *La cenerentola* with Supervia had to be cancelled, *La Bohème* substituted. The Norwegian soprano Eidé Norena was with the company that season and would have been asked to sing Mimì, but they suddenly recalled that she was being presented at Buckingham Palace, so of course it was out of the question. Then, says Miss O'Donnell, 'Sir Thomas had one of his inspirations. "Elisabeth Rethberg!" he said. "I was speaking to her today. I'm sure she'll help us out." The secretary managed to catch her on

218

the telephone and said how very much obliged Sir Thomas would be if she could consent to sing Mimì that evening.' Rethberg demurred that she had not sung the part for years, and the time was then 4.30pm. She came nevertheless, and stayed to sing also an Elsa credited with all sorts of subtleties by Ernest Newman, and then next season Sieglinde, the Marschallin ('consummate vocal range and artistry') and, once more, her Aïda.

This was her most famous rôle. She sang it sixty-seven times at the Met, and it was the part everybody most wanted to hear. At Ravinia Park the audience applauded her Nile scene with Martinelli for twenty minutes. At Covent Garden in 1936 it was still, according to 'Figaro', 'vocally glorious'. Yet there were limitations, both of temperament and voice. 'Figaro' had noted them ten years earlier, and so had old Herman Klein, who in the

219

Gramophone (August 1925) virtually warned her that this was not the voice for Aïda at all ('a lovely organ, skilfully managed', but 'too light'). In New York, other critics, Oscar Thompson and W.J. Henderson, had warned, more urgently but later in the day, that she should not be singing as heavy a rôle as Rachel in *La Juive*. That was in 1930, and the danger was probably not clearly audible then. But by the mid-1930s it was; and in 1934 she was only forty years of age.

There were other limitations. She was never much of an actress, though sometimes she would make a special effort and critics would claim to observe an improvement. To some extent she compensated with her voice. Here is that analysis of her performance as Elsa in *Lohengrin* written by Ernest Newman in 1935 and mentioned earlier. 'Only an artist of her intelligence could or would have known how to use a voice of the most absolute unsophistication for her first scene; a voice with more body, born of a new psychological assurance, for the Elsa who, having passed safely through her first overwhelming experience of the world, faces Ortrud in calm confidence; and yet a third voice, still more positive, more assured, and with a note of hard anger in it, for the later scene in which she realises Ortrud is her and Lohengrin's enemy.' That sounds to have been a real performance, yet in general either her hearers were less perceptive or she herself did not measure up to the dramatic conviction and subtlety of her Covent Garden Elsa.

One might wonder whether the concert hall was not, after all, her natural home, but here too the limitations appear. She gave a Lieder recital in London at the Queen's Hall on 19 July 1935, when *The Times* noted 'the exceptional beauty of everything save her more forceful notes ... when the tone took on too sharp an edge'. There were also 'musical intelligence and subtleties of phrasing', yet 'though versatility is suggested, the outstanding impression of her singing is undoubtedly in placid beauty'. Poor Rethberg! There seems always to come a 'but' or a 'yet'. In the late 1930s the decline accelerated, and in 1942 was brought up short in the face of her failure in a thoroughly misguided attempt to sing the *Siegfried* Brünnhilde. She retired, none too gracefully, that year.

'Touch very gently on her failings,' the conductor and accompanist Edwin McArthur once wrote. There was never, he felt, a more lovely singer than Rethberg, or a more devoted artist. Unhappily, a lot of pirated recordings from her later years exist to demonstrate the failings. Happily, there is a splendid legacy of recordings from 1924 to 1934, the years of her prime, and in these we encounter an art in the presence of which most 'but's and 'yet's are banished. We also hear a voice to fall in love with.

CHAPTER 45

Martti Talvela

As long as there are people who remember seeing him – and, after all, videos and photographs extend that prospect almost indefinitely – it will be the *sight* of Martti Talvela that first comes to mind when he is named; and by sight will generally be meant size. He was six foot seven inches (some say eight), and broad (some say 300 pounds in weight). On whatever stage he stood, and in whatever company he sang, he could dominate. In the rôles he made most completely his own – Sarastro, Inquisitor, Hagen, Boris, Dosifey, Paavo Ruotsalainen in Kokkonen's *The Last Temptations* – his physical stature was a bonus; nobody could think of it as incidental. Yet in another sense it was of secondary importance, and what should come first in the memory is his art. He worked within his physique, which while providing advantages and opportunities also prescribed limits. There are in fact many other ways in which he should be remembered: principally as singer and actor, of course, but also as a national figure and a supremely effective festival director, a sheep-farmer, and perhaps a priest manqué – maybe even a prophet.

'Singing,' he said, 'must be a passion, like the praying of a holy man.' Talvela (similar to Jon Vickers in this) was possessed of a strong conviction that the singer could, and should, be doing God's work. 'I think I have to say something in this life to people,' he remarked in an interview with his fellow-countryman Erkki Arni, 'and I can do it better with my singing voice than with my speaking voice …. The drama is important, but because it has something deep to say to people.' There was an intensity about him, that can certainly be heard in his singing and which, combined with his physique (that again), could make him a very formidable man indeed. He could be both gentle and genial, yet there was also a fierce urgency which in a restaurant would make the waiters move in silent-film double-speed time, and which, in serious matters, such as the financial needs of the Savonlinna Festival, could impress itself forcibly even upon the President of the Republic.

Savonlinna became for several years the centre of his artistic life, the focus of his crusade. It is not true to say that he founded the operatic tradition there, but he was certainly the key figure in its eventual triumph. Visitors to Finland, 'land of a thousand lakes', will usually take in

the south-east lake district, one of the historical sites of which is the fifteenth-century Olavinlinna fortress, or St Olaf's Castle. It was the soprano Aïno Ackté who first conceived of operatic productions there in the open courtyard. The story has often been told: she instituted the first festival in 1912, and after it lapsed, from 1930 to 1967, the local township restarted it as the Savonlinna Opera Festival, inviting Talvela to become Artistic Director in 1972. With his international reputation he was able to open what had been a national event (or perhaps not quite that) to world interest. For his first season he brought the producer August Everding over from Hamburg and with Toni Businger as stage designer mounted Mozart's *Taikahvilu* – or *Die Zauberflöte* in Finnish. He himself sang Sarastro, his 'lions' (Sarastro's customary retinue) being Olavinlinna's native black rams. His entrance, down four flights of stairs from the battlements, was probably the most impressive in the opera's history, but what struck foreign visitors still more forcibly was the excellence of the company as a whole and the great possibilities ahead.

In 1975 the castle's 500th anniversary was to be celebrated. *Die Zauberflöte*, which with its fairytale production had quickly become almost a Finnish national institution, was put on again; Aulis Sallinen's *The Horseman* had its premiere with Matti Salminen as the protagonist; and Talvela appeared as Boris Godunov. All seats were taken – and the courtyard could accommodate nearly three thousand. President Kekkonen attended, as did the Prime Minister and every member of the Cabinet. In 1977 the opera commissioned from Joonas Kokkonen, *The Last Temptations*, gave Talvela a rôle that was made for him: that of a revivalist preacher whose life is reviewed in flashbacks from his deathbed. It ran eventually for something like two hundred performances, to quote Erkki Arni, 'persuading the religious Finns that opera was not quite such a sinful entertainment after all'. Throughout all these years, Talvela worked hard, withdrawing for valuable months from the international circuit, and receiving (it was reckoned) something like one-tenth of the fee he commanded abroad.

It was of course an immensely distinguished international career that he had; and that career dated from almost the start. He made his debut in 1961 at Stockholm where Wieland Wagner heard him and invited him to Bayreuth. His first rôle there was Titurel in *Parsifal*, and in the same year, 1962, he joined the Deutsche Oper in Berlin. Over the next five or six years he acquired stage experience and repertoire (which eventually numbered fifty-five rôles). His reputation grew, with engagements in 1968 at Salzburg and the Metropolitan. Here he made an immediate and overwhelming impression as the Inquisitor in *Don Carlos* followed by Fasolt and Hunding, the rôles which two years later were to introduce him to audiences at Covent Garden. The real revelation in London, however, came a week later with the *Götterdämmerung*. In the *Financial Times*, Ronald Crichton wrote: 'The truth is that everyone on Saturday was

223

overshadowed by the Hagen of Martti Talvela.' 'The most imposing figure on stage and the most eloquent singer,' said *The Times*; and 'A great operatic discovery' was the verdict in the *Evening Standard*. On his return in 1972 Talvela confirmed all of this with an unforgettable Dosifey in *Khovanshchina*, sung for the first time at the house in Russian. Peter Heyworth of the *Observer* wrote that 'Martti Talvela once again shows himself to be one of the outstanding singers of the present day,' and Gillian Widdicombe in the *Financial Times*: 'His singing is so rich and powerful, combining dramatic expression with ideally focused vocal quality, that he effectively magnetises himself as the dominant personality.' At the Metropolitan a corresponding revelation came with his Boris Godunov there in 1974. On the dust jacket of David Hamilton's *Metropolitan Opera Encyclopaedia* (Thames and Hudson, 1987) the single photograph chosen to represent 'The World of Opera' is one of Talvela as Boris, with crown and sceptre, his giant figure attended by the Tsarevitch, Paul Offenkrantz. When he repeated the rôle at Savonlinna in 1976, now singing in Finnish, he went further and, according to Rodney Milnes reporting in *Opera*, revealed 'unsuspected reserves of eloquence, the scenes with the boy being almost unbearably poignant'.

Talvela retired from his Savonlinna directorship in 1979, at a time when his health had become a problem. His weight brought its own dangers and while in America for an earlier Metropolitan season he was found to be diabetic. He began to talk more about devoting himself to the sheep-farm in Juva, the maintenance of which was also something of a religion with him, though he also wanted to continue his career in a more concentrated fashion, limiting himself to some ten rôles and more song recitals: those, he said, would be enough to 'bring my message'. Always there was this sense of artistic-religious mission, in which, as he told Harlow Robinson, his interviewer for *Opera News* (February 1986), there is 'the human being who can see something mystical'. Lying ahead was also to have been a period as Director of the Finnish National Opera, a five-year term starting in 1992: but on 22 July 1989, dancing at his daughter's wedding, he dropped down dead. He was fifty-four years old, and Finland mourned as for the death of a hero.

For myself, recalling his performances in London, I see first in the mind's eye, as everyone does, the great figure on stage as Dosifey, Hagen or Fasolt reducing even our house giants, mighty men like David Ward and Michael Langdon, to normal dimensions. But I also remember his first song recital in the Royal Festival Hall, when he gave forth such magnificence of tone that it was quite enough simply to 'drink' the voice; yet next day *The Times* carried a review which accepted his Kilpinen, thought less of his Rachmaninov, sniffed at his Brahms and dismissed his Schubert – with no word about the voice. It might have been a little pipsqueak of a voice that had sung to us that evening: whereas here had been a true and

sumptuous bass voice, rare in itself, massive in power, gorgeous in quality, unique in character.

Records preserve this: a recent reissue of Kilpinen songs brought back with sudden and vivid fidelity the sheer marvel of that sound, particularly in its upper middle register, burnished gold in opulence and purity. There was an unpolished element in his singing too, yet I remember at the time it seemed to me that recordings exaggerated it. And certainly there were plenty of critics who did appreciate the beauty of his voice. Ronald Crichton, in the *Götterdämmerung* review quoted above, found himself at first 'overwhelmed by the superb vocal quality', and Peter Heyworth on his Dosifey concluded: 'I can recall few basses capable of such expressive and shapely legato singing.' Perhaps the fact that one of Talvela's early heroes on records was Ezio Pinza has some bearing on that. At all events and amidst all the memories of sight, career and character (and I'm sure, incidentally, that Erkki Arni is right in his recollection of Talvela's voice as having a kind of sadness inherent in the tone), it is worth emphasising that Martti Talvela was a singer to *hear*: that he was (and is), in short one of the *singers* of the century.

225

CHAPTER 46

Toti Dal Monte

'Toti Dal Monte ... whose art has a jewel-like delicacy and fineness that must be heard to be believed.' The words are those of Kaikhosru Sorabji (born Leon Dudley) whose cranky genius took several forms, one of which was to be the most outspoken critic of singers and singing in his generation. He wrote throughout most of the inter-war years on music in London, and in general his opinion of the current state of the art of singing was that it stank. Most of all he blamed the Italians. They had a birthright and a tradition – he worshipped at the shrines of Tetrazzini and Boninsegna, Caruso and Battistini – but the modern generation had betrayed its inheritance. Noise and clamour had usurped the thrones once occupied by melodic grace and well-schooled accomplishment. Exceptions were few; the shining one was Toti Dal Monte.

Such an opinion meant something, however immoderate its expression. Sorabji heard Dal Monte in her London season of 1925, then again in Italy where he was 'left breathless by the marvels of singing she achieved', then in the early 1930s when there appeared to be some suspicion of a decline – but no, for in 1935 she sang at the Queen's Hall and was marvellous as ever: 'Here was the ineffable perfection of *bel canto*, indescribably lovely, delicate and subtle phrasing, and a sense of style that can only be compared to the craftsmanship of a Fabergé in precious metals.'

That was in the songs and arias which opened her programme. Later came 'a dazzling performance of the Mad Scene from *Lucia di Lammermoor*, in which the sparkle and virtuosity of the florid work was strictly subservient to the essential musical-expressive purpose .... It is only artists of such consummate accomplishment who, having mastered the mere technical difficulties of this school of vocal writing, can pass on to the as-hard task of making an emotionally expressive matter of it.' The occasion was made doubly blissful by the participation of John McCormack, whose singing was 'the tenor counterpart of that of Madame Dal Monte'. This was verily the cup that runneth over, but next day Sorabji would awake to smite the degenerates who disgraced the tradition which 'two such supreme vocal artists in one and the same programme' had so nobly upheld.

The message was trumpeted loud and clear. Unfortunately the platform

Dal Monte as Lucia di Lammermoor

was not high enough (the *New English Weekly* having a limited circulation even among the intelligentsia), and at Dal Monte's next Queen's Hall recital, in the February of the following year, her audience was scanty. Among it sat Walter Legge, reporting for the *Manchester Guardian*. He liked the singing well enough but was more interested in the concert as a portent: 'A fashion is passing, and soon the *coloratura* soprano will disappear from our concert halls.' It was further evidence of what another critic of those days (Edwin Evans) had once called 'the passing of the top E flat'. Legge reflected that only a generation ago Melba and Tetrazzini were challenged by a host of aspirants, whereas then, in 1936, Dal Monte stood alone: 'No new Italian soprano has attempted to dispute her exalted position.' He was overlooking Lina Pagliughi and (French but in the same field) Lily Pons: the point still held. Dal Monte was seen as last in the great line. Hers was a dying art, doomed because the operas written for such singers were out of fashion and (it seemed) likely to remain so. The second half of the twentieth century, of course, has had a different story to tell.

Operas such as *Lucia di Lammermoor* and *La sonnambula* seemed in Dal Monte's time far more old-fashioned than they do now. There was limited demand (or support) for revivals, consequently a limited repertoire. Of the *bel canto* operas in which she was the specialist, Dal Monte sang only: *Il barbiere di Siviglia, La sonnambula, Lucia di Lammermoor, Don Pasquale, L'elisir d'amore, La figlia del reggimento* and *Linda di Chamounix*. Her Verdi operas were *Rigoletto* and *La traviata*, which were often seen as falling within the old-fashioned category too. She did sing other rôles, though not many (most important being the title rôles from Mascagni's *Lodoletta* and *Madama Butterfly*). Generally, like Pons and Galli-Curci, she was type-cast, in an era which, officially at any rate, considered the type archaic.

The odd thing is that the type itself was probably not Dal Monte's by nature. Certainly Gigli did not think so. In his memoirs (London 1957) he recalls that he first sang with her in *Lodoletta*, when 'she had a beautiful lyric-soprano voice, perfect for the romantic heroines of *La traviata* and *La Bohème*'. That was in 1918, at the start of her career. Her impresarios, he says, persuaded her to turn to the *coloratura* repertoire in which she achieved world fame. 'Then, after enduring the strain for years, her vocal cords finally slackened, and she found herself unable to sing *coloratura* any longer. Her natural, lyric-soprano voice was still intact, but her impresarios clamoured only for Lucia, and to the consternation of the public, she suddenly vanished into premature retirement.'

The account is partly misleading: for example, the rôle which Dal Monte sang most frequently in later years was not Lucia but Butterfly (recorded in 1939 with Gigli as Pinkerton). As for how 'premature' her retirement was, that depends somewhat on the date of her birth: the books used to give 1899, whereas it is now established as 27 June 1893. She sang in opera for the last time in 1947 (*Il barbiere di Siviglia* at Pescara), gave

Dal Monte as Rosalina in Giordano's *Il re*

concerts fairly regularly till 1951 and made a one-off appearance at Sofia in 1960. Still, an essential truth is there, well borne out by her records.

For myself, Dal Monte is one of the most cherished of singers on record; if some hitherto unpublished item were to appear on the lists I would immediately send off for it. Yet before playing I would offer up a silent prayer for the high notes. Not that she lacked them: they would be there, right up to Lucia's E flat. But one is aware of the adjustment as it is made. At her Covent Garden debut in 1925 the critic of *The Times* reported that, 'The high notes above B flat are a little hard.' As the decade advanced, the B flat itself would probably have been included, and perhaps a couple of notes below it. And possibly 'hard' is not quite the word, but rather some such description as 'strong and brilliant, but wanting in warmth and ease'. One of her loveliest records is of 'Ah, non credea mirarti' from *La sonnambula* (1929), almost ideal in its clear purity of tone and firm evenness of line. Yet even here one slightly regrets the high notes – A and A flat,

229

nothing higher, but just slightly less comfortable in production and resonance than they should be with a high soprano.

Another limitation to her work as a *coloratura* was that she had no trill.
Her *fioriture* were certainly graced with fluency and precision, but it is
strange to think such fine schooling (she studied with Barbara Marchisio,
teacher also of Rosa Raisa) should have left her without one of the
principal adornments of her chosen art. But then, perhaps at that time the
coloratura speciality was not in view.

She made her debut (1916) as Biancofiore, a secondary rôle in Zan-
donai's *Francesca da Rimini*, at La Scala. Then came Lola in *Cavalleria
rusticana* with Mascagni conducting. Among the operas of the next few
years are *La rondine* (as Lisetta), *Pagliacci*, *Loreley* (Anna) and *Ballo in
maschera* (Oscar, which would surely have been charming and was never
repeated). The decisive factor was that the rôle for which she came to be
most in demand throughout Italy in those early years was Gilda in
Rigoletto. When La Scala reopened after the war, in 1922, Toscanini chose
her for a production which entered the annals immediately as a revelation
and a model for all. Dal Monte herself shared in the revelation for, as she
described it later, Toscanini actually wanted his singers to *understand*
things (the reason for those rests in 'Caro nome', for example). Her Gilda
on that great occasion was prized for its penetration of the music's spirit,
transforming her exquisite vocalising into a higher form of art altogether.

After this triumph her fame spread before her. She was fêted in South
America and Australia, took her share of glory in the famous performances
of the Scala company under Toscanini in Berlin and Vienna, enjoyed a
success in Chicago (though only a short-lived one at the Metropolitan,
nipped in the bud, she believed, by the jealousy of Amelita Galli-Curci).
There were tours in Russia and the Far Fast, honours from heads of state,
tributes from fellow musicians such as David Oistrakh, who told her that
his ambition was to play the violin so as to sound like her singing.

She was, by all accounts, a charming, conscientious, courageous little
woman, a great spreader of happiness who yet had a core of seriousness,
even sadness, about her. That, I am sure, has something to do with the
special appeal of her singing. She may indeed have had about her a good
deal of her own intensely moving Madame Butterfly. The first impression
may be of something light and childlike; before long, we see through to a
sensitive heart and an inner strength.

CHAPTER 47

Robert Merrill

It sometimes happens that, for no particular reason, a singer drops out of one's listening-life for two or three years, and then resurfaces in some unexpected form or context when least looked for. So it was with Robert Merrill in my own curiously assorted schedule. He had been a favourite throughout the period in which his records were new, essentially the 1950s and '60s, but somehow the reissues had passed me by and occasions for fetching out the originals had not arisen. Re-acquaintance came through Bloch's *Sacred Service*, and there could not have been a better chance or choice.

It was a fairly late recording, first issued over here in 1972. Bernstein conducts, and does so with that sense of passionate involvement which, in the right music, would bind all the participants into a community of the spirit: a great surging exaltation, arising out of a profound yearning. Merrill's voice emerges from the introductory music with a dark richness that sets the listener tingling with the very first sound. It has all the remembered firmness and strong body of tone – that of a genuine singer, who knows how to bind the notes evenly just as Bernstein welds a perfect circle of emotion. But there is also something that memory captures only after a moment's pause for focus and recall. The voice, in those years, did take on quite a remarkable depth, remarkable at least in a Verdi baritone, which is what Merrill pre-eminently was. Here a listener without prior knowledge would be likely to say 'bass-baritone'. The darker hue adds greatly to the authority of the cantor: the voice of his people, and therefore the voice of the ages.

Merrill writes about the inspiration of this performance in his auto-biography, *Once More From The Beginning* (with Sandford Dody, New York, 1965). He attributes it to the conductor ('The melody always sings in Bernstein; he catches fire, and it spreads to the men and the boys.'). There is no doubt of its presence in the recording, or that Merrill has caught his full share of it. He sings like a man who has found his spiritual home. The cantor's tones of invocation, comfort and lament are movingly eloquent, and his technique makes smooth and easy the brief passages of melisma as it does the pervasive rich *cantabile*.

This was music he took seriously, and it was so with another work of

231

Bloch's, the 22nd Psalm, itself the subject of a telling paragraph in the book. He had married a pianist, and had been astonished to find that she practised eight hours a day, every day, including their first holiday abroad. It began to dawn on him (and he is quite frank about this) that, by the standards of a real musician, he had never thoroughly prepared anything. The Bloch, he decided, would be different. The two of them worked at it together, and after the first rehearsal with orchestra the maestro enquired into the identity of the European coach with whom the baritone had so impressively studied.

The conductor's remark, and the entire episode, cast their comment on the singer, his career and reputation. Merrill kept his place (and, after all, he was with the the the Met for thirty-one seasons) because he had a great voice and was, I imagine, a good guy. It could not be realistically assumed, however, that when he went home he would instantly, or in the course of, say, the next day or the following week, bury his head in a new score, study till he could sing it in his sleep, ponder fine points of nuance and expression, analyse the character's motivation and hidden feelings. On the whole, he enjoyed his music, but then he also enjoyed the good life, good food, the more popular entertainment of shows and radio, from which he also drew fame and fortune. Hence the pleasant surprise implicit in the conductor's remark on finding him so well prepared for Bloch's 22nd Psalm.

Returning to the *Sacred Service*, one finds Merrill's part in it, if not subtle, then at least plentiful in feeling, sensitivity and responsiveness. That was not always so, and 'subtlety' is not a term that figures prominently – if ever – in the critiques. Or rather, its presence is confined to sentences such as James Hinton's, 'He sang with fine tonal effect but without subtlety of style' (report on *Faust* in *Opera*, February 1954). Such criticisms also extended to his acting. Typical is a comment on his Gérard in *Andrea Chénier*. 'Mr Merrill has always been a stick as an actor and not too careful as a musician, but his magnificent voice and fluent singing carry the day' (Richard RePass, *Opera*, January 1962). In 1965 another critic, Martin Bernheimer, summed up: 'Although Scarpia is his newest rôle, it offers a good opportunity for appraisal of his characteristic strengths and weaknesses. His voice is as free and well produced today as it ever was. It has darkened slightly and grown more dramatic in quality, but it is still a gorgeous instrument. Few baritones can sing Scarpia with comparable ease and tonal richness. But Merrill remains basically a dull, monochromatic figure on the stage. He is insensitive to the meaning of what he is singing, and rather crude when it comes to dynamic modulation. His Scarpia therefore sounds just like his Germont, and is just as sympathetic as his Rodrigo. Merrill spent most of "Vissi d'arte" staring compassionately at Crespin, and no one would have been surprised had he led the applause afterwards.'

We in London did not hear him until 1967, when he made his only

Covent Garden appearance, as Germont, in *La traviata*. The only visual
memory I have is of his entry (though Elizabeth Vaughan's fragile Violetta
and Renato Cioni's Roman-profiled Alfredo begin to move in the mind's eye
when summoned). The sound was good and solid, much as hoped for; but
the stage figure remains blank. Later, in 1975, he gave a recital at Drury
Lane, and this was far more vivid. Again the voice surprised by its
darkness, but, though at the age of 58, he appeared to be in magnificent
vocal health, lavish with the arias (*L'africana, Don Carlos, Andrea*

233

Chénier, Zazà) and generous with encores. Here the singer's character established itself genially and expansively, but more so, if I remember rightly, in some of his songs than in the operatic excerpts. There was a fine group of spirituals at the end, and most of all one felt a real passion and refinement of his art in the *Three Hebrew Songs* of Ravel. More 'inner' and serious than anything else, these are performances I can 'hear' to this day, especially 'Mejerke, mein Suhn' with its urgent start and magical octave lift at the end.

The only other 'personal' experience I have is indeed a second-hand one but it clearly made such an impression that I almost think of it as my own. A friend, paying a short visit to New York, was whisked away by his hosts to the Met, where he found himself attending an indifferent performance of *La traviata*. Only with the first words of Germont, 'Madamigella Valéry', did he suddenly sit up and take notice: a singer unknown to him, he thought, and (as the rest of the scene confirmed) clearly in a class of his own and (also obviously) one to make note of for the future. The interval revealed the 'newcomer' to be Robert Merrill, then in his last season.

It is this kind of thing that renders much American critical writing on Merrill suspect in its balance, or even, at times, guilty of downright meanness. The reports have to be credited because they come from people who heard the singer month after month, year after year. Yet, cumulatively, the balance inclines towards the negative, and when I think of that voice I cannot believe the inclination to be just. Listening again, for instance, to his Nile Duet in *Aïda* with Leontyne Price, one wonders whether much of it has ever been more finely sung: 'Rivedrai le foreste imbalsamate', 'Pensa che un popolo, vinto straziato' are ideal in the sheer beauty of sound, and, while the declamation lacks verbal intensity, there is a positive aspect there too, for the voice is powerful but compact, its resonance thoroughly even, its tone never spreading. In his own time, Merrill's recordings had constantly to undergo comparison with Gobbi's, with results that were often unfair to both singers. Certainly, Gobbi's way was the more memorable, its humanity and individuality were supreme. Yet even in a rôle such as that of Michele in *Il tabarro*, which Gobbi made so much his own, it is possible to hear Merrill with appreciation of the voice and voice-production he brought to this music; and in the 'unpublished' aria, 'Scorri, fiume eterno', where Merrill's performance can stand alone, it does so with both musical and dramatic credit.

As to the man himself, or rather the man-artist, the very first thing I remember reading was that he had deserted the Metropolitan for Hollywood. This was 1951, and the writer had added, 'Can you imagine Giuseppe De Luca would ever have done that?' Well, no; but the comparison was facile (for one thing, to be in films had been the American's boyhood dream). More to the point was his repentance. More to the point still is a page in his autobiography which tells of the boy in his first job, as 'dress salesman', or dogsbody, at Uncle Abe's in Manhattan. Passing the old Met,

with his rack of 'Frocks by Bernstein', he saw the backstage door was open, and he crept in. Bori and Tibbett were rehearsing *Traviata*. 'When I was discovered by the assistant stage manager and removed from the sacred premises and led into the street, it wasn't the sudden change that made the sunshine harsh, the colours of the samples garish, and the din of 7th Avenue deafening. I couldn't articulate it then, but I somehow knew that inside the theatre there was form and that here in the street there was only chaos.' The 'articulate' element may quite possibly be the ghost-writer's; but that 'somehow' can only have been the grace of the Spirit.

Chapter 48

Dmitri Smirnov and
Leonid Sobinov

'Tweedledum and Tweedledee' we thought them: wrongly, as it happens. Smirnov and Sobinov stood shoulder to shoulder in the old His Master's Voice Historical Catalogue, and between them they comprised the sum-total of our knowledge of The Russian Tenor. I'm talking of a time just pre-war, 1938 or '39, and of a youthful time too, when pennies for records had to come more or less from heaven. So, in fact, most of the knowledge of those tenors at that time was hearsay, and was soon to be beyond our reach entirely as the horrendous deletions virus of wartime years made straight for the Historical Catalogue, and soon Dum and Dee, like Rosencrantz and Guildenstern, had gone into the dark. They turned up on dealers' lists at preposterous prices, and to the 35 shillings asked for Smirnov (a lot of money in those days) we could only say 'Nohow' and to the £2 for Sobinov 'Contrariwise!'

The truth was, as we came to discover, that these two Russians were remarkably unalike. On the face of it, their chance-coupling through apt alliteration's artful aid was supported by similarities of age, career, repertoire and reputation. Dmitri Smirnov (1882-1944) came to the Bolshoi in 1904 and introduced himself to western Europe two years later in Paris. Leonid Sobinov (1872-1934) made his official debut, also at the Bolshoi, in 1897 and appeared for the first time at La Scala, Milan in 1904. In the Russian repertoire they shared most of the principal lyric rôles – Lenski in *Eugene Onegin*, Vladimir in *Prince Igor*, Levko in *A May Night*, and so forth. Outside it, representative rôles were Faust and Romeo, Alfredo and the Duke of Mantua, Nadir in *Les pêcheurs de perles* and Rodolfo in *La Bohème*. Alike, they shunned the heavier commitments in Italian opera, though in Russia Sobinov became a familiar Lohengrin, and Smirnov made a recording of the Narration.

It was in timbre, taste and temperament that they differed most, also in their history as Russians in Russia, to which Smirnov rarely returned after the Revolution, while Sobinov remained as an artist held in the highest esteem, recipient at the time of his sixtieth birthday of the Red

Leonid Sobinov   Dmitri Smirnov

Labour Banner, a Soviet counterpart of the British Order of Merit. Sobinov, moreover, was always the favourite of public and critics alike.

At his death, some 30,000 attended the lying-in-state, and his coffin-bearers were principals of the Bolshoi, where he had sung for over three decades. Smirnov died, in comparative obscurity and (I should imagine) grimly unhelpful wartime conditions, at Riga.

To my mind, Smirnov is by far the more interesting singer, and not merely 'interesting' (for that can be a subtly belittling word). His recordings have about them a rare beauty, both of voice and of style, though certainly there are faults too. In Jürgen Kesting's monumental volumes, *Die grossen Sänger* (Düsseldorf, 1986) he is introduced under the heading 'Der Manierist', which I take to be the equivalent in noun-form of that poisoned adjective 'mannered'. By this account, Smirnov was a vocal sensationalist, a dealer in 'show-effects', with a touch of self-conscious, ingratiating show-off. Such an impression has its valid origins but is wide of the mark: or rather, it isolates a flaw and sees it as symptomatic, whereas another (and I think truer) way of looking at it is as the excess of a virtue, the virtue being that of an imaginative involvement in the music and in the means by which a singer can pleasurably share this with his listeners.

237

In July 1935 the *Musical Times* had a review of a late recital given by
Smirnov in England, at the now defunct Aeolian Hall. It deserves quoting
in full, for not only is it particularly well-written but it is as observant and
well-balanced a critique of a singer as I have read. The writer describes
him as 'big, of likeable presence' and still having it in his power 'to make
the world ring with his name'. Then he turns to the fascination of his
singing: 'You want to go on listening to Smirnov's voice, if only to see what
it will do next; to find out to what new turn of fancy it will choose to react.
Some of his effects are staggering, and it must be said that most of them
are legitimate. I have never heard a singer who is at once so completely
himself and at the same time so much an amalgam of everybody else.
When the fit moves him he can give you genuine thrills – thrills commu-
nicated through the medium of impassioned phrases piled one on top of
the other, welling in a long-drawn, full-throated stream to their climax.
The greatest Italian dramatic tenors might envy Smirnov this particular
gift. Then a different kind of fervour seizes him and with it a complete
shifting of his tonal and mental bases. A span of singing *à la Russe* (the
Tartar touch, perhaps) – petulant, plaintive; another *à l'Espagnol* –
tigerish, unconciliating; and then, wonder of wonders, he sets you thinking
of an English parish tenor, with singing that seems almost disembodied.
In the absence of an apparent *point d'appui*, his singing at such times is,
frankly, unpleasant. The whim passes, and there he is again, flighting his
voice, spinning, lightly touching, and "snatching graces" in the manner of
an old-time *bel canto* expert. "Falsetto" you say, as a mere filament of tone
passes his lips. It grows and grows, however, in its passage suggesting an
on-coming roll of thunder ... Smirnov throws his voice about like a juggler,
but it always returns handily for its owner's next trick.'

'Trick', we observe, and 'many regrettable things were done', the writer
concludes: 'He left frayed edges behind him.' It still sounds to me like a
concert to go right to the top of the 'sorry-I-missed' list.

Whether Sobinov did anything of this sort seems (for better or worse)
unlikely. Certainly he was an admirable singer. His voice had a natural
beauty that distinguished him right from the beginning: as a student he
sang in *Pagliacci*, not as Canio but Beppe whose patch of glory is Harlequin's Serenade, on this occasion encored thrice. He also studied in Italy,
which no doubt helped to prepare him for the success he enjoyed a few
years later at La Scala. There he sang first in *Don Pasquale* with Rosina
Storchio (the first Butterfly), Giuseppe De Luca and Antonio Pini-Corsi,
described by the *Corriere della Sera* as 'un quartetto che rimarrà celebre
e forme insuperabile'. Later, in *Fra Diavolo* he was dubbed 'esecutore
simpaticissimo', his other rôles there being Des Grieux in *Manon* and
Fenton in *Falstaff*. He also enjoyed some notable successes in Monte Carlo
and Madrid, with a return to La Scala in 1911; but essentially his career
was home-based, and after the Revolution almost exclusively so. No
recordings appear to be known from this later period: the last were made

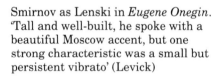

Smirnov as Lenski in *Eugene Onegin*. 'Tall and well-built, he spoke with a beautiful Moscow accent, but one strong characteristic was a small but persistent vibrato' (Levick)

Sobinov in lieutenant's uniform, 1905: 'I tell you in private, I feel very stupid in uniform. I feel a complete idiot ... there's not a lot of sense in all this.'

in 1911, the voice firm, even and virile, with signs of growth in his capacity as an expressive artist and in his ability to convey emotion through the impersonal recording medium.

Even so, his singing was never remarkable for its expressiveness on record, whereas that never seems to have been a problem for Smirnov. He recorded in a rather wider range of music than Sobinov, touching what is loosely called the *bel canto* repertoire (*Il barbiere di Siviglia*, *La favorita*, *L'elisir d'amore*), the contemporary Italian school (*Iris*, *Bohème*, *Tosca*, *Il tabarro*) and a rather more varied selection of songs, including some of Rachmaninov's and two popular Italian pieces, 'Mattinata' and 'Maria Mari'. This reflects the more cosmopolitan career, which may look more eventful than Sobinov's but ran a good deal less smoothly. His years at the Bolshoi and Mariinsky are placed by the invaluable chronicler of the

239

times, Sergei Levik, distinctly below Sobinov's, both in vocal quality and in reliability as an artist. In France he enjoyed an enduring spell of popularity at Monte Carlo, where he sang in brilliant casts including Selma Kurz, Frieda Hempel, Titta Ruffo and Chaliapin. He was also the Dmitri of the famous production that introduced Paris to *Boris Godunov* in 1908. There he made such an impression on Otto Kahn, great power at the Metropolitan, that a highly favourable contract was negotiated for a New York debut in 1910. His total of no more than twenty-two appearances in four operas (none of them Russian) over two seasons tells its own tale of disappointment. In London his debut in Rimsky-Korsakov's *May Night* in Beecham's Russian season was reported in *The Times* (27 June 1914): [of Levko's solos by the lake] 'They are charming songs and charmingly sung by M. Smirnov, a singer new to Drury Lane, whose tenor voice is pure and musical though not remarkably strong' (he reminded one listener of McCormack). After the war, his operatic appearances became fewer, with more concert work and a film debut as Peter the Great – silent, however. For a while in the 1930s he lived in London, where Gerald Moore recalled meeting him by chance one day and being shocked on seeing this fine handsome man distraught and quite broken in spirits by the death of his wife.

That must have been the same period as the song recital so vividly described in *Musical Times*. It is a pity that the critic could not have heard Sobinov on a similar occasion. I fancy that, if he had done so, his report would have been more simply favourable and much less interesting. It is so with the records. Both tenors are heard in a recent anthology of early Russian singers (*Great Singers at the Mariinsky*, Nimbus N17865). From Sobinov comes a perfectly good piece of uneventful singing in an aria from Rubinstein's *The Demon*. From Smirnov comes an atrocity – a high C inserted into Faust's last aria, 'Giunto sul passo estremo' from *Mefistofele*. It is indefensible – but very well done, and only one feature of a performance about which a whole essay could be written: a performance which has its share of faults in addition to the atrocity, but which is also a thing of rare beauty, with some exquisite shading and a conviction of *living* the music from moment to moment. 'The audience listened without breathing,' a reporter might say. Not true, of course: pure hyperbole. But you know what is meant, and it is what characteristically happens when Smirnov sings. For better or worse.

CHAPTER 49

Gundula Janowitz

'His head was still full of Gundula Janowitz, for her recital had been the highpoint of his holiday.' I think that must be my favourite first sentence in any English novel apart from *Pride and Prejudice* and with the possible further exception of A.N. Wilson's *Wise Virgin*. It comes from *Dismal Ravens Crying* by David Fletcher (Macmillan, 1989), the title itself sufficient attraction to the operatically-attuned reader who surveys the public library's crime fiction shelves in search of something for a spare evening. The phrase plays hide-and-seek for a while, but you hear it in your mind as a nasty voice intent on villainy. Purcell's *Dido and Aeneas*, of course, and the entry of the Sorceress and Witches ('who, like dismal ravens crying, Beat the windows of the dying'). Such sinister business is presently to claim Inspector Jolley, who for the moment is a happy man, his head also occupied with the sound of a voice, but a celestial one: 'To have heard her live at last still made him feel unreal, like a child given an unexpected half-holiday.'

Not many singers have been chosen for such a well-lit place in fiction, but it comes as no surprise that the object of the detective's enthusiasm (given its general direction) should be this particular one. She has a marked capacity for inspiring devotion. I personally know one devotee who after the best part of a lifetime in which the shining ideal of a singer was Frida Leider transferred some of that special feeling uniquely to Janowitz; and another, whose references to the 'Beloved' need no translation. A keeper of the archives has, I believe, recently passed away in Germany, but in this country a worldwide network of Janowitzians seems to have its centre, buzzing with activity and bursting with enthusiasm. As for the singer herself, she likes the appreciation and fellowship as anyone would, but the archive, the legend, is not her subject. 'I love singing,' she says, and that is it. Listening, analysing, studying other people's comments: no.

What, then, was it that so captivated that level-headed man Inspector Jolley and those many whom he represents? 'He sighed, his mind replaying a single phrase she had executed with unique grace.' That is all the writer provides by way of explanation. We ponder the identity of the phrase. Mozart's 'Porgi, amor, qualche ristoro' perhaps. But no, it had been a concert 'in a spartan Austrian hall'. Something of Schubert maybe: 'Still

241

sitz ich an des Hügels Hang, Der Himmel ist so klar.' That points the way, at any rate, for 'klar', 'clear', like the sky on Schubert's fine spring day, denotes well the character of the voice. But there is a better German word than that, and it comes in that same verse: 'Frühlingsstrahl', the 'rays of spring'. That is it: the radiance of voice, the 'Strahl'.

'A sparkling robe of joy', a phrase from Thomson's *The Seasons*; that also describes it, and suggests one reason why Janowitz's voice is so welcome and apt in Haydn, both in *The Seasons* and *The Creation*. 'Selig, wie die Sonne meines Glückes lacht', 'Blissful as the sun of my happiness laughs' – the opening of Eva's solo in the Quintet from *Die Meistersinger von Nürnberg*: there too is the Janowitz radiance. Singing these over in one's mind creates an appetite, a thirst rather, to hear the sound itself. That is another explanation of the Inspector's half-holiday excitement: it is the voice of refreshment, with the promise of more to come.

It is also a voice – strange to think – which arose out of the ruins of Berlin. Janowitz (German in spite of the name, the father having come

Janowitz as Agathe in *Der Freischütz*

242

from a place near the Austro-Hungarian border) was born there in 1937, and the years of her childhood were those of the soldiers and the speeches, the bombs and the destruction. After the war the family moved to Graz in Austria where music prospered even if their fortunes did not. The girl learnt to play the violin and found a voice; but there was no money, for instance, for records (the first records of singing she had were of *Aïda* and *Il trovatore* with Renata Tebaldi). From the Graz Conservatory she won a Wagner Society scholarship to Bayreuth, where Wieland Wagner recognized her talent and engaged her as a Flower Maiden in *Parsifal*. That was 1960. The previous year she had been spotted by the eagle eye of Walter Legge who recommended her to Karajan. Her career began at the Vienna State Opera, with the ideal debut rôle of Barbarina in *Le nozze di Figaro*. In 1961 *Opera* magazine's correspondent reporting from Bayreuth commented on 'a genuine vocal orgy' of Flower Maidens ('Never before have I heard such beautiful singing in this scene'). The cast-list was certainly impressive – it included Hilde Gueden and Annaliese Rothenberger – and was headed by the then unfamiliar name of Gundula Janowitz.

In those early ears Karajan played perhaps the most important part in shaping her career. Nowadays, when so much is heard in his disfavour, it is interesting to hear Janowitz tell of his consideration. He worked her very wisely within a light-voiced repertoire that gave her experience and exposure. Even in 1963 she could be heard in Vienna in quite small parts, in *L'incoronazione di Poppea* for instance, or the shepherd in *Tannhäuser*, which attracted notices such as 'Gundula Janowitz, who will certainly soon be heard in bigger things' (*Opera*, April 1963). The 'bigger things' included Pamina at Aix-en-Provence ('the great revelation of this festival') and that in turn led to her first British engagement, as Ilia at Glyndebourne in the 1964 *Idomeneo*, at which the other newcomer was Luciano Pavarotti. More influential than this was a visit to England made earlier that year when at the Kingsway Hall she recorded her Pamina in the great recording of *Die Zauberflöte* under Klemperer. Although, as Desmond Shawe-Taylor remarked in his Quarterly Retrospect for *Gramophone* (January 1965), her name 'is turning up everywhere just now', it was this recording that made it famous worldwide. Her voice, said Shawe-Taylor, 'is one of the purest and cleanest high sopranos to come from Europe for many years', and it became of immediate interest to Berlin and Salzburg (which with Vienna remained the cornerstones of her career) as well as the Metropolitan, La Scala and the Colón.

Shawe-Taylor's remarks were not entirely uncritical. 'Her instincts are very musical,' he wrote, 'but she is still inclined to sing separate notes rather than phrases, and to leave her words unclear or unmeaningful: the great cry of "Die Wahrheit!", for instance, needs to ring out more decisively.' Others had partly similar reservations, and at one time there appeared to be a consensus among English critics that she favoured sound more than sense. Reviewing an operatic recital record in 1968, Harold

244

Rosenthal wrote that Janowitz was 'fast becoming the German Sutherland – wonderful creamy tone, never an ugly sound, but almost complete uninvolvement in what she is singing, and often lots of vowels and very few consonants'. I would not have thought 'creamy' to have been quite the right word even then, but of course the criticism (uninvolvement, not enough consonants) is one which singers tend to incur almost by reflex if they make a habit of singing beautifully – some puritan streak urges critics to complain, in a world where ugliness is plentiful, of something conceived of as 'meaningless beauty'. If there ever was a fault of this kind in Janowitz it is not in evidence when she turns, as she did in a major recording project, to the songs of Schubert. It is true that in the notes to this edition she commits herself to the unfashionable proposition that 'the intelligibility of the text ranks second to the musical flow', but some of the great tests of expressiveness in singing are included here – such as Hagar's Lament and Gretchen's song at the spinning-wheel – and in every changing phrase the response is strong and vivid. So it is in her Strauss: the fine darkly brooding tone of her Ariadne ('Wo war ich?'), the lovely softening of the Countess's 'Du Spiegelbild' in the closing scene of *Capriccio*, the sensitivity to the depths as well as the soaring radiance of the *Four Last Songs*.

It was in some songs of Richard Strauss that I myself most recently heard her. She was singing for the first time in the concert hall at Birmingham with the City's Symphony Orchestra under Simon Rattle, and it must be said that Strauss (dearly as he loved the soprano voice) does not always give his singers an easy ride. The voice came through, in the start of 'Ruhe, meine Seele', as a small but bright and distinct point of sound in the texture. Never forcing a passage, it drew attention by maintaining a perfectly concentrated focus. She was then in her fifty-eighth year but the quality was youthful, at times almost girl-like. In the 'Wiegenlied' a gentle *portamento* soothed tenderly, and in 'Befreit' she called upon the greater reserves of dramatic tone to match the orchestral swell. It was a masterly lesson in the deployment of forces. It showed how a singer who puts first the essential business of singing (the purity of tone, the firmness, the musical flow) lives to sing another day. More than that: the 'Strahl' was still there, the 'sparkling robe of joy', and afterwards, on the homeward journey, one joined in imagination the internally singing detective, the admirable Inspector Jolley, as he drove towards the raven-cry of murder with a voice of morning sunlight ringing in his head.

CHAPTER 50

Joan Sutherland

On the eve of the great Sotheby's sale, when all the world had assembled for the private viewing, a husky voice of thrilling contralto depth cried: 'Lead me to The blood.' Everyone that evening made their pilgrimage to 'The blood': it was the movement of the moment. Up for sale were Sutherland's costumes, rich in colour as in memory, brocaded, bejewelled, and (some of them) weighing half a ton; but it was a flimsy bit of white stuff stained with red ink that stole the show. When next day the maculate garment was knocked down for a mere £5,000, going-going-gone, to the Royal Opera House Archive, the price and destination were both felt to be about right. Meanwhile the mind reverted to a sound and a sight legendary in our time.

The legend originated on the night of 17 February 1959, and, for once, I was there. These were the gallery days, though on that occasion I had promoted myself to the amphitheatre and sat in one of those front rows which are the best in the house. The opera itself was on trial as much as the prima donna. Most of us had never seen it, and most of us, I should say, hoped for vindication. As at an earlier, still more legendary performance of *Lucia di Lammermoor* (see E.M. Forster's *Where Angels Fear to Tread*, ch. 6), little ripples of excitement ran through the house (I have altered the words slightly – Forster has 'violent waves', but that was Italy). The prelude, we noted, was not rum-ti-tum but set the scene with poetic and ominous dignity. The curtain rose on Zeffirelli's magnificent production with that formidable flight of steps and the castle lights beyond. The music was good and the voices were not half bad. And then came the scene at the fountain, and our heroine: we knew her well of course, and hers was not a face that make-up could disguise, but, to our thinking, she looked as some tall, distinguished figure in a nineteenth-century print might look if brought to life, and when she began to sing it was at once apparent why this unlikely event in the Covent Garden of those years was taking place. This was the voice we had waited for.

We had heard Callas, but even at best that voice had never possessed the pure beauty and ease on high of this we were hearing now. In concert we may not so long ago have heard Lily Pons, but she had nothing of this power and fullness. On stage our *coloraturas* had been Wilma Lipp,

246

Mattiwilda Dobbs, Elda Ribetti – insubstantial in the big auditorium. We had gramophone records, but it was hard to translate the pre-electrical sound of Sembrich, Melba and Tetrazzini into actuality, and from more recent times the Italians Dal Monte and Pagliughi had brilliance but not the ingratiating softer grain of this young Australian's voice. Galli-Curci, yes, it was more like that in its limpid beauty, but surely more ample, rounder and warmer in expressiveness. So indeed it was the voice (at least in the way of *coloratura* sopranos), just as this was the evening (in the way of Italian grand opera), to which life had been tending.

The quality was utterly and completely pure, not the faintest hint of surface-scratch upon it. It was equally free from any kind of wobble or intrusive vibrato, and the high notes were heavenly. They came beautifully enough in 'Regnava nel silenzio', and in the decorated phrases of the *cabaletta* they were ecstatic. It also became evident that this was a real characterisation, that the arias in context had none of that vacuous prettiness which we suspected might be the limit of their charms. As the unfolding of the heroine's rôle proceeded, through duets to sextet, excitement and conviction grew steadily. Again as in Forster's novel, 'the climax was reached in the mad scene', when Lucia was similarly 'clad in white, as befitted her malady'. Strange to say, I remember no blood; but then there were other things to think about.

It was one of the most effective of all stage entries, in production worthy of an Eisenstein. After the Chaplain's harrowing narrative to chorus centre-stage, all turn suddenly towards the spiral staircase stage-right, and the woman then seen descending is a pitiful and shocking transformation. When she sings, there is a corresponding deathliness and pallor in the tone. As the imaginings of dementia warm and sweeten it, we hear singing of the utmost loveliness – but never as an object independent of the drama. In the cadenza of 'Ardon gl'incensi' the recollected tune of the love music is sung in a high arching phrase which in the score is broken off half-way, but by Sutherland was continued in unaccompanied notes of such beauty that any literalist who forbade them would simply have been a puritanical cheat. That phrase is the one which, of all, was the most wondrous and unforgettable.

Later, after the performance, I joined for an exasperating five minutes, a group of professional critics, urbanely amusing and apparently untouched by the wonder. There were also people like Victor Gollancz, who was overheard by the *Observer's* critic Peter Heyworth to say, 'My God, she's as boring as Melba.' It was atrophy. Somehow the elders wanted to play down, shrug off, this manifest success, which of course they could not do, for the judgment of the gallery was soon confirmed in the opera houses of the world.

Sutherland's triumph that night and in the years which followed was as genuine and as well justified as anything in the history of opera. But equally there is no doubt in my mind that things later went wrong. It was

247

Royal Opera House

COVENT GARDEN

HOUSE MANAGER . JOHN COLLINS

THE ROYAL OPERA HOUSE, COVENT GARDEN LIMITED

GENERAL ADMINISTRATOR . DAVID L. WEBSTER

in association with the Arts Council of Great Britain

presents

THE COVENT GARDEN OPERA

in

the first performance of a new production of

Lucia di Lammermoor

Opera in Four Acts

Music by GAETANO DONIZETTI

Text by SALVATORE CAMMARANO
after the novel by Sir Walter Scott

Scenery and Costumes by FRANCO ZEFFIRELLI
Costume Assistant: Alix Stone

Conductor: TULLIO SERAFIN

Producer: FRANCO ZEFFIRELLI

on

TUESDAY, 17th FEBRUARY, 1959

not in the development of her career, which was brilliant and enduring; nor in the choice of rôles, which was unfailingly sound. Nor was it the case (and this might well have happened) that the dramatic, expressive side of the work got neglected. Rather it seems that some basic features of style went awry. One of them was easily correctable, and to some extent was corrected; the fondness for a downward *portamento* which endowed the singing with a manner, or mannerism often described as 'droopy'. More fundamental was a way of inflecting individual notes to the detriment of a well-bound unity in the melodic phrase. The tone-quality itself was somehow involved in this, for a harder, thinner sound would have been more readily perceived as having firm definition. A more spritely effect might have been obtained had there not also been a tendency to round-out and dull the vowel-sounds. Then in later years came a loosening, never quite a wobble but a beat.

All of these negative features are, I believe, exaggerated in recordings. I suppose I must have heard Sutherland fairly regularly in London throughout her career, and it was only on the very last occasions that I found pleasure as a listener 'in the flesh' to be seriously diminished, as it had been for much longer by the singing as recorded. 'In the flesh' the

Sutherland as Lucia di Lammermoor

249

beauty of a thoroughly pure tone counted for more; in the perspective of a large opera house or concert hall, the vowels, the droops and fussy inflections settled down into the context and were less insistent than on record. On the other hand, in the flesh as in the recordings it became ever more true that the best things were the *cabalettas*, the brilliant second-half of the big solos, in which the virtuosity of her scales, trills and staccatos remained marvellous as ever. As for the recordings, I take increasingly the greatest pleasure in the earliest: or rather, in those which closely followed her initial triumph as Lucia, and most especially those imaginatively compiled anthologies up to the 'Romantic French Arias' of 1970. That is not to write off everything that appeared after that date (such as the last recorded of the *bel canto* operas, *Anna Bolena* which came as such a moving epilogue in 1988); in a sense, the judgement is a corollary to the enthusiasm described earlier. An enthusiast fears that people will unknowingly judge on inferior evidence. There is a story of Melba in her later years answering a woman who thought to compliment her by saying, 'My dear, you have never sung better.' 'Oh but my dear, I have,' she replied.

To play a sequence of those early recordings, from *The Art of the Prima Donna, Command Performance* and the first recital of all (made in 1959) is to recapture much of the wonder. Yet even they fail, I suspect, to give a true impression of the sheer size, the house-filling volume of her voice. One must not exaggerate: it was not a voice for Wagner (though she sang a promising Eva in *Die Meistersinger*) or for such a rôle as *Turandot* (though her recording makes one think again). Nevertheless, it was a voice that, left to itself, would expand and be everywhere, not a point in the spotlight on stage. The managers at Covent Garden knew that, and cast her (before Lucia) as Amelia, Aïda and Donna Anna, foreseeing a future in the lyric-dramatic field. Her husband, Richard Bonynge, saw farther and better, and therein lies the whole story.

Audiences at Covent Garden who had heard her in the *coloratura* of Jenifer's solo in *The Midsummer Marriage* may also have foreseen her ultimate achievement; so may those who went to the St Pancras Town Hall for *Alcina*. These no doubt prepared us, as well as her, for the great premiere of *Lucia di Lammermoor*. That was indeed a night of nights, and the costume that commemorates it went cheap at the price.

Dates, Books and Records

The singers are found here in alphabetical order. After the name (professional name only) their chapter number in this book is given in brackets, and the biographical information which follows is limited mainly to dates, names of teachers, place and rôle of operatic debut, important first appearances abroad, and world premieres. The list of books and records is selective. Autobiographies are included, though not all will be currently in print. The recordings listed are on compact disc unless otherwise stated, and catalogue numbers have been added where it is thought they may be useful; but of course many are deleted, often with a new reissue on a different number and sometimes another company label. The *Gramophone* Classical catalogue is the best guide to what is available. Of general reference books the most comprehensive is the *New Grove Dictionary of Music and Musicians* (Macmillan 1980) or for opera singers the *New Grove Dictionary of Opera* (1992). Among many other helpful books is the *International Dictionary of Opera* (St. James's Press 1993) which will be found to have interestingly written discursive articles on several of the singers listed here. On the earlier singers and their recordings Michael Scott's *The Record of Singing* (Duckworth, 2 volumes 1977, 1979) can usually be relied on for an informative and stimulating entry, and for the art on records of singers up to 1970 there is *The Grand Tradition* (Duckworth 1974, reprinted as second edition 1993) by the present writer. Where a number has been dedicated to a particular singer in this series, reference is always given to the *Record Collector*, an invaluable specialist magazine available on subscription and published quarterly. Information from the Editor, 111 Longshots Close, Broomfield, Chelmsford, Essex CM1 5DU, England.

ANDERSON, Marian (10) American contralto. b. Philadelphia 17 Feb. 1899; d. 1992. Studied w. Frank la Forge and Giuseppe Boghetti. Philadelphia Prize-Winner 1923. Concert debut 1925. Carnegie Hall 1929. European and American tours from 1930. Salzburg concert 1935. Lincoln Memorial concert 1939. Operatic debut Metropolitan 1955 (Ulrica, *Ballo in maschera*). Concert work with world tours till 1965. Delegate to UN 1957.
Autobiography: *My Lord, What a Morning* NY 1956. See also J. Sims-Wood: *Marian Anderson: An Annotated Bibliography and Discography* Westport 1981.
Records: RCA Victor. Seek spirituals, Sibelius songs, *Samson and Delilah* arias.

AUGER, Arleen (37) American soprano. b. Long Beach, Ca. 13 Sept. 1939; d. Netherlands 10 June 1993. Studied voice and violin Univ. Cal., later singing w. Ralph Errolle. Audition-winner Vienna State Opera. Debut VSO (Queen of Night,

Zauberflöte 1967). Frankfurt 1974. Salzburg, La Scala, Metropolitan, City of London Fest (*Alcina* 1985). Prolific concert and recording artist.

Records: seek Schubert (Hyperion CDJ33009) and Wolf recitals, *The Art of Arleen Auger* (Koch 37248-2), Mozart and Haydn arias (Decca 414 2DM), Bach cantatas (on Hänssler), *Alcina* (EMI), Strauss *Vier letzte Lieder* (Telarc).

AUSTRAL, Florence (36) Australian soprano. b. Richmond nr. Melbourne 26 Apr. 1894; d. Newcastle, Australia 15/16 May 1968. Studied Melbourne Conservatoire and NY (1918). Debut Cov. Gdn. 1922 (Brünnhilde, *Walküre*). Berlin 1930. Concert tours Europe, America, Australia. Retired 1940.

See: D. White: *Florence Austral* (*Record Collector* 14 1/2).

Records: seek excerpts *Ring des Nibelungen* (Pearl CDS9137), solos from Brahms's *Requiem*, *Golden Legend*, *Stabat Mater* (Rossini), Church sc. *Faust* w. Chaliapin. Solo recital Pearl GEMM CD9146.

BERGONZI, Carlo (19) Italian tenor. b. Polisene nr. Parma 13 July 1924. Studied Parma Conservatory. Baritone debut Lecce 1948 (Figaro, *Barbiere di Siviglia*). Tenor debut Bari 1951 (Andrea Chénier). Scala 1953. Metropolitan 1956-1988. Cov. Gdn. 1962. Retired 1992. Instituted Bergonzi Verdi Prize at Busseto.

See: G. Gualerzi: *Carlo Bergonzi* (Opera March 1978).

Many recordings: complete operas inc. *Aïda* (Decca, Karajan), *Ballo in maschera* (RCA, Leinsdorf), *Don Carlos* (Decca, Solti), *Bohème* (Decca, Serafin). Seek also *Verdi, 31 Tenor Arias* (Philips 432 486-2PM3) and early recordings (Cetra *Pagliacci* and *Simon Boccanegra*).

CALVÉ, Emma (2) French soprano/mezzo. b. Decazeville 15 Aug. 1858; d. Millau 6 Jan. 1942. Studied w. Mathilde Marchesi and Rosine Laborde. Debut Brussels 1881 (Marguerite, *Faust*). Paris 1884. Scala 1887. World premiere *L'amico Fritz* (as Suzel) Rome 1891. Her first Carmen Opéra-Comique 1891. Metropolitan 1891. Cov. Gdn. 1892. Anita in Massenet's *Navarraise* (1894) written for her. Continued occ. concert appearances till 1938.

Autobiographies: *My Life* NY 1922 (reprint 1977), *Sous tous les ciels j'ai chanté* Paris 1940. See also: D. Shawe-Taylor: *Emma Calvé* (*Opera* Apr 1955).

Records: a nearly complete edition on Pearl CDS9482. Seek 'death-bed message' and Mapleson Cylinders from Met. 1902 on LP.

CEBOTARI, Maria (34) Austrian soprano of Russian birth. b. Kishinev, Bessarabia 10 Feb. 1910; d. Vienna 9 June 1949. Studied at Kishinev Conservatory and with Oskar Daniel (Berlin). Opera debut Dresden 1931 (Mimì, *Bohème*). Aminta in world prem. Strauss's *Schweigsame Frau* (1935). Berlin 1936. Vienna 1946. Cov. Gdn. 1936. Lucile in world prem. von Einem's *Dantons Tod* (Salzburg 1947), Iseut in Martin's *Vin herbé* (Salzburg 1948). Films 1933-1941.

See: A. Mingotti: *Maria Cebotari: das Leben einer Sängerin* (Salzburg 1950).

Records include many wartime broadcasts (BASF/Acanta), complete *Rigoletto*, *Traviata* excerpts, pre-war solos Parlophone-Odeon, post-war HMV (good selection on Preiser 90034).

CHALIAPIN, Feodor (3) Russian bass. b. nr. Kazan 13 Feb. 1873; d. Paris 12 Apr. 1938. Studied w. Usatov in Tblisi. Worked first in chorus travelling comp. Debut 1890 Ufa (Stolnik in *Halka*). Mariinsky, St Petersburg; Mamontov Company Moscow, 1896. Salieri in world premiere Rimsky Korsakov's *Mozart and Salieri* 1898. Bolshoi 1899-1914. Scala 1901. Metropolitan 1907. Diaghilev seasons Paris 1908 (inc. *Boris Godunov*). London, Drury Lane 1913, Cov. Gdn. 1926, Lyceum 1931. Title-rôle world premiere *Don Quichotte* Monte Carlo 1910. Films: *Ivan the Terrible* (silent), *Don Quixote* (1930). Concerts worldwide till 1937.

Autobiographies: *Pages from my Life* London 1927, *Autobiography as told to Maxim Gorky* London 1968, *Man and Mask* London 1932. See also: V. Borovsky: *Chaliapin* NY and London 1988.

Records: many collections, Pearl, Nimbus, EMI. Seek live recordings Covent Garden (*Boris Godunov*, *Mefistofele*, *Faust*) and Albert Hall (*Mozart and Salieri*).

CHRISTOFF, Boris (23) Bulgarian bass. b. Plovdiv 18 May 1914; d. Rome 18 June 1993. Scholarship from the Gusla and Cathedral Choirs, Sofia. Studied w. R. Stracciari. Debut Rome 1946 (Colline, *Bohème*). Cov. Gdn. 1949 (*Boris Godunov*). Scala 1947. US debut San Francisco 1956. Also Buenos Aires. Last recordings 1980.

See: A. Bozhkoff: *Boris Christoff* London 1991.

Recordings inc. *Boris Godunov* (1952 cond. Dobrowen, 1962 Cluytens), *Don Carlos* (1954), *Simon Boccanegra* (1957), Nielsen's *Saul and David*. Complete Mussorgsky songs. Seek also early recordings 1949-52, Sofia concerts (1979/80).

CORTIS, Antonio (30) Spanish tenor. b. aboard ship 12 Aug. 1891; d. Valencia 2 Apr. 1952. Studied Madrid Conservatory. Debut 1915 small parts. Buenos Aires 1917. Rome 1920. Chicago 1924-32. Verona 1927. Scala and Cov. Gdn. 1931. Returned to Spain 1935. Retired 1951.

See: F.V. Grau: *Antonio Cortis: Il piccolo Caruso* Valencia 1988. J. Dennis & J. Leon: *Antonio Cortis* (*Record Collector* 20, 1971).

Recordings: good selection transfers Preiser (89043), Nimbus (NI 7850).

CRESPIN, Régine (20) French soprano. b. Marseilles 23 Feb. 1927. Studied w. S. Cesbron-Viseur and G. Jouatte (Paris). Debut Mulhouse 1950 (Elsa, *Lohengrin*). Paris 1950. Bayreuth (Kundry, *Parsifal*) 1958. Glyndebourne 1959. Cov. Gdn. 1960. Metropolitan 1962. Salzburg 1967. Mezzo rôles from 1977. Concert tours. Retired 1989.

Autobiography: *La Vie et l'amour d'une femme* Paris 1982. See also: A. Tubeuf: *Régine Crespin* (*Opera* April 1963).

Recordings: *Rosenkavalier* (Decca, Solti), *Walküre* (as Sieglinde, Decca, Solti). Recitals inc. *Nuits d'été* (Decca 417 813-2DH), Italian arias (Decca 440 416 2DM).

CROSS, Joan (28) English soprano. b. London 7 Sept. 1900; d. Aldeborough 12 Dec. 1993. Studied Trinity Coll. Mus. London. Chorus Old Vic 1924, Cherubino (*Nozze di Figaro*). Sadlers Wells 1931-46. Cov. Gdn. 1931. World premieres of Britten's *Peter Grimes*, *Rape of Lucretia*, *Turn of the Screw*, *Albert Herring*, *Gloriana*. Recital, oratorio work. Retired 1954.

See: Harewood: *Joan Cross: A Birthday Celebration* (*Opera*, 1990). Many refs. in biographies of Britten and Pears.

Recordings: *Grimes* excerpts, complete *Turn of the Screw*, near-complete *Rape of Lucretia*. Seek also pre-war solos, esp. *Otello*.

DAL MONTE, Toti (46) Italian soprano. b. Mogliano Veneto 27 June 1893; d. Treviso 25 Jan. 1975. Studied w. A. Meneghelli and B. Marchisio. Debut Scala

1916 (Biancafiore, *Francesca da Rimini*). 1922 *Rigoletto*, Scala (c. Toscanini). Metropolitan 1924. Cov. Gdn. 1925. Also S. America. World premiere Giordano's *Il re* (Scala 1929). Tours inc. Australia. Films. Retired opera 1947, finally 1950.

Autobiography: *Una voce nel mondo* Milan 1962. See also: G. Pugliese: *La Toti* Italy 1993.

Recordings: complete *Madama Butterfly* (HMV). Representative collections on Preiser 89001, Pearl GEMM CD9493. Passages 'live' from Vienna State Opera (Koch).

DE LOS ANGELES, Victoria (26) Spanish soprano. b. Barcelona 1 Nov. 1923. Studied Barcelona Conservatory. Debut Barcelona 1944 (Mimì, *Bohème*). Winner Geneva Competition 1947. Paris Opera 1949. Cov. Gdn. and Scala 1950. Metropolitan 1951. Bayreuth 1961. Colón, Buenos Aires. World concert tours; still singing 1994.

See: P. Roberts: *Victoria de los Angeles* London 1982. Also G. Moore: *Am I too Loud?* London 1962.

Recordings inc. complete *Bohème* and *Carmen* (EMI, Beecham), *Madama Butterfly* (1954 c. Gavazzeni, 1960 c. Santini), *Faust* (1954, 1958 c. Cluytens), *Pelléas et Mélisande*. Seek collections of early recordings, Spanish songs. Also Wigmore Hall 1990 recital (Collins Coll 1247-2).

DE LUCA, Giuseppe (40) Italian baritone. b. Rome 25 Dec. 1876; d. New York 26 Aug. 1950. Studied w. Persichini, Rome Academy. Debut Piacenza 1897 (Valentin, *Faust*). Scala 1903. Colón 1906. Cov. Gdn. 1907. Metropolitan 1915-40. Michonnet in world premiere *Adriana Lecouvreur* (Milan 1902), Sharpless in *Madama Butterfly* (Milan 1904), Paquiro in *Goyescas* (NY 1918), title-rôle *Gianni Schicchi* (NY 1918). Retired 1946.

See: N. Douglas: *Legendary Voices* London 1992, also *Record Collector* vols 5 and 11.

Recordings: complete recordings 1902-1930 Pearl GEMM CDS9159, 9160 (2 vols, 3 discs each). Representative collection 1917-30 on Preiser 89036, 89073. Seek also Golden Jubilee Concert 1947.

DE LUCIA, Fernando (9) Italian tenor. b. Naples 11 Oct. 1860; d. Naples 21 Feb. 1925. Studied Naples Conservatory. Debut Naples 1885 (*Faust*). London (Drury Lane) 1887, Cov. Gdn. 1892, Waldorf 1905. Metropolitan 1893. Also S. America, Russia. World premieres *L'amico Fritz* (Rome 1891), *I Rantzau* (Florence 1892), *Iris* (Rome 1898). Sang last in public 1924.

See: M. Henstock: *Fernando De Lucia, Son of Naples* London 1990.

Recordings: (ed. Henstock) 1902-1921 (3 discs) Pearl GEMM CDS9071, songs Opal CDS9845. Also Symposium 1149. Seek LP album: The G & T Recordings Rubini RS305, *Barbiere di Siviglia* Rubini SJG121.

DI STEFANO, Giuseppe (14) Italian tenor. b. nr. Catania 24 July 1921. Studied w. L. Montesanto (Milan). Debut Reggio Emilia 1946 (Des Grieux, *Manon*). Scala 1947. Metropolitan 1948-65. Cov. Gdn. 1961. World tour w. Callas 1973-4. World premiere Pizzetti's *Calzare d'argento* (Scala, 1961).

Recordings: w. Callas include *Puritani, Rigoletto, Ballo in maschera, Bohème, Tosca*. Seek early recordings, esp. LP album *The Young Giuseppe Di Stefano* EMI RLS765.

254

FARRAR, Geraldine (17) American soprano. b. Melrose, Mass. 28 Feb. 1882; d. Ridgefield, Ct. 11 March 1967. Studied Boston, NY, Paris, finally w. Lilli Lehmann. Debut Berlin 1901 (Marguerite, *Faust*). Monte Carlo 1904. Metropolitan 1906-22. World premieres *Königskinder* (Met. 1910), *Suor Angelica* (Met. 1918). Films (silent).

Autobiography: *Geraldine Farrar: The Story of an American Singer* NY 1916; *Such Sweet Compulsion* NY 1938. See also: W.R. Moran: *Geraldine Farrar* (*Record Collector*, vols 13, 14, 22).

Recordings, mostly Victor, inc. several w. Caruso (e.g. Puccini, Nimbus NI7857). Seek *Carmen* excerpts and 60th Anniversary Issue IRCC CD810.

FERRIER, Kathleen (13) English contralto. b. Higher Walton, Lancs 22 Apr. 1912; d. London 8 Oct. 1953. Studied w. J. Hutchinson and R. Henderson. Oratorio debut Newcastle 1942 (*St Matthew Passion*). Opera Glyndebourne 1946 (world premiere *Rape of Lucretia*). Also Gluck's *Orpheus* Glyndebourne, Holland and Cov. Gdn. Recitals inc. Edinburgh, Salzburg, Vienna, NY.

See: ed. N. Cardus: *Kathleen Ferrier: A Memoir* London 1954, W. Ferrier: *The Life of Kathleen Ferrier* London 1955, M. Leonard: *Kathleen* London 1988, P. Campion: *A Career Recorded* London 1992.

Recorded for Decca: many collections and reissues current, inc. folk songs, Mahler, Holland Fest. *Orpheus*.

FISCHER-DIESKAU, Dietrich (32) German baritone. b. Zehlendorf, Berlin 28 May 1925. Studied w. G. Walter and H. Weissenbrun. Debut Freiburg 1947 (Brahms's *Requiem*). Opera Berlin 1948 (Posa, *Don Carlos*). Vienna Opera and international concert career 1949. Salzburg 1952. Bayreuth 1954. Cov. Gdn. 1965. Retired 1993. World premieres *Elegy for Young Lovers* (Schwetzingen 1961), Britten's *War Requiem* (Coventry 1962), Britten's *Songs & Proverbs of Wm. Blake* (Aldeborough 1965), Reimann's *Lear* (Munich 1978).

Autobiography: *Echoes of a Lifetime* London 1989 (also books on Lieder esp. Schubert, and on Wagner and Nietzsche). See also: K. Whitton: *Dietrich Fischer-Dieskau* NY & London 1981. G. Moore: *Am I too Loud?* London 1962.

Probably largest recorded output of all comparable singers. Seek esp. *Winterreise* (w. Moore, Demus or Brendel), Wolf Goethe Lieder, *Fliegende Holländer*, *War Requiem*.

FLAGSTAD, Kirsten (21) Norwegian soprano. b. Hamar 12 July 1895; d. Oslo 7 Dec. 1962. Studied w. mother, E. Schytte-Jacobsen, G. Bratt. Debut Oslo 1913 (Nuri, *Tiefland*). 1917 operetta, then opera in Scandinavia. Bayreuth 1933. Metropolitan 1935. Cov. Gdn. 1936. Scala 1948. London, Mermaid (*Dido and Aeneas*) 1951. World premiere Strauss's *Vier letzte Lieder* London 1950. Director Oslo Opera 1958-60.

Autobiography: *The Flagstad Memoirs* (w. L. Biancolli) NY 1952. See also: E. McArthur: *Flagstad: A Personal Memoir* NY 1965.

Recordings: *Tristan und Isolde* (1952), *Rheingold* (as Fricka, 1958). Many collections. Seek *Wesendonck Lieder* w. Moore, *Haugtussa* w. McArthur, Sibelius orch. songs, and many pirated stage perfs.

GALLI-CURCI, Amelita (5) Italian soprano. b. Milan 18 Nov. 1882; d. La Jolla, Ca. 26 Nov. 1963. Studied piano Milan Conservatory. Mainly self-taught as singer.

Debut Trani 1906 (Gilda, *Rigoletto*). Buenos Aires 1910. Chicago 1916. Metropolitan 1921. World concert tours till 1935.

See: C. Le Massena: *Galli-Curci's Life of Song* NY 1945; A. Favia-Artsay: *Galli-Curci* (*Record Collector* vol. 4).

Recordings: complete edition pre-electrical recordings 1916-1924 Romophone 81003-2, 81004-2. Others on RCA, Nimbus, Pearl.

GOBBI, Tito (6) Italian baritone. b. Bassano del Grappo 24 Oct. 1913; d. Rome 5 March 1984. Studied w. G. Crimi. Debut Gubbio 1935 (Count, *Sonnambula*). Rome 1938. Scala 1942. San Francisco 1948. Cov. Gdn. 1951. Chicago 1954. Metropolitan 1956. World premieres inc. Ghedini's *L'ippocrita felice* (1956). Films inc. *Rigoletto, Pagliacci, Barbiere di Siviglia*. Directed in London and Chicago.

Autobiography: *Tito Gobbi: My Life* (w. I. Cook) London 1979.

Many recordings inc. several w. Callas (e.g. *Rigoletto, Aïda, Tosca*). Early recordings on Testament SBT1019. Seek LP album (3 recs) EMI RLS738.

HISLOP, Joseph (16) Scottish tenor. b. Edinburgh 5 Apr. 1884; d. Berryside, 6 May 1977. Studied w. G. Bratt. Debut Stockholm 1914 (*Faust*). Naples 1919. Cov. Gdn. 1920. Chicago 1920. Scala 1923. Colón 1925. Paris (Op. Comique) 1926. World concert tours, operetta, film. Retired 1937, then taught Stockholm and London.

See: M. Turnbull: *Joseph Hislop: Gran tenore* Aldershot 1992; M. Bott: *Hislop* (*Record Collector* vols 23, 25).

Recordings: selection on Pearl GEMM 9956. Seek LP album (2 recs) Rubini RS308 (w. *Manon Lescaut* excerpts).

IVOGÜN, Maria (8) Hungarian soprano. b. Budapest 18 Nov. 1891; d. Beatenburg, Switz. 2 Oct. 1987. Studied Vienna and Munich. Debut Munich 1913 (Mimì, *Bohème*). Chicago 1921. Berlin 1925. Cov. Gdn. 1924. Retired 1935. Taught Vienna, Berlin. World premiere *Palestrina* (as Ighino).

See: A. Frankenstein: *Maria Ivogün* (*Record Collector* vol. 20).

Good selection of recordings Nimbus NI7832.

JANOWITZ, Gundula (49) German soprano. b. Berlin 2 Aug. 1937. Studied Graz Conservatory. Debut Vienna 1960 (Barbarina, *Nozze di Figaro*). Bayreuth 1960. Glyndebourne 1964. Metropolitan and Salzburg 1967. Paris 1973. Cov. Gdn. 1976. Retired opera 1990. International concert tours.

Many recordings inc. Haydn *Creation, Seasons*, Schubert songs, *Nozze di Figaro* (DG, Böhm), *Arabella, Ariadne auf Naxos, Capriccio, Vier letzte Lieder*. Seek live ('pirate') recordings *Attila* Berlin 1971, Verdi *Requiem* Munich 1974.

LAURI-VOLPI, Giacomo (18) Italian tenor. b. Rome 11 Dec. 1892; d. Valencia 17 March 1979. Studied Rome Academy w. A. Cotogni, later E. Rosati. Debut Viterbo 1919 (Arturo, *Puritani*). Rome 1920. Scala 1922. Metropolitan 1923. Cov. Gdn. 1925, also S. America. Retired 1956.

Autobiographies: *L'equivoco* Milan 1938, *A viso aperto* Milan 1955. See also: Lauri-Volpi: *Voci parallele* Milan 1955, Williams & Hutchinson: *Lauri-Volpi* (*Record Collector* vols 9, 12, 20), L. Bragha: *La voce solitaria* Rome 1982.

Recordings: collections on Nimbus, Pearl, Preiser. Seek LP Rubini GV500 (early recordings) and Tima 25 (later curiosities).

LUDWIG, Christa (31) German mezzo-soprano. b. Berlin 11 March 1928. Studied with mother and F. Hüni-Mihacsek. Debut Frankfurt 1946 (Orlofsky, *Fledermaus*). Vienna 1955. Chicago and Metropolitan 1959. Bayreuth 1966. Cov. Gdn. 1968. Extensive concert tours till 1994.
See: C. Osborne: *Christa Ludwig* (Opera 1973).
Many recordings inc. *Così fan tutte* (1955, 1962, both w. Böhm), *Fidelio*, *Lohengrin*, Mahler cycles. 1993 recital (*Farewell to Salzburg*) RCA 09026 61547 2.

MELBA, Nellie (7) Australian soprano. b. Richmond, Melbourne 19 May 1861; d. Sydney 23 Feb. 1931. Studied w. M. Christian and P. Cecil in Australia, M. Marchesi, Paris. Debut Brussels 1887 (Gilda, *Rigoletto*). Cov. Gdn. and Paris 1888. St Petersburg 1890. Scala and Metropolitan 1893. Australian tours w. own opera company. Retired 1926.
See: W. Moran (ed.): *Nellie Melba: A Contemporary Review* Westport, Ct. 1985; J. Hetherington: *Melba* Melbourne 1967; D. Shawe-Taylor: *Nellie Melba* (*Opera*, Feb. 1955).
Recordings: complete Victor recs. 1907-16, Romophone 81011-2. Other transfers Pearl, RCA. Seek LP boxed set EMI RLS719 (complete London recordings) and deleted CD, EMI CD7 61070.

MERRILL, Robert (47) American baritone. b. Brooklyn, NY 4 June 1917. Studied w. S. Margolis. Debut Trenton 1944 (Amonasro, *Aïda*). Metropolitan 1945 (-75), Venice 1961. Cov. Gdn. 1967. Also S. America. World concert tours, films, popular broadcast programmes.
Autobiographies: *Once More from the Beginning* (w. S. Dody) NY 1965; *Between Acts* (w. R. Saffron) NY 1977.
Many recordings inc. *Traviata* and *Ballo in maschera* c. Toscanini. Puccini: *Trittico* (Decca). Collection VAI 691116.

McCORMACK, John (25) Irish tenor. b. Athlone 14 June 1884; d. Dublin 16 Sept. 1945. Studied w. V. O'Brien and V. Sabatini. Won National Competition 1903. Opera debut Savona, Italy 1906 (Beppe, *L'amico Fritz*). Cov. Gdn. 1907. Naples 1909. NY (Manhattan) 1909 (Metropolitan) 1910. Monte Carlo 1921. Concert work till retirement 1938, then again in wartime.
See: L. Strong: *John McCormack* London 1941; G. Ledbetter: *The Great Irish Tenor* London 1977; N. Douglas: *More Legendary Voices* London 1994.
Many recordings w. transfers on EMI, RCA, Nimbus, Pearl. Seek: LP boxed set (6 recs) Pearl GEMM165-60 (*The Years of Triumph*).

NILSSON, Birgit (27) Swedish soprano. b. Vastra Karups 17 May 1918. Studied w. J. Hislop. Debut Stockholm 1946 (Agathe, *Freischütz*) Glyndebourne 1951. Bayreuth 1954. San Francisco 1956. Cov. Gdn. 1957. Scala 1958. Metropolitan 1959. Retired 1984.
Autobiography: (English ed.) *My Life in Pictures* NY 1981. See also *Opera News*, articles by J. Young (vol. 34), S. Wadsworth (44).
Recordings inc. *Ring* cycle (cond. Solti), *Tristan und Isolde* (Bayreuth 1966), *Turandot*. Seek 'live' *Turandot* Met. 1961. Also Scandinavian songs (Decca, BIS, Bluebell).

PATTI, Adelina (24) Italian soprano. b. Madrid 19 Feb. 1843; d. Craig-y-Nos, Wales 27 Sept. 1919. Studied w. E. Barilli. Concert tours USA as child-prodigy.

Opera debut NY 1859 (*Lucia di Lammermoor*). Cov. Gdn. and Berlin 1861. Paris 1862. Scala 1877. Metropolitan 1887. S. America 1888. European and American tours. Retired opera 1897, last concert 1914.

See: J. Cone: *Adelina Patti* Portland 1993; H. Klein: *The Reign of Patti* NY & London 1920.

Records: Pearl GEMM 9312. Seek LP album EMI RLS 711.

PERTILE, Aureliano (29) Italian tenor. b. Montagnana 9 Nov. 1885; d. Milan 11 Jan. 1952. Studied w. V. Orefice. Debut Vicenza 1911 (*Martha*). Scala 1916. Colón 1918. Metropolitan 1921. Cov. Gdn. 1927. Berlin and Vienna 1929. Retired 1944. World premieres *Nerone* (Boito, 1924; Mascagni, 1935).

See: complete ed. of recordings w. book by M. Tiberi. Tima 1994; B. Tosi: *Pertile: una voce, un mito* Malipiero 1985; P. Morby (*Record Collector* vol. 7).

Representative collections of later recordings on Preiser.

PINZA, Ezio (12) Italian bass. b. Rome 10 May 1892; d. Stamford Ca. 9 May 1957. Studied Bologna Academy. Debut Soncino 1914 (Oroveso, *Norma*). Scala 1922. Metropolitan 1926. Cov. Gdn. and Salzburg 1934. Also films, musicals and concert tours.

Autobiography: (w. R. Magidoff) *Ezio Pinza* NY 1958. See also: *Record Collector* vol. 26; N. Douglas: *Legendary Voices* London 1992.

Recordings include Verdi's *Requiem*. Many collections (RCA, EMI, Pearl, Preiser, Nimbus). Seek live recordings from Metropolitan and Salzburg.

PONSELLE, Rosa (35) American soprano. b. Meriden Ct. 22 Jan. 1897; d. Green Spring Valley, Balt. 25 May 1981. Studied w. R. Romani. Debut Metropolitan 1918 (Leonora, *Forza del destino*). Cov. Gdn. 1919. Florence 1933. Retired 1937. Director Baltimore Civic Opera.

Autobiography: (w. J. Drake) *Ponselle: A Singer's Life* NY 1982. See also: *Ponselle at 80* (*Opera*, Jan. 1977); J. Steane: *Voices, Singers & Critics* London 1992; J. Hines: *Great Singers on Great Singing* NY 1982; N. Douglas: *Legendary Voices* London 1992.

Recordings: complete Columbia acoustics on Pearl GEMM CDS9964; Victors on Romophone 81006-2 and 81007-2. Seek also *Traviata* 'live' and post-retirement recordings on RCA.

POPP, Lucia (41) Austrian soprano of Czech birth. b Uhorska Ves; d. 15 Nov. 1993. Studied Bratislava Academy. Debut Bratislava 1963 (Q. of Night, *Zauberflöte*), also Vienna and Salzburg. Cov. Gdn. 1966; Metropolitan 1967. Member Cologne Opera. Concert tours.

See: A. Blyth: *Lucia Popp* (*Opera*, Feb. 1982).

Many recordings inc. *Zauberflöte*, Strauss *Intermezzo, Rosenkavalier, Vier letzte Lieder*. 5 collections on EMI. Schubert songs (Hyperion CDJ33017). Seek also videos.

RETHBERG, Elisabeth (44) German soprano. b. Schwarzenberg 22 Sept. 1894; d. Yorktown Heights NY 6 June 1976. Studied Dresden Conservatory. Debut Dresden 1915 (Arsena, *Zigeunerbaron*). Salzburg and Metropolitan 1922. Cov. Gdn. 1925. Many seasons Chicago, San Francisco. Many concerts. World premiere *Aegiptische Helena* (Dresden 1928).

See: Herschal, Hirst & Friedrich: *Elisabeth Rethberg: Ihr Leben und Kunster-*

tum Schwarzenberg 1928 (reprint 1977); *Record Collector* vol. 8; J. Steane: *Voices, Singers & Critics* London 1992.

Recordings: complete 1924-9 on Romophone 81012-2, 1927-34 Romophone 81014-2. Selection 1920-5 on Preiser 89051. Seek also 'live' *Otello* Metropolitan 1937 and *Aïda* excerpts Cov. Gdn. 1936.

RUFFO, Titta (33) Italian baritone. b. Pisa 9 June 1977; d. Florence 6 July 1953. Studied w. V. Persichini. Debut Rome 1898 (Herald, *Lohengrin*). Buenos Aires 1902. Cov. Gdn. 1903. Scala 1904. Russia 1905. Colón 1908. Chicago-Philadelphia 1912. Metropolitan 1922. Retired 1933.

Autobiography: *La mia parabola*, Milan 1937 (re-edited w. discography 1977; Eng. trans, Dallas 1995); A. Farkas (ed.): *Titta Ruffo: An Anthology* NY 1984; N. Douglas: *More Legendary Voices* London 1994; W. Legge: *On and Off the Record* London 1982; J. Mouchon: *Les enregistrements du baryton Titta Ruffo* Marseilles 1991.

Recordings: complete edition on Pearl. Many collections inc. Nimbus, Preiser.

SCHUMANN-HEINK, Ernestine (42) Austrian contralto. b. Lieben nr. Prague 15 June 1861; d. Hollywood 17 Nov. 1936. Studied in Graz. Stage debut Dresden 1878 (Azucena, *Trovatore*). Berlin and Hamburg 1882. Bayreuth 1896. Cov. Gdn. 1897. Chicago 1898. Metropolitan 1899; last appearance 1932. Concert tours USA. Film *Here's to Romance* (1935). Klytemnestra in world premiere *Elektra* (Dresden 1909).

See: M. Lawton: *Schumann-Heink: Last of the Titans* NY 1928 (reprint 1977); J. Howard: *Schumann-Heink* (*Record Collector* vols 17, 25); J. Howard: *Schumann-Heink: Her Life and Times* Sebastopol Ca. 1990.

Recordings: good selection (1906-29) Nimbus NI7811. Seek also *Trovatore* duet w. Caruso.

SCHWARZKOPF, Elisabeth (3) German soprano. b. Jarotschin nr. Poznan. Studied w. L. Mysz Gmeiner (Berlin) later w. M. Ivogün. Debut Berlin 1938 (Flower Maiden, *Parsifal*). Vienna 1945. Cov. Gdn. and Salzburg 1947. Scala 1948. San Francisco 1955. Metropolitan 1964. World concert tours. Retired opera 1972, concerts 1979. Ann in world premiere *Rake's Progress* (Venice 1951).

See: Schwarzkopf (ed.): *On and Off the Record* NY 1982; A. Sanders: *Elisabeth Schwarzkopf: A Career on Record* London 1995; J. Steane: *Voices, Singers & Critics* London 1992; G. Moore: *Am I too Loud?* 1962. A. Jefferson: *Elisabeth Schwarzkopf* London 1996 won headlines with its 'revelations of the past': its methods and the suggestibility of its approving reviewers would make an interesting study.

Many recordings inc. *Meistersinger* (Bayreuth 1951), much Mozart, Strauss, Wolf, operetta. Seek wartime recordings (Acanta), Salzburg recitals, duet recital w. Seefried.

SCOTTI, Antonio (22) Italian baritone. b. Naples 25 Jan. 1866; d. Naples 26 Feb. 1936. Studied Naples and Salerno. Debut Malta 1889 (Amonasro, *Aïda*). S. America 1892. Scala 1898. Cov. Gdn. 1899. Chicago, Metropolitan 1899. Formed Scotti Grand Opera Touring Co. 1919. Chim-Fen in world premiere Leoni's *L'oracolo* (London 1905).

See: W. Hogarth: *Antonio Scotti* (*Record Collector* vol. 28); M. Bott: *On Tour with Scotti* (*Opera* vol. 27).

Recordings inc. several w. Caruso. Good selection of solos Pearl GEMM CD 9937.

SMIRNOV, Dmitri (48) Russian tenor. b. Moscow 19 Nov. 1882; d. Riga 27 Apr. 1944. Studied w. E. Pavlovskaya. Debut Moscow 1903 (Gigi in premiere of Esposito's *Camorra*). Bolshoi 1904. Mariinsky 1910. Paris 1906. Monte Carlo 1908. Metropolitan 1901. London (Drury Lane) 1914. Much concert work.

See: J. Stratton: *Dmitri Smirnov* (*Record Collectior* vol. 14).

Recordings: good selection Pearl GEMM CD9106. Also 1 disc in the 3-disc *Singers of Imperial Russia* vol. 3 Pearl GEMM CDS9000004-6. Seek LPs, Rubini GV74, 75.

SOBINOV, Leonid (48) Russian tenor. b. Yaroslavl 26 May 1872; d. Riga 14 Oct. 1934. Studied Moscow Academy. Small rôles w. Italian Opera Co. in Moscow. Bolshoi 1897. Mariinsky 1901. Further study Italy 1905. Scala 1904. Monte Carlo 1906. Madrid 1908. Extensive Russian tours. Retired 1934.

Autobiography: *Memoirs* (2 vols) Moscow 1970; J. Robertson: *Leonid Sobinov* (*Record Collector* vol. 24); *The Levik Memoirs* London 1995.

Recordings: one of three CDs in *Singers of Imperial Russia* vol. 1 Pearl GEMM CDS9997-9.

SUTHERLAND, Joan (50) Australian soprano. b. Sydney 7 Nov. 1926. Studied Sydney and London. Debut Sydney 1947 (Dido in concert performance of *Dido and Aeneas*). Stage debut Sydney 1951. Cov. Gdn. 1952. Vienna 1959. Paris 1960. Scala and Metropolitan 1961. Australian opera tour 1965. Opening New Sydney Opera Hse. 1974. Many US, Australian tours. Retired 1990.

See: N. Major: *Joan Sutherland* London 1987 (rev. 1994); E. Greenfield: *Joan Sutherland* London 1972.

Many recordings inc. *Lucia di Lammermoor* (1961 c. Pritchard, 1971 c. Bonynge). Most recital items are available though 'redistributed' in CD collections on Decca. Seek also 'live' recordings e.g. *Huguenots* and *Semiramide* from Scala.

TALVELA, Martti (45) Finnish bass. b. Hiitola 4 Feb. 1935; d. Juva 22 July 1989. Studied at Lahti Academy and w. C. Oehmann at Stockholm. Debut Helsinki 1960 (Sparafucile, *Rigoletto*). Stockholm 1961. Bayreuth and Berlin 1962. Metropolitan 1968. Cov. Gdn. 1973. Director Savonlinna Fest. 1972-9.

See: H. Robinson: *Believer* (*Opera News* vol. 50).

Recordings include *Boris Godunov* in original version, *Don Carlos* (Inquisitor, Solti). Songs by Mussorgsky and Kilpinen.

TAUBER, Richard (1) Austrian tenor (nat. British). b. Linz 16 May 1891; d. London 8 Jan. 1948. Studied w. C. Beines. Opera debut 1913 Chemnitz (Tamino, *Zauberflöte*). Dresden 1913. Berlin 1919. Vienna 1922. London (Drury Lane) 1931, (Cov. Gdn.) 1938. US and world tours. Also conductor and composer.

See: J. Dennis: *Richard Tauber* (*Record Collector* vol. 18); J. Steane: *Voices, Singers & Critics* London 1992; N. Douglas: *More Legendary Voices* London 1994.

Many recordings and transfers inc. EMI, Nimbus, Pearl. Seek also: 'off-the-air' transcripts and LP boxed set *The Art of Richard Tauber* 1916-46 EMI RLS7700.

TETRAZZINI, Luisa (15) Italian soprano. b. Florence 29 June 1871; d. Milan 28 Apr. 1940. Studied w. sister Eva T. and at Florence Institute. Debut Florence 1890

(Ines, *L'africaine*). Buenos Aires 1892. Warsaw and St Petersburg 1896. Moscow 1900. San Francisco 1905. Cov. Gdn. 1907. NY (Manhattan) 1908, (Metropolitan) 1911. Retired opera 1914. Many US and British concert tours till 1934.

Autobiography: *My Life of Song* London 1921. See also: C. Gattey: *Luisa Tetrazzini, The Florentine Nightingale* London 1995; D. Shawe-Taylor: *Tetrazzini* (*Opera* vol. 14); N. Douglas *Legendary Voices* London 1992.

Recordings: complete London recordings EMI CHS7 63802. Complete edition Pearl GEMM CD9221-5; single disc Nimbus NI 808.

VICKERS, Jon (43) Canadian tenor. b. Prince Albert, Sask. 29 Oct. 1926. Studied Toronto Conservatory. Debut Toronto 1952 (Duke, *Rigoletto*). Cov. Gdn. 1957. Bayreuth 1958. Vienna 1959. Metropolitan 1960. Retired 1988.

See: J. Williams: *A Sense of Awe: the career of JV as seen in reviews* (*Opera Quarterly* 1990); N. Goodwin: *Jon Vickers* (*Opera* vol. 13).

Many recordings inc. *Fidelio, Les Troyens, Otello, Tristan und Isolde, Peter Grimes*. Good collection on VAIA 1016 (Italian arias), also VAIA 1007 (*Winterreise*).

VISHNEVSKAYA, Galina (39) Russian soprano. b. Leningrad 25 Oct. 1926. Studied w. V. Garina. Debut Leningrad Light Opera Co. 1944. Bolshoi 1952 (Tatiana, *Eugene Onegin*). Metropolitan 1961. Cov. Gdn. 1962. Scala 1964. Concert tours. Films (inc. Shostakovich's *Katerina Ismailova*). World premieres: Prokoviev's *War and Peace* (1959) and *Semen Kotko* (1970); also Shostakovich Symphony 14, Britten's Pushkin cycle *The Poet's Echo* and soprano part in his *War Requiem* written for her.

Autobiography: *Galina* London & San Diego 1984, now the subject of an opera (premiere Lyon 1996) by Marcel Landowski.

Recordings inc. recitals of Russian song with Rostropovich, *Eugene Onegin, War Requiem*.

ZANELLI, Renato (11) Chilean baritone, later tenor. b. Valparaiso 1 Apr. 1892; d. Santiago 25 March 1935. Studied w. A. Querze. Baritone debut Santiago 1916 (Valentin, *Faust*). Metropolitan 1919. Scotti Touring Opera 1922. Concert tours N. & S. America. Restudied in Milan. Tenor debut Naples 1924 (Raoul, *Huguenots*). Cov. Gdn. 1928. Scala 1930. Title-rôle in world premiere Pizzetti's *Lo straniero* (Rome 1930).

See: J. Dzazopulos: *Renato Zanelli* (*Record Collector* vol. 31).

Records: complete baritone & four tenor recordings Pearl GEMM CD9028. Fragment from *Tristan* 1930 Scala on Symposium 1102 (*Opera at La Scala*).

ZENATELLO, Giovanni (38) Italian tenor. b. Verona 22 Feb. 1876; d. NY 11 Feb. 1949. Studied as baritone Verona. Debut Belluno 1898 (Silvio, *Pagliacci*). Tenor debut Naples 1899 (Canio, *Pagliacci*). Scala 1902. Buenos Aires 1903. Cov. Gdn. 1905. NY (Manhattan) 1907. Opening Verona Arena (*Aïda*) 1913. Retired 1928. Taught NY, 'discovered' Lily Pons and Maria Callas. World premieres *Madama Butterfly* (Scala 1904), Giordano's *Siberia* (Scala 1902).

See: T. Hutchinson & C. Williams: *Giovanni Zenatello* (*Record Collector* vol. 14); N. Consularo: *Giovanni Zenatello* Verona 1976.

Recordings collected almost complete on Pearl GEMM CDS9073, 9074 (4 discs each). The few remaining on Symposium 1102. Electrical recordings Preiser 89038.

261

Index of Singers

Main entries are given in **bold** type.

General Index

References to operas and other large-scale works are given under their composers. When the text names an operatic character or an aria that also is indexed as a reference to the opera.

271